DATE			

EXCESS PROFITS

RONALD FERNANDEZ

EXCESS PROFITS

The Rise of United Technologies

▲▼ **Addison-Wesley Publishing Company**
Reading, Massachusetts • Menlo Park, California
London • Amsterdam • Don Mills, Ontario • Sydney

Copyright © 1983 by Ronald Fernandez

Library of Congress Cataloging in Publication Data

Fernandez, Ronald.
   Excess profits.

   Includes bibliographical references and index.
    1. United Technologies Corporation — History.
2. Conglomerate corporations — United States —
History.   I. Title.
HD9503. F47   1983   338. 7'62904'0973   83-3760

ISBN 0-201-10484-9

Production and typesetting by Wm. J. Richardson Associates, Inc.,
Dix Hills, New York. This book was typeset in 11–point Electra.
Jacket design by Marshall Henrichs.

ABCDEFGHIJ-DO-8543

First printing, May 1983

For Brenda Harrison

AUTHOR'S NOTE

On November 4, 1981 I wrote to United Technologies Director of Public Relations, requesting interviews with Chairman Harry Gray and other high officials of the corporation. In response I was told that United would not assist anyone doing an unauthorized history of the company. In addition, United's executives had no time to see me.

On November 24, 1981 I wrote to Harry Gray personally, explaining that the main reason I sought the interviews was "to empathize, to see the corporation's history from the point of view of its most significant corporate officers."

Mr. Gray referred my letter to Francis Murphy, then United's Vice President for Public Relations and Communications. Mr. Murphy reiterated United's refusal to help anyone doing an unauthorized history; and he also told me that United's executives had no time to assist anyone in such a large project.

I am sorry that United's executives refused to air their views.

ACKNOWLEDGMENTS

This book could not have written without the help of many librarians. At the Connecticut State Library my biggest debt is to Ted Wilson. Ted showed me how to locate information in the government maze and never failed to answer my questions when I was often unable to find what my footnotes said did exist.

Thanks, too, to Al Palko and Nancy Blount. They were unfailingly kind in my innumerable visits to the State Library.

At Central Connecticut State University, June Mazzei processed my many requests for interlibrary loans. She made it much easier for me to complete this book. Thanks, too, to June's assistant, Ms. Judy Cunningham.

At Central's "copy center" Marie Kascus, Faith Merriman, and Barbara Sullivan said yes even when they wanted to say no. They were especially helpful in repairing a microfiche machine that broke down with each and every use.

My student assistant at Central, Jeffrey Adams, provided many leads. I thank him for the time he spent with the Readers' Guide to Periodical Literature.

Mrs. Cary Mead sat through my many questions about the corporation's early years. She was very helpful and hopefully someone will soon write a book about her. She is an extraordinary woman.

At Addison-Wesley, thanks first to Doe Coover. She gave me the chance to do this book.

Brian Crockett saw the manuscript through its first draft. He never stopped asking for more facts, and his positive influence is reflected in the final manuscript.

Chris Kuppig is a superb editor-in-chief. He is concerned, he has an open ear, and he has an acute sense of what is most important to anyone writing a book such as Excess Profits.

Thanks to Robin Manna for her encouragement and assistance.

Ms. Tobie Sullivan edited this book. Tobie is intelligent, conscientious, and easy to work with. I thank her for taking so much time with my, originally, never-ending book.

Burt Baldwin, Bill Donovan, Bill Kerr, Kathy and Rich Kaplan, Jack Lucas, and John Rommel all read parts of the manscript. They bear no responsibility for the final product but their comments were helpful, their criticisms to the point.

With love, this book is dedicated to Brenda Harrison. I don't think it would have been finished without her.

Ronald Fernandez

CONTENTS

EXCESS PROFITS

PROLOGUE

Senator Hugo Black was outraged. In 1934, with millions of Americans unemployed and the Western world devastated by the worst depression in history, Black's Special Investigating committee easily demonstrated that many aviation companies had earned extraordinary amounts of the public's tax money flying the nation's mail.

Although almost every major figure in the aviation industry appeared at the Senate hearings, Black devoted special attention to Frederick Rentschler, president of the United Aircraft and Transport Corporation, by far the most successful aviation company in America.

Black began his interrogation mildly enough with an enumeration of United's fourteen associated operations. The Boeing Airplane Company? Yes, that was a United subsidiary. The Boeing Air Transport Company? Yes, that was a United subsidiary. The Sikorsky Aviation Corporation, Pratt & Whitney Aircraft, Chance Vought, Hamilton-Standard, Varney Air Lines, the United Aircraft Airports of Connecticut? Yes, each one was "wholly owned" by United.

Oddly, the senator ignored United Air Lines, one of Rentschler's most imaginative creations, but compensated for the oversight by concentrating on salary. Did United's president earn $431,544 in 1929? Rentschler confirmed that he had paid taxes on that figure but stipulated that only part of it was salary; over $300,000 was a bonus from Pratt & Whitney, and some came from director's fees for other aviation responsibilities. Were Rentschler's total personal earnings from 1929 to 1933 over 1½ million dollars?

When Rentschler admitted that was "about right," Black turned to other matters, content simply to let the numbers sink in—and the Depression-crippled nation react. The next day, the *Hartford Courant* in United's home town headlined its story "Rentschler's Fat Salaries Under Fire," and Senator Shipstead of Minnesota announced "that it was these people who were robbing the American people and ruining business."

Hugo Black agreed; his persistent questions regarding stock transactions revealed that in 1925 Rentschler had helped found the Pratt & Whitney Aircraft Company with a personal investment of $253. Three-and-a-half years later, his stock in the company had a market value of $35 million. Then there was his fancy footwork just before he and William Bocing joined forces in 1929. For a Boeing share that sold at six cents in 1927, Rentschler realized as much as $162 in 1929— a profit of 254,000 percent in less than two years. During the hearings, Black implied again and again that even if Rentschler had broken no laws, he was morally guilty of gouging the American people; legally or illegally, no businessman had a right to that great a return on any investment. Even worse, United's astronomical profits came from federal subsidies of its manufacturing companies, which supplied airplanes for the military, and its transport companies, which carried mail for the Post Office.

Black, who was determined to throw the money changers into the street, intended to impose the stiffest possible penalties. Despite his diligent efforts, however, he found no outright violations of the law— Rentschler was clearly a smart operator, but there was nothing illegal about fulfilling the American dream while one's fellow citizens were struggling to survive.

Ultimately, Frederick Rentschler was punished for the sin of success. Soon after his public condemnation as a profiteer, the United Aircraft and Transport Corporation was forcibly divided into three separate entities; Congress passed a law limiting profits on military contracts to 10 percent; and new postal regulations stipulated that no airline carrying mail for the government could pay even its top executives more than $17,500 per year.[1]

By 1982, almost fifty years later, United Aircraft had become United Technologies. A company that once had specialized in aviation now produced elevators as well as helicopters, computer chips and air conditioners and automobile paint along with jet engines. Soon after joining United in 1971, Harry Gray, as of 1983 its chairman, president, and chief executive officer, earned a reputation as a "takeover artist" and the "grand acquisitor" of corporate America.[2] Over ten years, he had purchased so many businesses— including the Otis Elevator Company; the Carrier Corporation and Essex Industries— that United grew from a company with $2 billion in sales in 1971 to nearly $14 billion in 1982. United Technologies is now the seventh largest manufacturing corporation in America.

Although Harry Gray and Frederick Rentschler are superficially quite different men— one having built a giant aviation corporation from scratch, the other preferring diversification through purchases— the underlying dynamic fueling each is identical: a complex and dramatic love-hate relationship with the federal government. For over sixty years, the primary business of United Technologies has been the imaginative use of federal funds to avoid dependence on federal funds.

From its beginnings as Pratt & Whitney Aircraft in 1925 until the mid-1980s, United has relied on Washington so consistently, if reluctantly, that its history constitutes a feverish run around a vicious circle. The government gives United an order; industrial capacity is created; and the corporation is burdened with that capacity unless the government reorders. The men who have managed the corporation have sought to avoid this dependency through exports, the cultivation of commercial customers and, after 1971, diversification. Still, whenever the going gets tough, tough aviation executives get going — right to Washington.

The government, however, may refuse to help or, especially after 1945, help too much with excessive military business. When United accepts the government's orders to ensure its survival, the vicious circles of dependence increase in size. Substantial new orders mean new capacity, which only aggravates the basic problem. Over the years, the corporation has been forced to run harder and harder to remain on the same endless loop. In the late fifties, economist John Kenneth Galbraith described this as "the dependence effect." Success breeds capacity; if production is to continue, much less increase, it may become necessary to create needs that currently do not exist: two cars in every garage, for example, or more shoes than one can wear, or extra wings of fighter planes.[3]

A company such as United that relies on Congress for ongoing production inevitably confronts the issues that make this story a matter of vital contemporary interest. What exactly constitutes excess profit? United's history reveals a double standard. It is considered acceptable for a private corporation to exploit private sources, but when the same corporation benefits from public contracts, it may risk condemnation.

If a company manufacturers weapons, should its profits be limited more stringently than those of a company providing neutral products? Because arms provoke outrage, United has frequently been subject to exceedingly close federal supervision. Ironically, one of the most vigorous enforcement periods came during the sixties, the worst decade in United's history.

Which comes first— the company's or the nation's interest? During World War II and during the fifties, United helped arm America only after the government reluctantly offered substantial tax breaks. By placing profits ahead of patriotism, were United's executives reprehensible or merely responsible to their stockholders?

If a company is needed, should it be allowed to profit from the public's need? During World War II, United legally earned what Eugene Wilson, then its president, called "unconscionable profits;" some of Sikorsky's best years were at the height of the Vietnam War.

Is the government responsible for the rescue of a private company whose existence is threatened by its own mistakes? Since 1975, the American people have paid half a billion dollars to repair what Air Force generals deemed a "design deficiency" in United's F-100 engine. After all, federal legislation dating back to 1925 implies that Washington is obligated to assist manufacturers essential to the industrial base required for war. But in exchange for its subsidies, what control can the government demand? During 1982, along with over $4 billion worth of prime military contracts, United Technologies received more than half a billion dollars of government money for research and development.

Finally, and most important, what is the appropriate relationship between a private company and the federal government? The United States is stalled at a business crossroads. If we are to compete effectively with nations such as Japan, we must reach a consensus on the role of government in the realm of private enterprise. The story of United Technologies illustrates that unless these issues are finally resolved, the battles between corporations and the government will continue —and America will remain at a disadvantage in commerce and, perhaps, in war.

1

RIGHT COMPANY,
RIGHT PLACE,
RIGHT TIME

"On April 6, 1917, the United States entered the
war. On June 8, 1917, public announcement was
made that a great fleet of 25,000 aeroplanes was
about to be created and would be decisive of the war
months before an effective Army could be put in
Europe."

Senate Committee on Military Affairs,
August 1918

Twenty-Five Thousand Planes

In June of 1917, aviation became—almost overnight—a significant part of the American industrial scene. President Woodrow Wilson called for the nation to produce twenty-five thousand planes in a single year. This was an incredible demand, considering that American planes to that time had been handcrafted by a small band of aviation devotees working in barns and sheds across the American countryside.

In 1913 and 1914 these pioneers built a grand total of 92 airplanes. The figure climbed to 178 in 1915, but despite the enduring magic of the Wright brothers' success at Kitty Hawk in 1903, most Americans still wanted nothing to do with flying. Let the sportsmen—the early birds, as they called themselves—monopolize the air while sensible people kept their feet on the ground, their bodies in one healthy piece.

In dollar terms toy balloons produced more sales than planes, so the early companies were risk ventures in every sense of the term. In Seattle, William Boeing founded the Pacific Aero Products Company in early 1916, but, to provide a "parachute" for his investment, Boeing made sure that the articles of incorporation allowed his company to produce a wide variety of nonaviation products.

The two companies truly in the business of manufacturing "aeroplanes"—Wright-Martin and the Curtiss Airplane and Motor Corporation— had translated their control of patents into orders that had not yet reached a hundred, much less a thousand, planes at a time. In fact, Wright had only merged with the Glenn Martin

Company because a French order for 450 engines overwhelmed it; and even then the combined Wright-Martin effort failed to deliver the goods on time.[1]

In 1916, however, the war in Europe abruptly—and somewhat unrealistically— transformed the American public's perception of what modern warfare involved. Before 1914, nations rarely had mobilized more than 1 percent of their populations; by 1917, the major European powers had placed 10 percent of their men in uniform. Satisfying the huge appetites of these mechanized armies demanded unprecedented control of productive resources, and resulted in measures ranging from rationing to the recruitment of women for factory work to restrictions of pub hours in England.

But it was the advent of new military technology and the obvious need for enormous quantities of the most advanced weaponry that most impressed American observers. When the war began, for example, reconnaissance pilots protected themselves with shotguns and, later, machine guns. In mid-1915, the Dutch airplane designer Fokker developed a gear that allowed a machine gun to fire through a revolving propeller, thereby lending the Germans an instant edge— until the Allies discovered the device on a captured plane and subsequently used it themselves.

American patriotic groups such as the National Security League and the Aero Club lobbied vigorously for equivalent technological progress at home. Although aircraft production ranked low among military priorities, air-power advocates felt confident that Europe's experience would work to America's advantage in the event of war. The nation would need planes, and even a small slice of the military appropriations pie would mean unheard-of business for the infant aircraft industry.[2]

But whatever happened, Edward Deeds— the financial godfather of what was to become the United Technologies Corporation— was poised to take advantage of the business opportunities that might develop.

As a founder of the National Cash Register and Delco (Dayton Engineering Laboratories) corporations, Deeds was among Ohio's most prominent and controversial businessmen. In 1912, after he had been sentenced to one year in jail "for bribery and criminal methods in driving competitors out of the cash register business," the Circuit Court of Appeals set aside the conviction on technical grounds. Deeds was free to operate, and add to, his diverse business holdings. In April of 1915, in partnership with Charles Kettering and the father-son team of Harold Talbott Sr. and Jr., he established the Dayton Metal Products Company to supply war-torn Europe with munitions equipment.

Dayton Metals was soon making fuses for the British government and, as America prepared for war, the Army and Navy. In short order, the new firm was seeking investment opportunities for its surplus cash. Deeds did not look far: Dayton was also home to the Wright brothers. Although Wilbur had died and their original company had been sold, Orville had formed a second operation to pursue his own interests. Dayton Metals purchased this second Wright Airplane Company to exploit the Allies' potential need for aircraft— and the government contracts sure to come if America went to war.[3]

On April 9, 1917, three days after America declared war on Germany, Edward Deeds and his associates incorporated the Dayton-Wright Airplane Company. The prospects for plane manufacturers looked quite promising because the Army had already asked for fifty million aviation dollars and the Army's fierce competitor, the Navy, also had its eye on large airplane appropriations. The $50 million was itself three times the Army's total expenditure (up to 1917) on planes.

By April 12, the military's projected aviation budget had skyrocketed to $300 million. According to President Wilson's Council of National Defense, three years of war lay ahead. The "maximum attainable capacity" projected for the aviation industry was thirty-seven hundred planes in 1918, six thousand by 1919, and nine thousand by 1920. The figures were astonishing, but enthusiastic Americans suspended rational judgment. Preparations for an air armada proceeded at a feverish pace.[4]

Edward Deeds was delighted to be of assistance. At the government's request, he had been functioning as an industrial advisor since early 1917. Directly after the declaration of war, he sold Washington the acreage (some of it swampland) for the huge, new Wilbur Wright airfield in Dayton, Ohio. He even introduced the builder of the new facilities to Army procurement officials.

By May, Deeds was formally a member of the government's Aircraft Production Board. Once again he was glad to assist when

French Premier Ribot cabled an unexpected request for twenty-five thousand airplanes and thirty thousand engines, insisting that American compliance "would allow the Allies to win the supremacy of the air."

Although in normal times such an outrageous request might have provoked laughter, in June of 1917 it produced a public relations campaign. Addressing newspaper editors at a briefing luncheon, Howard Coffin, head of the Aircraft Production Board and vice president of the Hudson Motor Company, said, "The future history of the world's nations may be influenced by your action... The sea may be mined and netted and the submarine lurks in its depths. But the highways of the air are free lanes, unconquered as yet by any nation. America's great opportunity lies before her. The road to Berlin lies though the air. The eagle must end this war."

As if invocations of partiotism were not enough, the editors also received practical assurances from another board member. Edward Deeds, who was now overseeing the procurement of equipment, told the audience that "if we start immediately we can put 10,000 aviators on the French front by this time next year and win the war. We are convinced of this. If we can put through the program as provided in the bill soon to be introduced to Congress, we will get there next spring to win the war."[5]

Along with their lunch, the editors ate up these prophecies of production miracles and military victory. In a June 10 editorial, *The New York Times* assured its readers that the planes "can be rapidly built. We have the aviation fields and the hangars. We have the men. Money is all that is lacking." The *Times* suggested an immediate appropriation of half a billion dollars, with another half billion to follow. Forty thousand planes were needed at once "to enable the American air service in France to put this country foremost in a branch of warfare in which it should be supreme."[6]

Between June 10 and July 23, the *Times* printed thirteen similar appeals. The combined support of the newspapers and advocates in Congress resulted in the largest appropriation ever passed for a single purpose. To the $50 million already budgeted in May and July, on August 12, 1917, Congress added — without amendments and without a roll-call vote— $640 million for over twenty-five thousand planes. Now all the fledgling aviation industry had to do was produce, in twelve months, twenty-five more planes than America's total production up to 1917.

Flaming Coffins

By September, Mr. Edward Deeds had been commissioned as Colonel Deeds to expedite the implementation of his orders. One of the colonel's first assignments upon accepting his commission was to oversee orders for the Dayton-Wright Airplane Company, which that month signed a cost-plus contract for four thousand British-designed de Havilands at nearly $30 million. Total fixed profits came to almost $4 million but, because actual costs had yet to be determined, another $2½ million was available. Dayton's contract set a "bogey cost" of $7,000 per plane; if production expenses were less (and in fact they were $2,600 less), the manufacturer would keep 25 percent of the difference. In theory, the bogey was a sensible idea; in practice, it permitted the aviation industry to exceed the 12½ percent fixed profit considered adequate by the government.

With its first contracts signed, Dayton-Wright still lacked both a factory and the capital with which to build or buy one. To remedy this situation, Deeds and his colleaque Charles Kettering decided to sell to Dayton-Wright a plant that the Domestic Building Company, which they co-owned, was building for Delco. To permit Deeds to stay in the background, a syndicate composed of Kettering and the Talbotts bought the plant for *unsecured* notes of nearly $700,000, then traded it with Dayton-Wright for $1 million worth of its capital stock. The first two transactions neatly cancelled each other out.

Meanwhile, the syndicate sold the Dayton-Wright stock to the Dayton Metal Products Company, another property of Deeds and Kettering, in exchange for a set of securities that Dayton Metal Products sold to the syndicate. By the end of this ingenious series of deals, in which less than fifteen hundred dollars actually changed hands, Dayton Metals held all of Dayton-Wright's stock; and now that Washington had agreed to advance over $2 million to tool up the Dayton-Wright plant, Deeds and Kettering were in even better financial shape.[7]

When plane construction finally began, hasty and ill-advised decisions led to delay and disaster throughout the aircraft industry. The few de Havilands that reached Europe were built so poorly that many officers refused to permit Americans to fly them. For one thing, the conspicuously placed fuel tank offered such an inviting target to enemy gunners that pilots labeled the planes "flaming coffins"— a man got in but he rarely got out. The SJ-1 training planes, some four hundred of which were produced at Dayton-Wright, were condemned soon after delivery because the plane and its incompatible engine proved to be a lethal combination. Thousands of the Bristol fighters made by the Curtiss Airplane and Motor Corporation were condemned even before they were delivered. Along with faulty construction, a major problem was the Liberty engine, which had been partially designed by Edward Deeds and which was to have a profound effect on the development of the Pratt & Whitney Aircraft Company.

When the United States declared war in April of 1917, it possessed no engines suitable for military service. American officials rejected European models, which promised more problems than benefits; inevitable delays in transporting designs and samples would render them obsolete before they reached the Western front. The Allies' manufacturing methods, moreover, differed considerably from those employed in America; adapting new means of production would incur further delay. To speed production, Deeds decided to help the Packard Motor Company redesign the promising power plant it had exhibited at a New York aeronautical show in January. By July, Packard's prototype Liberty engine was ready for testing, and in September Deeds placed orders for over fifteen thousand Liberties on the government's behalf, only six thousand of which were to come from Packard.

Because the aircraft manufacturers were unable to cope with such massive demands, the colonel mobilized the automobile industry. In November and December, Ford and General Motors received substantial orders. But the first— and most controversial— order went to a brand-new company, Lincoln Motors, that had been established specifically to build the Liberty. On August 31, Edward Deeds had put in an order for six thousand engines despite the fact that his Dayton Metal Products owned $100,000 worth of Lincoln's stock. What's more, he mandated use of the Delco ignition system on the first twenty thousand Liberties produced— by transferring his Delco stock to his wife's name, he eliminated any conflict of interest.[8]

Or so the colonel thought. The other contractors, snubbed by the "Dayton-Detroit Gang" and willing to air their grievances, violently disagreed. By early 1918 the heat grew so intense that

Deeds resigned as the chief procurer of America's aviation equipment. Nevertheless, the controversy did not subside. Despite the Liberty's fancy financing, it actually was a reliable engine; the problem was that neither Deeds nor his colleagues had determined whether it meshed with European-designed airframes. On the de Haviland planes, the powerful but heavy Liberty greatly impeded maneuverability. As war ace Eddie Rickenbacher later told a congressional committee investigating aircraft production, ". . . During one brief flight over Grand Pre I saw three of these crude machines go down in flames, an American pilot and an American gunner in each flaming coffin dying this frightful and needless death."[9]

Along with the deaths, America was shocked by Colonel Deeds' flagrant failure to deliver the goods. By July 1, 1918, American aviators were so restless with nothing to fly that Washington purchased over 500 planes from the Allies. By the time the Army developed a workable system for transporting its planes to the Western front, the war was over. All told, the United States spent over half a billion dollars for 13,991 military aircraft. All told, 213 flaming coffins made it to Europe.

The scandal swept across the country with such force that Woodrow Wilson felt obligated to appoint a special presidential commission to investigate all aspects of aircraft production. Headed by Charles Evans Hughes, Wilson's Republican opponent for the presidency in 1916, the commission interviewed hundreds of witnesses, visited all major plants, and scrutinized the account books of the prime contractors. The evidence was overwhelmingly negative. Hughes cited "defective organization of the work," "serious lack of competent direction of the work," and "delays and waste" at all levels. As for Edward Deeds, his conduct was of such "a reprehensible character" that "there were certain acts shown, not only highly improper in themselves but of especial significance, which should lead to disciplinary measures."[10]

With no legal basis for action against Deeds, Hughes recommended a court martial; Attorney General Thomas Watt concurred. In late 1918 it looked as if the notorious Deeds actually might stand trial— until Secretary of War Newton Baker intervened. In an unprecedented move, Baker, an Ohioan like Deeds and the press's scapegoat for aviation's failures, asked the Judge Advocate General to hear other witnesses on Deeds' behalf. Not only was this request granted but a new report exonerating Deeds was quickly issued, and

General Squier, head of Army aviation, hosted a Washington banquet in praise of the colonel's achievements. As the Army now saw it, Deeds was a public-spirited American who had voluntarily sacrificed money and position to serve the nation— and instead of vilifying him, the country should thank him.[11]

Despite the colonel's patriotism, the nation now owned nearly fourteen thousand brand-new planes and more than twelve thousand high-powered Liberty engines for which it had no use. Supply greatly exceeded any conceivable demand and, to make matters worse, Washington immediately cancelled all war contracts when peace was declared in November of 1918. Some aviation firms closed their doors; others struggled desperately to survive. In Seattle, William Boeing, grateful he had anticipated nonaviation products, turned to furniture and sea sleds while waiting out the bad times. In New Jersey, the Wright-Martin Company was purchased by Mack Truck, renamed the Wright Aeronautical Corporation, and put to work at reduced levels of operation to fill the Navy's need for medium-sized engines for its smaller planes.

America's aviation industry was paralyzed by the peace. Congress was unlikely to fund new planes with fourteen thousand surplus on hand. The commercial prospects, too, appeared dismal until the government found at least one peaceful use for aircraft. To supply the new air mail service, established in May of 1918, Washington slowly began selling the ships to itself. By giving its planes to the Post Office at cost, the War Department laid the groundwork for a system that was to prove essential to the profitability of American aviation— and, ultimately, to the profitability of what was to become United Technologies.

Air Mail Tries to Take Off

From the outset, the United States Air Mail— and the aviation industry— encountered several seemingly insurmountable problems. To provide reliable service and establish a commercial market for planes it was necessary to furnish sturdy aircraft, decent airports, workable communications systems, and a network of beacons to allow night flyers, many of whom had already experienced crashes, to determine where they were going. In the meantime, the air service offered few advantages over trains. Congress therefore kept appropriations low, which compelled the Post Office to purchase the huge overstock of flimsy war-surplus planes. Thus, the surviving firms of the aircraft industry were deprived of the only apparent customer for an improved peacetime product.

Postal officials traveled (by train) all over the country trying to cajole, bargain with or, if worse came to worst, threaten cities into building airports. Although appropriations were low in 1921 to 1923, officials hinted that the Post Office eventually would reimburse municipalities that helped provide the necessary facilities. Lying to the one city about the activities of its neighbors and vice versa, they promised prestige as well as profits.[12]

Air fields slowly began to dot the land, but pilots literally flew in the dark. Without lights to guide them to emergency fields, they often abandoned ship wherever they could. On one memorable air mail flight, Charles Lindbergh took off from St. Louis, bound for Peoria. When a haze settled in near Springfield and his stock of flares failed to help him locate a landing field, the pilot "dove over the left side of the cockpit while the airspeed registered above 70 miles an hour and the altimeter 13,000 feet." Luckily for Lindbergh, his parachute functioned perfectly, but "the last I saw of the de Haviland was as it disappeared into the clouds . . ." (The next day he found it close to a farmhouse.)[13]

Because such crashes instilled little public confidence in the air mail or in airplanes, postal officials used $500,000 of federal funds to establish emergency landing fields every 20 miles across the country. Each field was equipped with a revolving light atop a windmill tower so that pilots would always have a safe landing place in reasonable range. Standard "airport" fields, placed at 250-mile intervals, contained boundary lights that flooded the landing strips with as much illumination as possible.

By 1924, enough lighted fields existed to initiate regular night flights across most of the continent. The Post Office's success impressed Representative Clyde Kelly of Pennsylvania so much that, in response to railway mail clerks' anger over heavy air-mail subsidies, he suggested a bill authorizing the relinquishment of mail routes to private carriers. Assistant Postmaster Paul Henderson recommended that Kelly wait one more year, until lighted airfields covered the entire nation. At that point, the Post Office could quell any skepticism that its six years of hard work had resulted in neither a profitable service nor a reliable source of business for the aircraft manufacturers.

Congressman Kelly complied. But for an air industry drowning in red ink, patience felt like penance; in 1923, they produced only fifty-six commercial ships, and sixty in 1924.[14]

In addition to footdragging by the Post Office, the fact that no other lucrative peacetime market for airplanes had materialized nearly bankrupted the industry. Except for soldiers and stunt fliers, nobody wanted to fly. Manufacturers blamed Washington for refusing to regulate air traffic to eliminate the chaos in America's skies and soothe the fears of potential passengers. For years the War Department had kept the best planes for itself and the Post Office had sold defective aircraft to unlicensed amateur pilots. Throughout the early 1920s, newspapers routinely reported items such as the following:

Red Bank, New Jersey, January 15, 1922. Pilot utilizes ice-covered Shrewsbury River as landing field. Plane plows into crowd of ice skaters, killing woman, maiming man and knocking down a score of other spectators.

Jackson, Michigan, September 10, 1922. Air tourists, incorrectly informed as to landing field, crash plane on house, knocking off chimney and putting hole in roof.

Grand Rapids, Michigan, April 29, 1923. Pedestrian walks into propeller of plane being warmed up in city alley.

Media, Pennsylvania, June 30, 1923. Controls of government-surplus plane do not respond. Pilot, to miss crowd, lands in side wind and crashes.

New York, New York, August 5, 1923. War-type machine crashes. Four people injured.[15]

Although Congress patiently listened to the pleas of air-safety advocates for effective regulation, each year legislators sat on the bills that were introduced, and each year aviators continued to kill themselves and innocent victims. When Congress finally acted, the impetus came neither from concern for the public nor for the air mails. It came from national defense. The last straw was Army Air Corps General Billy Mitchell's open accusation of Admiral Billy

Moffett, chief of the Navy's Bureau of Aeronautics, of "treasonable neglect" of American aviation.

War Between (and in) the Army and the Navy

From the vantage point of the 1980s, early aviation seems like high adventure— double-winged planes, open cockpits, dashing aviators in white silk scarves executing daring stunts in equipment held together with wire; but in the 1920s, aviation spelled competition for the Army and the Navy. Pilots were the butt of jokes and were discriminated against by the military establishment— especially after pilots had the audacity to publicly proclaim the vulnerability of infantry and ships to air attacks and to suggest that fliers could destroy cities from the air.

As if the aviators' longstanding battles within the services were not enough, the Army's air arm objected to the Navy's air arm. Agreed, sailors might use up some of the surplus planes stifling new development but, far more important to the Army, naval aviation forced a sharing of the small amounts Congress appropriated for new airplanes. Moreover, the ultimate aim of many Army air officers was an independent air force, which seemed far less likely if the Navy had its own planes.

The Navy had established a Bureau of Aeronautics in August of 1921 under Admiral William Moffett. The crafty admiral offered a ready list of reasons to support a Navy air arm, including the preservation of what he called the "friendly competition" between the services, each of which had its own special needs. In the long run America would benefit from the developments each service separately sponsored; progress would be hampered by an Army monopoly on military aviation. What's more, regulations stated that "the Navy shall control all shipping, including convoys, communcations, sea lanes, and scouting." In coveting reconnaissance missions, the Army was treading on Navy turf. If Congress gave the Army the job, the unity of command necessary for effective coordination would be irreparably damaged— imagine the services arguing about who was in charge when a coastal city was threatened with enemy attack.

Given all that, Moffett still had one more card to play. "Naval aviation is an integral part of the fleet," he insisted to any reporter willing to listen. "Naval aircraft must go to sea on the backs of the fleet." To do that, aviators required precise training in the basic principles of naval warfare and naval tactics. And to take aviation to sea, the Navy needed special planes designed for use on water, where runways were nonexistent and big bombers useless.[16]

Although Moffett was an able politician, his arguments neither diminished the fierce competition between America's air arms nor got the Navy the special planes necessary to solve its aviation problems. On twenties ships, space was at a premium. The bigger the plane, the fewer could fit on any Navy ship — and the less likely they would be to get into the air. In 1919 maneuvers, the Navy had mounted a 60-foot run on top of a battleship's forward gun turrets. If it was pointed into the wind, a small plane with the most powerful engine then available could barely gain flying speed by taxiing to the tip of the platform, diving clear of the ship, and climbing just before it slammed into the ocean.[17]

Sometimes the planes did hit the water, so catapults were devised as a alternative to shoot the plane into the sky. Despite protests from ship's officers that these big compressed air guns shed grease over the teak decks, they did yeoman's work while the Navy awaited carriers that would actually let aviators go to sea on the backs of the fleet— but even then, space would be an issue because the planned carriers would be reconverted battle cruisers. They would give pilots a runway, but for the foreseeable future the Navy's best weapon against the Army could only be a small, light, powerful plane. While designs for an appropriate plane existed in many shapes and forms, all were burdened with at least one supposedly insurmountable problem: heavy water-cooled engines. Adding horsepower (radiators, plumbing, pumps) meant extra weight, which in turn increased the size of the airframe and made a light, powerful plane impossible.

Hope came, however, with the concept of an air-cooled engine. With the plumbing and water eliminated, a power plant weighed in at an acceptable level, and a body could easily be designed around it. Although the Army (and the government research facilities it owned) offered some help, its principal experience was with the thousands of liquid-cooled Liberties. In desperation, Admiral Moffett turned to private enterprise— and strong arm tactics.

Because the Navy was clearly the most promising source of

potential business for the postwar engine industry, almost singlehandedly, Moffett was in a position to call the shots. When the Lawrence J— a small but promising 200 horsepower air-cooled engine— appeared, he authorized a second try after it failed Navy qualification tests. And if Lawrence was given a production contract even before the second exam, that too was acceptable.

Although the Lawrence Aero-Engine Corporation eventually produced fifty acceptable engines, Moffett was reluctant to bet his and the Navy's aviation future on one small company. When he approached Wright Aeronautical its president, Frederick Rentschler, explained that Wright's research focused on the bigger power plants and that profits came from a 200 horsepower liquid-cooled engine. In mid-1922, the firm had neither the time nor the personnel required to produce another engine.

Moffett, who refused to take no for an answer, threatened never to buy another liquid-cooled power plant. In fact, instead of obtaining spare parts from Wright, the Navy would cannibalize its existing engines.

Aside from an Army contract that carried it through 1922, Wright had no big orders on its books. Rentschler either accepted the admiral's "proposal"— which now had escalated to include provisions for an outright purchase of Lawrence by Wright— or he went out of business.

Wright bought Lawrence for half a million dollars in mid-1923, a merger that eventually fostered some solid technical developments: The Whirlwind, an altered version of the Lawrence J engine, propelled Lindbergh across the Atlantic. But with Wright as its main source of supply for air-cooled engines, the Navy had its back to the wall. When Commander Eugene Wilson, the new chief of the Navy's Bureau of Aeronautics Engine Section, first met Rentschler in June of 1924, he pressed for progress on a 400 horsepower air-cooled engine to power the planes on the new "aircraft carriers" about to enter service.

After politely displaying the larger engine then under development, Rentschler uttered heresy: he suggested a new liquid-cooled engine. Considering the dependence on Wright, the Navy had brought upon itself, it now had to accept the company's timetable for the air-cooled model and to swallow its anxiety when Rentschler resigned Wright's presidency soon after meeting with Wilson because the Wright board of directors refused to fund sufficient basic research to suit him. What's more, the board saw even less reason than Rentschler to speed the development of a large air-cooled engine for the Navy.[18]

It seemed as if the Navy was spinning its wheels, and Army General Billy Mitchell also was thoroughly frustrated. Military aviation was a mission, with Mitchell its self-proclaimed prophet. If Congress and his superiors wouldn't approve a well-funded, independent air force, then Billy Mitchell would take his case to the American people.

Billy Mitchell and Calvin Coolidge

Asked to deal less controversially with Army old-timers, General Billy Mitchell smiled and said, "When senior officers won't see the facts, you've got to do something unorthodox, perhaps an explosion."

The general liked explosions. To demonstrate to his implacable colleagues and to the public his belief that air power could singlehandedly win the next war, he published an article as early as March of 1921 detailing the devastation aerial bombing could achieve. Four months later he followed up with a mock bombing of New York City, during which a fleet of seventeen planes theoretically "dropped 21 tons of gas, flame and fragmentation bombs over the lower city." According to officers, effects were felt as far as Time Square, and "those of the inhabitants who survived the bombs' deadly effects were scurrying toward Yonkers."

After Mitchell requested that reporters tell the American people how he had paralyzed New York, *The New York Times* obediently headlined its story "City Wiped Out in Big War Game," and *The Herald* wrote, "City in Theoretical Ruins from Air Raid. Survivors Flee Stricken Island Seeking Shelter in the Country. General Mitchell Says So."[19]

The general's superiors, to prevent him from saying so again, ordered him to publish nothing without the explicit permission of Secretary of War John Weeks. And though Mitchell tried to curb controversy in order to retain his command, by late 1924 he was as desperate as his rival Billy Moffett: he wanted change, and he wanted it yesterday. When the *Saturday Evening Post* asked him to publish a series of five articles on *"The Air Force and Air Power"* Mitchell agreed— if President Coolidge gave permission.

During the subsequent meeting, Coolidge reaffirmed his interest in aeronautics. If General Patrick, Mitchell's boss, agreed, Coolidge would approve the articles. Patrick, when informed by Mitchell that the president had said yes, quickly seconded the authorization. Secretary of War Weeks had not been consulted, and Mitchell had neglected to tell Patrick about a letter from Coolidge qualifying his approval with this comment: "I cannot speak for your superior officers. The matter should be taken up with them and their decision in relation to the articles followed."

To compound Weeks's rage at the predictably controversial articles, Mitchell told Congress in early 1925 that the organization of American aviation was "fundamentally wrong" and that the Navy was concealing information about the vulnerability of its ships to air attack. In Mitchell's opinion, the Navy should be closely questioned about its attempt to deceive the American people.

Secretary Weeks, who finally had had enough of Mitchell's "explosions," announced that the general would not be reappointed second in command of the Army's air service. He would be banished to an unimportant post in Texas and would also be demoted to colonel. Short of court martial, Weeks had taken every disciplinary step he could.

Mitchell nevertheless refused to keep quiet. Without asking the department's permission he published the *Post* articles as a book, "Winged Defense," then publicly announced that battleships were obsolete: "What is keeping them up as much as anything else, and largely preventing open and free discussion of their uses, are the propaganda agencies maintained by the navies . . ."[20]

Despite Weeks's renewed fury, Mitchell did have a valid point about the Navy and its incessant combat with the Army. As Eugene Wilson later admitted, "During the Mitchell controversy, the Navy Bureau of Aeronautics ceased to function as a material bureau to become a propaganda agency."[21] To counter the general's criticisms, for example, Admiral Moffett sent the dirigible Shenandoah on a series of "public relations" flights scheduled to coincide with county fairs all over the West. The scheduled flights also coincided with thunderstorm predictions. But to confess a weakness in lighter-then-air craft, Moffett's pet project, was to retard their development and, not incidentally, to support the convictions of Billy Mitchell.

When the Shenandoah crashed on September 3, 1925, eighteen men lost their lives. From his Texas exile, Billy Mitchell issued the charges that finally moved President Coolidge and Congress to take notice. The Navy, the now-colonel complained, was guilty of "treasonable neglect," and the Shenandoah presented a grisly illustration of what that neglect could produce.

All summer Calvin Coolidge had hesitated, ignoring pleas from industry representatives to appoint a presidential commission to analyze air power. Coolidge had not wanted to feed the controversy created by Mitchell but, with eighteen men dead, he had no choice. Within two weeks of the Shenandoah tragedy Dwight Morrow, a well-known Wall Street financier and friend of the President, had been appointed chairman of a committee whose single task was "to make a study of the best means of developing and applying aircraft in national defense."[22]

Coolidge demanded quick results: because the long and bitter battle between the Army and Navy had undermined public confidence in the military services, the sooner America established a definitive aviation policy the better it would be for all concerned.

In Hartford, Connecticut, the trio of businessmen— Frederick Rentschler, engineer George Mead, and Edward Deeds— who had incorporated Pratt & Whitney Aircraft two months previously heartily applauded the president's call to action. If the Morrow Board actually were to sanction a forward-looking policy, they would possess a priceless guarantee denied to their industry predecessors: primarily because of Billy Mitchell's criticisms, the Navy would finally have sufficient funds to buy their wares.

Of course, the Morrow Board had yet to formally approve a long-range spending program, and Pratt & Whitney Aircraft had yet to produce an engine; but if and when if did, it would be the right company, at the right time, in the right place.

2

A NEW FIRM: PRATT, WHITNEY, RENTSCHLER, AND MEAD

"I longed to do something new and on my own account."

Frederick Rentschler, 1925

"This was, for us, the opportunity of a lifetime. . . . No one but a craven fool would pass up such a golden opportunity to. . . give aviation the real shot in the arm it needed, and for which the time was right."

Mrs. George Mead, *Wings Over the World*

When Calvin Coolidge established the Morrow Board in September of 1925, he hoped to finally end the wars between and within America's army and navy by putting the power and prestige of his office behind one comprehensive aviation policy.

That was good news for the industry— and great news for Frederick Rentschler and George Mead, who had established their engine business two months previously. Although they would have preferred waiting until the government's policy was in place, the Navy demanded a new engine at once, and they were reluctant to risk losing their only sure customer for the revolutionary power plant they were about to introduce.

The two men bet their futures on Admiral Moffet's promises of engine orders, but they did it with other people's money. Backed by the influential Colonel Deeds, they convinced the Pratt & Whitney machine-tool company of Hartford, Connecticut, to fund the manufacture of George Mead's newly invented engine. Years later Rentschler would explain that they had chosen Hartford because of its local pool of trained mechanical talent; in fact, they chose Hartford because Pratt & Whitney had acres of unused space filled with scores of idling machines.

The Two Pratt & Whitneys

In 1925, Pratt & Whitney was an established firm experienced in the manufacture of weapons. Founded in 1860 by Francis Pratt and Amos Whitney (a cousin of Eli's), it owed its existence to Sam Colt and the Civil War.

Pratt & Whitney met while working at Sam Colt's Hartford pistol factory. In the 1850s six-shooters made six-figure profits, and Colt's success attracted ambitious tool workers who came to be trained, then left to start their own businesses.

When fire destroyed Pratt & Whitney's first shop in 1861, they set up another small operation. Their many innovations in machine tools enabled them to quickly produce so many accurate guns for the Union Army that throughout the Civil War their business prospered; by 1865, the firm moved into a larger three-story factory on Hartford's Capitol Avenue.

Even after the war, orders kept coming. But to boost sales, Pratt & Whitney took their American ingenuity to other nations and other continents. In 1870 they signed contracts to stock three complete arsenals for the Imperial German government. As its reputation for quality spread, the firm eventually got orders for tools or arsenals from Russia, Canada, Chile, Italy, Spain, and Greece. As Pratt, the firm's salesman, explained, "The world was the company's field, and it was only necessary to seek business in a liberal and intelligent way to secure it every time in the open market."

In 1901, its global success prompted an offer to buy Pratt & Whitney. Though they might have rejected such a bid twenty years before, Pratt at seventy-four and Whitney at sixty-nine agreed to sell their company to Ohio-based Niles Bement Pond, at that time "the largest and most aggressive machine tool manufacturing and sales organization in the world." Niles' instructions to Pratt & Whitney were direct: focus all efforts on machine tools, cutting tools, and gauges. Let others make weapons— the company's only job was to stock armories and factories with as many machine tools as a customer desired.

Pratt & Whitney followed orders and prospered under Nile's rule. When America entered World War I, the Capitol Avenue facilities were expanded to expedite rapid construction of new armories. By producing the tools that made the nation's cannons, Pratt & Whitney successfully laid the mechanical groundwork for war. As with aviation, however, peace caused problems. Directly after the Armistice, Washington cancelled all contracts.[1]

Because it was competing unsuccessfully with its own war-surplus tools, Pratt & Whitney took the only sensible course: it shut down its machines and used this dormant period to redesign and revise its offerings. The only way to find new business, Pratt & Whitney executives argued with the Pond board, was to manufacturer products far superior to those already stocking the nation's armories and factories. At the same time, to generate revenue from now-idle space, the company rented out large portion of its facilities to the Connecticut Valley cigar industry. By 1925, the factory bulged with tobacco leaves; peace had reduced parts of Pratt & Whitney to a storehouse for tomorrow's stogies.[2]

Enter Frederick Rentschler, who was pondering his future after his resignation from Wright in 1924. He was thirty-seven, unemployed, extremely ambitious, and intent upon avoiding his family's foundry in Hamilton, Ohio.

Rentschler had had enough of that as a young man. For eight years later his graduation from Princeton, he had dutifully labored at Hooven, Owens, Rentschler Company. When the war beckoned, he enlisted in the Army and used his experience with tools to inspect airplane engines at the Wright-Martin Aircraft Co. in New Brunswick, New Jersey. Away from Ohio and on his own, he enjoyed the work immensely. During the firm's reorganization after the Artistice, the young man assumed the vice presidency with the promise of the top job if he managed day-to-day operations successfully. Although Rentschler's management prowess soon earned him the presidency, his achievements did not save him from constant battles with Wright's board of directors. In his opinion, these men knew nothing about aviation, nor did they care to learn. They were merely investment bankers focusing on the bottom line.[3]

Rentschler's eye was on the same place, but he was rebuffed when he tried to explain that big money would come only in time and through years of expensive research and development efforts. Even then there was no assurance of profit. Even if a new engine or plane was not, like the wartime de Havilands, a dud, new goods sold only if they were technically superior to their predecessors. If you didn't invest in research and development, you watched people flying products that worked too well and lasted too long to provide continuing business to a producer. (As late as 1963, the Air Force cancelled a multimillion-dollar contract with Pratt & Whitney for 136 new engines because those in the B-52 bomber had lasted much longer than expected.)

For a while Rentschler actually considered returning to the family business. His father had died in 1924, and his older brother

Gordon was about to leave Ohio for a vice presidency at Manhattan's National City Bank. If nothing else, heading up the foundry promised security, prestige and wealth at a much lower risk.

By January 1 of 1925, however, Rentschler had detemined that he would be happy only if he continued in aviation. His problem was how. To start a new firm, he needed at least a quarter of a million dollars. He had no intention of turning to investment bankers, with whose money went control the company. Another potential source was the federal government— The Navy funded research and development of engines at Wright; perhaps they would do the same for Rentschler.

Admiral Moffet said no. Whereas Wright was a going concern with years of experience and many proven engines, Rentschler's aviation company was only a vision. But if Rentschler did somehow manage to develop a powerful air-cooled engine, Moffett could guarantee— at least verbally— that the Navy would buy it in volume and underwrite initial research and development by setting aside ninety thousand dollars for the purchase of six experimental engines. To sweeten these promises, the admiral assured Rentschler that, when the production contract was drawn up, the price of the engine would be high enough to amortize the entire cost of development.[4]

Rentschler thereupon consulted the two men who eventually made his dream a reality: Edward Deeds, an old friend of his father's and chairman of the board of Niles Bement Pond, and George Mead. Then chief of engineering at Wright Aeronautical, Mead had a well-deserved reputation for excellence and originality. Since his graduation from MIT in 1915, he had excelled at the Wright-Martin Corp. He previously had managed the power-plant laboratories of the Army Air Services in Dayton and had left, at Rentschler's urging, to take over Wright's engineering in 1920. Mead's experience with air-cooled engines was virtually unsurpassed; he was eager to join Rentschler in a new venture; and he already had a vital contribution to make: an original design for a large radial air-cooled engine.[5]

Edward Deeds, meanwhile, was well aware of Pratt & Whitney's idle capacity and large surplus of wartime profits. Given the saturated market for machine tools, he endorsed that company's desire to invest in an industry that promised real growth. After the three men solidified their ideas in a series of meetings, the colonel enlisted the aid of Niles Bement Pond's board of directors in producing George Mead's engine. Because Rentschler's brother Gordon was a board member and the corporation's president, James Cullen, was another close Rentschler family friend, Deeds had little trouble. Nevertheless, without the colonel's power and prestige behind him, Rentschler might have taken that dreaded trip back to Ohio.[6]

Instead, he went to Hartford to explain to Pratt & Whitney executives the Navy's desperate need for an air-cooled engine and to stress his assurances from Admiral Moffett. Moreover, he indicated that his small staff would be composed of the very best people from the Wright Aeronautical Corp. Soon only a skeleton would remain in New Jersey, offering feeble competition to Rentschler's new enterprise.

Rentschler's minimum financial requirement from Pratt & Whitney was $250,000. If the new engine proved itself, another half million dollars would be necessary for the first production run, but with orders then on hand, that money would never be at risk. The real gamble lay with the development funds. Despite the Navy's agreement to reimburse the company for those costs, the money would come through only if George Mead's engine did. (This was, after all, 1925. In 1981 United Technologies received, up front, nearly half a billion dollars from Washington for research and development.)[7]

Rentschler's proposal was approved within a matter of days, and by mid-July a brand-new company, Pratt & Whitney Aircraft, was incorporated in Delaware. "The arrangement simply was that Pratt & Whitney had the money," Rentschler recollected years later. "We though, we had the experience, and our business deal with them was that they would only have half of the common stock of the company; half was ours. It was their obligation to put up the money and ours to run the company."[8]

Rentschler had the control he wanted. The machine-tool company agreed to an initial advance of $250,000 for development, for which they would receive 7 percent interest on their capital. If the engine succeeded, Pratt & Whitney Aircraft would issue preferred stock "for all cash advances, materials and machinery and equipment theretofore furnished. . ." Other than that, Rentschler was home free. Although 50 percent of the common stock did rest with the tool company, he and Mead held the other 50 percent. For a total investment of five hundred dollars (Rentschler's 1,375 shares of stock at twenty cents per share and Mead's 1,125), the two men had the chance of a lifetime. And four years later, when their stock had a street value of nearly $60 million, Frederick Rentschler and George Mead had succeeded far beyond their wildest expectations.[9]

The Beehive

By early August, Pratt & Whitney Aircraft had displaced the tobacco farmers in the tool company's Capitol Avenue factory. An area the size of a tennis court became a beehive of activity for Mead, his able engineering assistant Andrew Wilgoos, and the eight or nine others who composed the company's first payroll.

Their shop was spartan at best. Walking through the halls that led to the "factory," the workers marched single file or else brushed against the tobacco stored through and over and under the wire partitions. But despite the crowded conditions, no one seemed to mind. These men, who had worked together for years, had the greatest respect and admiration for one another's skills. For a short period of time, the overwhelming desire to complete this one job dominated their lives. Naturally each sought personal gain from his labors, but camaraderie, dedication, and enthusiasm characterized these early months.[10]

Rentschler and Mead conscientiously informed the Navy of their progress. A month before Pratt & Whitney's incorporation, Mead and Eugene Wilson, the head of the Bureau of Aeronautics' Engine Section, already had discussed the engine's design, and from then on Rentschler visited the bureau as often as possible. Some of this was pure politics; with only one customer, the merchant was obliged to stroke those issuing the orders. But Rentschler also needed the Navy's approval of Mead's engine and hoped to check— and, with luck, to control— the design changes the Navy inevitably mandated.

Fortunately Rentschler, Mead, and Wilson hit it off, and their friendship fostered agreement on the details of the engine. Problems over the power plant were indeed minimal. The trouble came from an Army committed to liquid-cooled engines.

After years spent flying Colonel Deeds' Liberty, Army pilots strenuously resisted a power-plant revolution. Rentschler learned the strength of Army lobbyists in early October of 1925, when Wilson called to announced the Morrow Board's threat to recommend unified procurement of supply and design. If the Army were to control who bought what, all bets on air-cooled engine contracts were off; with Congress about to assign procurement to a new agency, Admiral Moffett would be reluctant to sign an order for hundreds of engines. In essence, Wilson suggested that Rentschler change the Morrow Board's mind or forget about a sure market.[11]

Rentschler got the point. To keep Congress on his side he enlisted his competition for the Navy's business, most of whom were in favor of the separate procurement system. On the same day Wilson called him, Rentschler phoned friends, Chance Vought and Bill Boeing among them, to ask them to appear before the Morrow Board to promote the Navy's point of view.

While Boeing sent the company's president, Philip Johnson, Chance Vought came to plead his case (and Rentschler's) personally. Vought's small but successful Long Island-based operation hinged primarily on the production of Navy reconnaissance planes. For months Vought had discussed Pratt & Whitney's new engine with Rentschler and Mead because the three were friends and because the Navy wanted it installed in Vought's new plane, the famous Corsair fighter. As Rentschler later commented, "Mead and I had worked very closely with Vought in determining the specification of the new engine and were greatly dependent on his judgment as to what a theoretical engine could do in the air."[12]

Vought's testimony before the Morrow Board reads like a hymn to the Navy. Any success in aviation, he testified, rested on the ability "to conceive and produce the required equipment for the government." The young aviation industry appreciated that "to the broad-minded policy and forward judgement of the Navy Department must go the credit for the development and maintenance of an engine industry in this country since the war."

In tandem, industry and the Navy had produced the progress that American aviation enjoyed, and any change in this very successful system made sense to no one— except perhaps the Army.[13]

With the deletion of one or two paragraphs, Rentschler's written statement to the committee is an exact duplicate of Vought's speech; Rentschler probably wrote it and Vought, because of his prominence as an aviation pioneer, was selected to read it. Whatever the case, both men applauded the Navy.

With his Washington work done, Rentschler help Admiral
Moffett organize a private dinner at New York's Waldorf Hotel.
Intent on leaving no stone unturned in gathering press support for
the Navy's position, Moffett had contacted George Wheat, Rentschler's public relations counsel, who in turn had invited the aviation writers for New York dailies to meet with Moffett and the
Navy's main contractors.

Although the journalists initially kept their distance, things
perked up after Moffett boasted of regularly outsmarting Army
General Billy Mitchell, and the admiral was asked the question he
most wanted to answer: Why was he opposed to unified procurement, which to the layman seemed a natural way to avoid duplica-
tion of effort, reduce expenses, and prevent competitive bidding
between the Army and Navy for the same products?

What the layman may not have taken into account was the
"friendly competition" between the services. Moffett cited the
example of General Motors. If any company needed central purchasing, General Motors did, yet it granted all its divisions complete
autonomy and even encouraged competition between them. The
company's success resulted from the stimulus of that competition;
and if competition and separate procurement were good enough for
General Motors, they were good enough for the Navy.[14]

Moffett never gave up. But for now, he and Rentschler were
forced to wait while the Morrow Board continued to hear
testimony. It would be at least two weeks before they could gauge
the effect of their assault on Congress and the press.

Meanwhile, Mead and company labored to produce the engine
that Moffett wanted— but perhaps would not be allowed to have—
by a target date of Christmas 1925. In early October Colonel Deeds
had cabled from Havana, "Get an engine ready by Christmas and
Deeds would give a turkey and all the fixings to every man in the
shop." On that day, the Pratt & Whitney staff marched to the Hartford market to charge the biggest turkeys they could find to Deeds'
account.

With Christmas dinner as bait, they resumed struggling to
shape the engine's parts. They also struggled to find a name for
Mead's creation. Wright had Whirlwinds and Cyclones; the colonel
had called his engine the Liberty; and now the team at Pratt &
Whitney Aircraft sought a name that was appropriate and distinc-
tive enough to encapsulate the aviation history they were making.

A consensus soon developed for "something in the bee line" to reflect their great pride in their busy-as-a-bee characterization. A year later Mead and his colleagues were to call the company newspaper "The Beehive"; in December of 1925 they decided that Wasp was the perfect name for their new engine.

Now all they had to do was successfully run one.

As the new year approached, the workforce had expanded to 33. The Wasp would soon be on a test stand, ready for cranking up, and Mead had already begun work on another, larger engine.

But even if the Wasp roared into action, what about Congress? How had things worked out at the Morrow Board?

Aircraft in National Defense

The Morrow Board submitted its recommendations to Calvin Coolidge on December 10, 1925, in a report entitled "Aircraft in National Defense." In thirty concise pages, the board presented a policy that quickly became the basis for the growth and development of American aviation; as a by-product very much a Christmas gift to the industry, it set the stage for profits and stability in the manufacture of commercial as well as military airplanes.

The Morrow report argued that aviation companies were failing as often as the reconverted de Havilands. The industry's precarious position threatened national security— victory in modern warfare hinged on soldiers' easy access to the best aviation equipment. According to the board, since "the strength of the aircraft industry will depend— for some time to come— on the number of new airplanes ordered by the services," the government was obliged to support an otherwise invalid industry. Long-term procurement programs (exactly what United Technologies' CEO Harry Gray was to request of Congress of 1980) were necessary to provide a stable market.

Aside from five-year guarantees to manufacturers, the board suggested that production orders be given "only to companies which maintained design staffs of reasonable size and kept them active," thereby eliminating hundreds of fly-by-nights. In theory, competition was desirable; in practice, it might deprive America of the best weaponry.

Above all, America must adequately fund research and

development of inevitable technological changes. Prototype agreements "should be awarded at a liberal price, high enough to cover all the overhead expense involved in the upkeep of the design and experimental departments." Moreover, government factories, in which the Army and Navy had manufactured planes for years, should be eliminated to give the extra business to private industry. As for commercial aviation, the board suggested that Congress regulate the airways by creating a bureau of air navigation within the Department of Commerce as well as "the progressive extension of the air mail service" to private operators.

The Morrow Board ended its report by stressing its "unanimous and undivided support" for each and every recommendation. President Coolidge and the nation should appreciate that it had approached its work "in a spirit of mutual accommodation"; the members earnestly hoped that "the same spirit may prove helpful to those charged with the grave responsibility of developing the policies in regard to the use of aircraft in national defense and to those who encounter the hazards of actual operations on the air." In other words, the Army, the Navy, and the aviation industry ought to call a truce and cooperate in implementing one national aviation policy.[15]

In general, the Morrow Board got its wish. Only the diehards who wanted a separate air force "yesterday" were dissatisfied. No one seemed to notice that the report had skirted a dilemma that was (and is) inherent in any capitalist society: because every taxpayer's money paid for national defense, the government could not allow the free market to determine who did and did not get defended. The use of public funds implied a subsidy for aviation. Although capitalists such as Frederick Rentschler insisted that industrialists paid their own way and competed for business in the open market, the truth is that from the Morrow Board on, the federal government openly subsidized aviation because the planes were needed— and because the factories were needed.[16]

Thus began the vicious circle that characterizes United Technologies', and for that matter, the entire aviation industry's fate. Acting upon the board's conviction that "whatever was done to increase the use of aircraft, to spread familiarity with aircraft among the people, and in general to develop 'airmindedness' would make it easier to build up an expanded airpower if an emergency arose," the government might inadvertently create too large an industrial base. And if the stimulation of commercial aviation created a bubble that burst, Washington, first in for a penny, might then be in for a pound. It would still need aviation factories for the next war, yet if those factories grew far larger than expected, the government might have to spend huge amounts of money to sustain them. Most people would deal with this fundamental, still unresolved dilemma by avoiding it. Businessmen would deny the subsidy; critics would complain about war-mongering capitalists; and the average American would obediently pay the piper.

At a time when buoyant optimism was the rule and citizens often ignored voices pleading for restraint, warnings about the unintended consequences of federal assistance to aviation were regarded as the pessimestic theories of naysayers. Besides, aviation did need immediate help. Calvin Coolidge had no choice but to step in; the Morrow Board would tell Americans what was necessary; and for now citizens would forget about the dilemma of using public funds to create (and possibly institutionalize) private industrial capacity.

The Wasp Takes Off

In Hartford, Frederick Rentschler and George Mead read the Morrow Board's recommendations with a massive sigh of relief. If Congress heeded the board, the aviation industry would boast its own Magna Carta. If not, at least no one had mentioned the creation of a separate air force controlling the procurement of all aviation equipment. Admiral Moffett was sure to obtain the money for hundreds of Wasps, and Pratt & Whitney aircraft was sure to obtain one of the largest peacetime engine orders ever placed— if, that is, George Mead's engine worked.

By Christmas Eve, workers had fully assembled the first Wasp, thus earning their Christmas turkeys. Yet there was still no proof the Wasp could meet the Navy's specifications in the forthcoming series of stiff qualification tests. With the Morrow Board pressure off, the test pressure seemed greater than ever. If the design proved inadequate, nearly a quarter of a million dollars, six months of ferocious effort, and many careers went down the drain. To Mead, the 650-pound Wasp weighed a ton— and it rested on his shoulders.

Now, in January of 1926, Mead advised caution. If the engine turns over, he said, hold it at 360 horsepower and see what happens. His colleagues, who disagreed, coaxed him into a first try at 380 horsepower. When the engine roared with all the confidence of a veteran, they went for 400. It delivered 410. On a third try, the Wasp hit 425 horsepower.

The delighted staff now prepared for the formal Navy qualification tests, which at that time took fifty hours. When Rentschler and Mead had worked at Wright Aeronautical in a rural New Jersey setting, tests were run over three days with no concern about noise. But because Pratt and Whitney's factory lay close to residential areas in the center of Hartford, tests were conducted during he day and took an excruciatingly long week to complete. And Mead, anxious to begin with, was expecially tense because the Wasp, designed for 350 horsepower, was being tried for a rating of 425. If the engine succeeded, so did the company. If not, it meant that Mead should have stuck to his guns and settled for achieving his original goal.

As in the informal tests, the Wasp passed without a hitch and with the highest marks. Finally, Hartford residents could stop complaining about the noise, and George Mead could stop driving himself to the point of exhaustion. He had 425 reasons for jubilation; the Navy added another when it cabled congratulations and the suggestion that the first Wasp be earmarked for the honor of a permanent exhibit at Philadelphia's Franklin Institute.[17]

Although the Navy's thought of enshrining the prototype might seem presumptuous in view of the fact that no Wasp had yet powered a plane, all concerned sensed the significance of a new type of engine that had exceeded all expectations; actual flight was merely a matter of more time and effort. On March 20, the Navy demonstrated its faith by ordering six experimental engines for delivery on April 8. As promised by Moffett, the price —ninety thousand dollars— would partially underwrite development costs.[18]

On March 31, Rentschler and a much-less-nervous Mead had already terminated Pratt & Whitney Aircraft's experimental period. With the Wasp roaring and the Hornet —the new, larger engine— looking just as promising, the board of directors voted for a quick business takeoff. To cover the experimental work on the engines, Pratt & Whitney Aircraft issued $200,000 worth of preferred stock to the Pratt & Whitney Tool Company, in exchange for which the tool company agreed to furnish the half million dollars required for large-scale production of Wasps and, eventually, Hornets.[19] This transaction was a gamble, because flight tests on the new engine were still to come. The Navy had agreed informally to buy engines; and Congress seemed certain to approve —with big appropriations— the Morrow Board's policy recommendations. But if just one card failed to fall into place, the factory might once again be storing tobacco.

On May 1 the Rentschler and Mead families drove to Washington for the flight tests. It took two days to make the trip, but Mrs. Mead recollects that they sang all the way: given Rentschler's reputation as a "sobersides," this must have been a unique period for the main actors.[20]

The Navy had chosen Wright Aeronautical's Apache plane for the tests. After Chance Vought installed a Wasp in it at his Long Island factory, it was transported to Washington for its exams. Even the least superstitious spectator must have considered the pilot's name— Champion— a good omen.

It proved to be just that. It was immediately apparent that the Wasp offered the Navy everything that Admiral Moffett had sought for so long. With its military equipment in place, Apache weighed three hundred pounds less than its liquid-cooled competitors, yet landed at speeds of only 56 miles per hour. This was slower than other planes and, given the short runways at sea, the slower the better. The Wasp-powered Apache also outclassed the competition on climb and ceiling and, as a bonus, reached speeds of 180 miles per hour.

With so much success on the Apache, the Navy decided to try the Wasp on Curtiss' Hawk and Boeing's Fighter, both of which had been designed for liquid-cooled engines. No major modifications were permitted during installation. When tests were held in June, the Wasp once again triumphed. As Eugene Wilson testified before the Delaney Committee on Naval Affairs eight years later, "When the Pratt & Whitney Wasp engine was developed, it incorporated. . . fundamental changes in the principles of design. Those fundamental designs have since been proved to be sound. The difference between success and failure is how much you have to spend on your product after you get it out of the factory. . . I believe that Pratt & Whitney's success can be ascribed to the fact that the engine has proved an amazing success at home and abroad, with the result that they have not spent a lot of money on service."[21]

George Mead had got it right the first time. The engine's remarkable reliability was demonstrated when the Navy dispatched a Wasp-powered plane on a seven-thousand mile trip. Servicemen stationed at refueling stops had nothing to do; the Wasp crossed the continent and back with no need for repairs.

On June 28, the Navy signed a contract for six more experimental engines for another ninety thousand dollars. With no production orders in hand, Pratt & Whitney already had recovered almost all the money spent on development. Now, as with the Wasp, the company could really take off if Admiral Moffett would only produce that promised contract for two hundred engines.[22]

Moffett would have, if it hadn't been for Congress' delay in passing the Navy's five-year procurement program. To get things moving, the admiral instructed Commander Wilson to issue a press release stating that "the greatest step forward in the history of aviation was taken today when Congressman Butler, Chairman of the House of Naval Affairs Committee, announced approval of the Moffett five-year Naval Aviation Building Program."

Although Butler had never even seen the plan, Moffett insisted that "when Butler read his name in the afternoon *Star* and looked at the editorial Mac [Marvin MacIntyre of the *Washington Star*] would get us, Butler would think he'd invented it himself." The admiral then rushed a copy of the plan to Butler's office in hopes that the congressman would approve the program the *Star* was about to anounce he already had approved.

Moffett won hands down. "With a whoop and a holler," said Moffett, the Naval Aviation Building Program sped through Congress. As of July 1, 1926, the admiral was awarded a 400 percent increase in his procurement budget. From 1920 through 1924, the Navy spent only $19 million on new planes; by 1926 to 1931, the total budget amounted to $85 million— pin money today but a staggering sum in Moffett's time. Over the five-year period, the Navy was to purchase 1,614 new planes, with 235 to come within the first year. Moffett ordered airframes from Boeing, Curtiss and Vought. The contract for large power plants, however, went only to Pratt & Whitney, which quickly obtained its order for 200 engines plus spare parts.[23]

Negotiating this first contract required time and patience. Because large air-cooled engines had never been produced in volume, there was no precedent on pricing— but the price had better not be too much. After the World War I scandals, the Navy was sensitive about alleged arms profiteering. Rentschler, with Edward Deeds on his board of directors, also favored discretion. If he could help it, no one would ever call him an unpatriotic, money-hungry capitalist.

Nevertheless, he and Mead were entitled to a fair profit. Despite Moffett's promises, they had risked a great deal of Pratt & Whitney's money. Mead's engine, moreover, ran like the finest clock. What was a fair reward for a very original achievement? How much was too much? These issues confronted Rentschler and the Navy with a problem as thorny in 1925 as it will be in the future. In many arms contracts, and invariably in new arms contracts, it is difficult to impose hard-and-fast prices on technology that may never before have seen the light of day. Manufacturers resist set costs because of potential loss; the services try to avoid them because, as Deeds exemplified in World War I, they may result in "unconscionable profit."

Rentschler protested the Navy's ultimate decision to price the Wasp in line with liquid-cooled engines of the same power, but the customer's will prevailed, especially in the face of a threatened Congressional investigation. This first order, signed on October 5, 1926, specified $8,750 per plane, of which $8,000 was for the engine and, as Moffett had promised, $750 for development costs. To the $180,000 already received for the twelve experimental engines, Rentschler now could add another $150,000 to the Wasp's research and development costs, thereby covering total expenditures. And if the company could improve productivity as the engine order progressed, it could easily net a handsome profit on an order that exceeded two million dollars. Whether or not they profited, however, the Navy's solid commitment to the Wasp assured Pratt & Whitney's short-term survival— and, not incidentally, the elimination of its competitors in the large-engine market.[24]

Flying the Mail with Bill Boeing

With the Wasp order in hand, Frederick Rentschler looked elsewhere to supplement Pratt & Whitney's military business.

Although air-passenger travel constituted an as yet untapped market, Rentschler assumed it wouldn't be exploited for years. Congress had just passed the Air Commerce Act in May of 1926, but even the best federal regulations would not soon erase the popular perception that flying was dangerous. And even if people determined to take the risk, airfares were high and open cockpits inhospitable.

But if passengers offered no hope for profit, Rentschler saw definite possibilities in their mail. Since the passage of the Kelly Act in 1925, private carriers had been transporting mail by air. Now Congress was promising to compensate for weaknesses in the original bill, which restricted carrier's fees to no more than 80 percent of the government's postal revenues. If air mail volume was high, the existing system might have made sense. As it was, the public's rejection made it a financial disaster. Although a letter sent from Boston, say, to St. Louis for twenty-five cents traveled through three separate mail zones, the theoretical speed of the process justified the high price. In practice, the carrier in the heavily traveled Boston-to-New York Zone received seven cents of the government's dime. From New York to Chicago, the carrier got four cents and, from Chicago to St. Louis, eight cents. Because each and every letter was hand-counted at each and every stop, the only advantage of air mail, speed, had disappeared long before the letter reached St. Louis. When customers realized they were paying more and receiving less they stopped using air mail, and the carriers stopped realizing profit. The first Kelly Act had failed.[25]

Congress amended the Kelly Act in June of 1926 to make mail weight the basis of carrier revenue. Forty stamped envelopes equalled one pound of mail, which to Washington meant four dollars' worth of stamps. To the carriers, however, it promised a maximum of three dollars for every pound transported (80 percent of four dollars actually equalled $3.20, but Congress, sensitive to accusations of subsidy, rounded the figure off). If a plane flew farther than one thousand miles, the carrier received a maximum of thirty cents more per pound for each additional hundred miles. Thus, a carrier might earn as much as $3.60 per pound on a twelve-hundred-mile route.

Under the new rules, with letters weighed rather than counted, the air mails once again promised speedy delivery. With intense lobbying on the carriers' parts, stamp prices would probably fall, whereupon increased volume might well result in large profits for businessmen such as Fred Rentschler.

The trick was to stay aloft long enough to reap the rewards of reduced mail rates. Some firms survived by imaginatively abusing the new system. Because postal authorities simply weighed a load and sent it on its way, companies began transporting stoves, lead shot, or flat irons. One outfit instructed employees to send one another registered letters on every scheduled flight — the registered mailbag required a one-pound lock that translated into three dollars of pure profit. Carriers eventually convinced the Post Office to use an even larger lock for extra fifteen ounces of revenue.[26]

These angles were unlikely to sustain the air mails for long, so some people considered legitimate ways to make money. One possibility was remodeling the war-surplus de Havilands powered by the war-surplus Liberties that most carriers still used. The planes were unreliable, unsafe and, even worse from their owners' point of view, heavy. A lighter engine could mean as much as five hundred pounds more mail and perhaps a passenger or two. The ideal, a new plane with a new engine, did not exist in 1926 — until the idea men at Pratt & Whitney and Boeing Airplane simultaneously conceived of installing a Wasp on a plane that Boeing had designed for a 1925 Post Office competition.

In joining forces, Fred Rentschler and William Boeing built on a friendship dating back to 1918, when Lieutenant Rentschler inspected the engines used in Boeing's World War I planes. After the Armistice the two men kept in touch, but it was only when each had what the other wanted that they became a powerful team.

The Boeing Airplane Co., like most aircraft makers, barely survived the peace. Although Boeing supplemented his aviation activities with his substantial lumber inheritance, he was about to close up shop after losing nearly $300,000 by 1920. Then, by markedly underbidding the competition, he was able to keep the company aloft with an Army contract for two hundred pursuit planes. During the early twenties, Boeing thrived by designing bombers for the Army and rebuilding nearly three hundred de Havilands for a variety of customers, including the Marine Corps and Cuba; in 1924, it won a Navy contract for forty-nine new training ships.

That same year, the Post Office launched a competition for experimental mail planes that would replace old de Havilands but utilize leftover Liberty engines. Boeing's entry was the Model 40, which flew well enough but, like its competitors, offered few improvements; no company won.

In 1926, inspired by Fred Rentschler's hard sell, Bill Boeing asked his engineers to design a new fighter plane around the new Wasp engine. The Boeing Model 40A was already in the air when the Post Office announced that, as of June 1927, transcontinental routes would be taken over by private enterprise, and that bids should be entered as soon as possible. Rentschler and Boeing simply shifted their attention from the fighter to a Wasp-powered mail plane. Whereas the maximum payload on a Liberty-powered ship was three to four hundred pounds, a Wasp could increase the payload by nearly a thousand pounds and evenly split the extra weight between mail and passengers. Ideally, the carrier would double its mail revenues and, by attracting just two passengers per trip, increase receipts by perhaps another three hundred dollars. With a big increase in mail volume, a shrewd operator could net more than a thousand dollars on each flight.[27]

Boeing's new mail plane incorporated two enclosed seats to accommodate passengers, but even without them air mail business would be profitable because the overhead was being paid by Washington. He could use the military's money to help underwrite the development of a new company —Boeing Air Transport— and then let the transport company provide orders for his airplane factory. Ultimately, Boeing would have used the military funds to end his reliance on the military market.

Unfortunately, Boeing needed twenty-five Wasp engines immediately to make his Post Office bid, but Pratt & Whitney's entire 1927 output had already been spoken for by the Navy. In explaining his problem to Commander Eugene Wilson, Boeing underscored Pratt & Whitney's desire for this first commercial order. Happily for all concerned, his scheme meshed with the Navy's policy of assisting manufacturers in securing commercial business and consequently lowering prices for their own purchases. What's more, the military's five-year procurement program was intended to create an industrial base for emergency plane production; were the Navy to refuse Boeing's plea for special treatment, it would undermine the very policies it had lobbied so hard to establish.[28]

So Boeing received his twenty-five engines. If he also had his overhead paid, well, that was just an unintended consequence of building planes for the federal government.

Soon afterward, Bill Boeing bid for a large chunk of the

transcontinental postal route— the heavily traveled two-thousand-mile run from Chicago to San Francisco. At $2.89 per pound ($1.50 for the first thousand miles and fifteen cents for each additional hundred miles), Boeing's bid was not only the lowest, but it made those of his competitors look like "skyway robbery." Bill Stout, a veteran operator, had asked for $5.09 per pound. Along with his colleagues, he advised the Post Office to reject Boeing's bid; for that kind of money, Boeing would be out of business within months, thereby further undermining the public's already shaky confidence in aviation.

Postal officials also were skeptical of Boeing's figures, but the Post Office, like the military, was subject to Congressional scrutiny. Though they did have the option of rejecting low bids from companies with neither resources nor experience, Boeing had both, and his partner, Eddie Hubbard, had been regularly flying the mail since 1919. With little room to maneuver, the Post Office risked the future of transcontinental service on Boeing's absurd bid but demanded that he post a half-million-dollar bond to assure performance of his contract. That was a large sum even for a rich man, yet Boeing willingly complied. By February 1927, the Boeing Air Transport Company was off and flying.

Wasp-powered Boeing 40A's both carried the mail at a profit and cemented the business ties between William Boeing and Frederick Rentschler. The commercial success of Boeing's mail plane and Rentschler's engine were inextricably linked. In the merger-packed twenties, it could come as no surprise were these two very ambitious men to join forces on a more permanent basis.

Back in Hartford

By anyone's standards, 1926 had been a banner year for Pratt & Whitney Aircraft. A remarkable new engine had impressed every important customer: the Navy had responded with a large order on very favorable terms and the Federal government had established air mail policies that laid a solid basis for stability and profits. As a later president of Pratt & Whitney aptly summarized the situation: "The link between military and commercial production was a stimulus and basic cause of our success." Pratt & Whitney did the research and developed the engines for a military market and then sold the "benefits of the discoveries" to the air-mail carriers and anyone else who could pay.[29]

To exploit his booming business, Fred Rentschler quickly made a number of important changes. To increase manufacturing capacity for the large Navy order, the company moved from quarters the size of a tennis court to those the size of a football field, eliminating the tobacco forever. The ten men who knew one another like brothers had grown into a staff of two hundred, producing fifteen Wasps each month by February of 1927. Rentschler firmly believed that, long before the Navy order was filled, his new employees would be occupied with the additional business needed to keep their enlarged facilities humming.

One major reason for Rentschler's optimism was George Mead's success with a second new engine: the Hornet. Developed to suit Admiral Moffett, who had requested torpedo planes and heavy bombers for America's aircraft carriers, the Hornet had a maximum weight of 750 pounds and a goal of 525 horsepower. By March of 1927, the Hornet was ready for the Navy's formal qualification tests. When it hit 570 horsepower in the final five hours of the exam, its weight-to-horsepower ratio easily outclassed that of the liquid-cooled competition. As a bonus for the Navy, more than half the Hornet's parts were interchangeable with those of the Wasp, simplifying maintenance and conserving space.

Initial funds for the Hornet's development came from Pratt & Whitney Tool Co. Although the Navy had agreed to underwrite development, as with the Wasp, it came through only after George Mead's engine. Now, the Navy's new contracts for seven experimental engines of $140,000 just about covered all developmental costs. The rest came from the Army. Lured by the Wasp's phenomenal success and the Hornet's great promise. Army officials paid over $50,000 for three experimental engines. Pratt & Whitney's ultimate research and development costs totaled $276.53.[30]

At this point, Pratt & Whitney stood virtually alone —with the exception of Wright Aeronautical, potential customers had no alternatives. And in a country about to champion Charles Lindbergh, a shared monopoly on the production of large airplane engines was, as oil is today, a very valuable asset. Yet, as with oil today, success depended on the manner of exploitation. Pratt & Whitney's short-term profits were assured, but an increase in manufacturing capacity beyond the market's long-term needs could result in greater production precisely when customers needed less. Despite Pratt & Whitney's competitive edge, its future rested on Fred Rentschler's ability to profit from the Lindbergh boom without getting caught in the inevitable bust.

The Lindbergh Boom

The twenties was an intense decade. Americans moved unceasingly from one passion to another, eagerly embracing everything from cars to con men. In 1920, for example, Charles Ponzi offered investors 50 percent interest in ninety days. Within a year, forty-thousand people had submitted $15 million. They never saw any interest, but Ponzi was cheered wherever he went. Even after he was jailed for fraud, the money kept rolling in.

In the mid-twenties, when thousands of Americans suddenly hungered for land in the "American Venice," some— quite deliberately— bought Florida property that lay underwater. And on the day Henry Ford introduced the Model A, crowds began gathering on New York's Broadway at 3:00 A.M. The *Herald Tribune* estimated that a million people showed up just to catch a glimpse of Ford's creation.[31]

On May 20, 1927, Charles Lindbergh had taken off from Long Island, bound for Paris in a less-than-fully tested plane that was to cross the Atlantic in slightly over thirty-three hours. He returned to America twenty days later as a national hero. The American ambassador to France, Myron Herrick, compared him to Joan of Arc and Lafayette. "He was the instrument of a great ideal, and one need not be fanatically religious to see in his success the guiding hand of Providence," Herrick gushed. "For he was needed, and he came at the moment which seemed exactly preordained."

Whether God guided the *Spirit of St. Louis* remains an open question, but Americans accorded Lindbergh such an overwhelming welcome that the confetti landed on anything remotely connected with aviation. When word reached New York that Lindbergh had landed safety in Paris, Mayor Jimmy Walker called every city department whose plants had steam whistles; within minutes a "bedlam" of blasts screamed through the city. Boats in the harbor picked up the tune, quickly followed by fire engine sirens. *The New York*

Times wrote that "If by that time there was anyone in New York unaware of Lindbergh's success, the shriek of fire sirens appraised them of something unusual."

Unusual was hardly the word for this ongoing acclaim. In June, Lindbergh landed a plane on New York's Hudson River with nearly four hundred boats crowding his runway. This time the whistles and sirens filling the air were joined by the horns of ocean liners. When Lindbergh attempted to address a radio audience estimated at 15 million, only the deafening din of "sirens, shrill tooters and full-throated whistlers" could be heard.

Wall Street, meanwhile, was enjoying the formidable profits generated by Lindbergh's success. Wright Aeronautical, which supplied his engine, saw its stock jump nearly thirty-five points in a week. Curtiss also benefited from a one-week rise of thirty-five points, and buyers clamored for shares of Seaboard Air Line, which happened to be a railroad.[32]

In Hartford, Frederick Rentschler, who had been in aviation too long to trust the sudden boom, watched the frenzy with skepticism. Once large orders for commercial engines began cascading in, he intended to look hard before making even the slightest leap. Let others have the "advantage" of a head start on Pratt & Whitney Aircraft; Rentschler would analyze the facts before tossing money into the Lindbergh wishing well. Rumor had it, for example, that Americans soon would park planes beside their cars. Pratt & Whitney made no engines suitable for private planes— a market then estimated to be potentially as big as for automobiles— and, according to Rentschler, had no need to. Even if such planes were manufactured, who would buy them? And where would they be parked? Or landed? Or serviced? Private planes were, at best, a big gamble for small winnings.

The issue of expansion, on the other hand, deserved careful consideration. The obvious benefits of self-sufficiency were outweighed in Rentschler's mind by one simple fact: a manufacturer who refused to share the wealth was unable to share the risks. He reluctantly decided to cover his flank by subcontracting 50 percent of Pratt & Whitney's work to small manufacturers and soon initiated agreements with the best suppliers that allowed all parties to expand and contract with the demands of the market. In general, he chose one primary source for parts, materials, or tools and kept another as a backup in case orders exceeded expectations or a company failed to deliver.

A final decision concerned inventories, which Rentschler kept to a minimum. Money in the warehouse was money out of Pratt & Whitney's treasury; large inventories, moreover, multiplied risk. Thus, Rentschler instructed his staff to maintain "a very strict control over inventories and at no time permit our commitments to be in excess of 200 to 300 engines above the actual orders we have on hand." In this way, Rentschler bet on the past. Pratt & Whitney would never be stuck with goods that, unlike the market for engines, refused to disappear.

Sharing 50 percent of the production load was a successful strategy that Rentschler never changed (when World War II began, in fact, federal officials suggested that other manufacturers follow his lead). But in 1927 he still had to determine how far to increase capacity. Beginning on August 1, he doubled factory floor space and created one of the world's largest plants devoted exclusively to the manufacture of airplane engines by annexing one of the Pratt & Whitney tool company's empty buildings. Nearly 100,000 square feet housed separate departments for connecting rods and cylinders, crankshafts and screw machines, enameling and polishing. Everything was arranged "so that the materials could travel in sequence of operations," and photographs show endless rows of aproned workers, many in clean white shirts, dutifully tending to their machines. The aisles, with their neatly painted white lines, looked like narrow highways. With a place for everything and everything in its place, including a separate floor for executive offices, the new Pratt & Whitney Aircraft mirrored the industrial ideology of the time.[33]

Rentschler's exceedingly efficient operation also lacked serious competition other than Wright Aeronautical. In later years General Motors' Allison division would become a competitor, as is General Electric today, but the size of their parent companies indicates the resources necessary to challenge the established engine manufacturers. Prospective engine makers unwilling to bet on a vastly increased market or unequipped with another Wasp up their sleeves soon invested elsewhere.[34]

Pratt & Whitney's gross revenues for 1927 exceeded $2.5 million on sales of 271 engines. Approximately 15 percent of this business came from commercial customers (especially Boeing), 4 percent from the Army and the balance, 81 percent, from the huge Navy order. The company averaged 25 percent profit, over $644,000, which was lower than necessary because Rentschler actually refunded money to the Navy.

To Rentschler's surprise, profits on the Navy's business proved so "embarrassingly high" that he asked the Navy what to do with it; his books, like those of the military, were subject to Congressional scrutiny and with Colonel Edward Deeds on Pratt & Whitney's Board of Directors, he felt vulnerable to criticism for profiteering. The Navy instructed him to return what it determined was excessive and permitted Pratt & Whitney a net profit of over $400.000 (21 percent on sales) on it first large order. To both the Navy and Rentschler, this seemed a fair rate of return in the absence of established norms. Of course, Congress might think otherwise, since here was a private business and an arm of the military deciding what was right and wrong to do with taxpayers' funds.[35]

But when Rentschler took what the Navy offered, he did so with at least two rationales. First, he and Mead were pioneers who had created a superb engine and who deserved a substantial return on their investment. Second, Congress had its eye on Navy profit margins. If he let greed get the better of him, he could easily jeopardize a secure and profitable future; in November, for example, he had signed another Navy contract worth over $3 million. Better to accept a Navy compromise and avoid any comparisons with Colonel Deeds.

In any case, Rentschler had no difficulty accepting a 24 percent profit on his Army business and a 35 percent profit on his commercial orders. He could rest content with a year that made Pratt & Whitney the most successful manufacturer of aviation engines in the United States.

A South American Bandit's Scalp

Once he'd closed the books on 1927, Rentschler finally had time to attend to the one neglected side of Pratt & Whitney's business: exports. Through the twenties, foreigners had offered a market for aviation products that increased as fast as did enthusiasm for planes. In 1922, America's total export sales of aviation equipment came to slightly more than $150,000. In 1926 the figure was nearly a million dollars; it doubled in 1927, and promised to double yet again in 1928.[36]

Rentschler chose to claim a part of this growing market for several reasons. In good times exports added customers; in bad times, they helped stabilize volume. And, as Don Brown, Pratt & Whitley's factory manager, put it, exports at all times "maintained an established American aeronautical industry readily available to meet the needs of a national emergency." Yet another benefit was profits without the discounts customarily given at home. Pratt & Whitney sold engines in South America and Europe at a price "several hundreds of dollars higher than the same engines were sold to our own government."[37] Even with a small sales volume on exports, the company could easily equal the profits from even a large Navy or Army order. In 1927 and 1928, export money only iced an already rich cake, but Rentschler understood that if times changed, an export market that composed 20 percent of sales might equal, at the bottom line, 50 percent of profits.

The military wholeheartedly supported the export trade because the more advanced equipment remained in America until manufacturers supplanted it. Foreigners received only obsolete goods, contributed to America's air-power overhead, and subsidized the research and development from which the services benefited.

One of Rentschler's first agreements was with BMW, the German automotive company, which sought a license to manufacture Wasps and Hornets for sale in Europe. The deal was signed by 1928 but, in the year or so it would take BMW to produce an engine, they would be forced to buy American. The publicity from the agreement, not incidentally, was bound to stimulate a larger market for Pratt & Whitney's products.

Rentschler also saw a ready market in Cuba, Mexico, and Central and Latin America. Mexico, Argentina, and Peru seemed interested in buying whole squadrons of Wasp-powered Corsairs. The February 1928 issue of the *Beehive*, Pratt & Whitney's company newspaper, lauded sales engineer Steve McClellan who, while serving with the Marines in Nicaragua, also acted as a Pratt & Whitney sales representative. Everyone wished him well and "put in an order for a bandit's scalp."[38]

The *Beehive* never mentioned whether McClellan succeeded. But he did try, as did another ambitious aviator named Ralph

O'Neill, who wanted to create an airline stretching from New York to Buenos Aires. To finance his business travels, he became a South American representative for Pratt & Whitney, pushing products while moving through the Americas setting up air mail and passenger service.

Rentschler accepted O'Neill's proposal because his friend William Boeing had already furnished a plane for the venture and requested that Rentschler put up the engine. That way, O'Neill could use Wasp-powered seaplanes to demonstrate to South America the fine quality of Boeing's and Pratt & Whitney's products.

When O'Neill visited Hartford, Rentschler became so intrigued with possibilities that he called his brother Gordon at the National City Bank in New York and asked him to see O'Neill. When Gordon also liked what he heard, he supplied O'Neill with letters of introduction to every National City branch manager along his proposed route from Havana to Buenos Aires to Santiago. In addition, to help O'Neill meet the right people wherever he went, Gordon Rentschler set up interviews with heads of various American companies in South America.

On his new protege's behalf Fred Rentschler also contacted Thomas Hamilton, owner of a prosperous Milwaukee propeller company, to suggest a South American representative for his wares. O'Neill left for South America in March 1928, holding contracts to represent three of the best aviation companies in America: Pratt & Whitney, Boeing, and Hamilton Propellor.

A very happy Ralph O'Neill expected to take the continent by storm. At first he did— his flying demonstrations in Rio de Janeiro impressed officials so much he was confident orders would be forthcoming. But on the way to Buenos Aires, O'Neill crashed. Although he survived, the plane did not. Nothing was left of the Wasp-powered seaplane— nor of O'Neill's relationship with Boeing and Rentschler.

In the hospital after the accident O'Neill received, instead of a get-well card, a cable from Seattle tersely cancelling his contract. He had cost his employers twenty-five thousand dollars, and that was enough.

O'Neill felt let down. Why spend time and money helping him get started and then, after one accident, leave him hospitalized in the middle of South America?[39]

One reason was patience. Rentschler and Boeing could wait to conquer the South American market. Granted, they had great ambitions— why else support O'Neill so generously?— but they also knew that, in 1928, exports couldn't add much to their domestic military and commercial business. Their loss had been substantial; if they sent O'Neill another plane what would happen if he crashed again? Additional crashes would cost more money and surely do little to generate orders. It would be better to temporarily restrain their ambitions, settle for laying an export groundwork, and focus all efforts on a new, quite promising piece of domestic business: Fred Rentschler and William Boeing were talking merger.

Bullish on Boeing

The primary factor motivating Rentschler and Boeing to unite was the quick success of the Boeing Air Transport Corporation. In twelve months the new company had earned solid profits and promised even more through mail and passenger revenues and large orders for Boeing's planes and George Mead's engines.

Boeing had launched its air transport operations on July 1, 1927, with twenty-five Wasp-powered planes readied for twenty hours' flying time over two thousand miles. If they arrived on schedule, their mail service would be three times faster than the trains'. If they proved reliable, they might attract Americans eager to follow Lindbergh into the air. Designed to supplement the mails, the two-passenger "lounges" might be in real demand.

When the first Boeing 40A's crossed the Great Plains, the engines overheated while penetrating "a pillow of extremely hot air" hanging over the land; even an air-cooled engine was no match for that hellish sky. Mead and engineering assistant Wilgoos quickly devised small radiators to circulate the oil necessary for cooling, and Mead went to Omaha to supervise installation. Cartoons depict him perched on the plane's wing, listening to the engine's roar or taking its temperature with a thermometer! Despite the possible inaccuracy of these images, he did solve the problem.[40] Through 1927 Boeing Air Transport averaged about 130,000 pounds of mail per month.

This promising start inspired William Boeing to imitate his colleague Fred Rentschler by attempting to double his business and seeking new markets. By January of 1928, he had purchased Pacific

Air Transport, which held the lucrative Los Angeles to Seattle route and naturally would order its planes from Boeing and its engines from Pratt & Whitney.

Impressed by the performance of the Hornet engine, Boeing next adapted his mail fleet to increase payload and profits through the new power plant. At the same time, he developed a new plane— the four-seater 40C— to exploit Pacific's passenger traffic. Although a 40C's pilot still flew in an open cockpit and passengers still climbed a narrow ladder to the wing, where they weaved their way through the struts into very cramped quarters, Boeing pioneered in providing reliable service to anyone with the gumption to pay up and fly. In 1928 Boeing's transport operations averaged ten passengers each day and his net profit (on all operations) totaled nearly seventy-five thousand dollars a month.[41]

In May of 1928, Congress delighted the mail carriers by replacing their previous four-year contracts with ten-year route certificates; as long as they complied with postal regulations, carriers would hold their franchises indefinitely. Now large investments made sense especially after Congress reduced postal rates by half in August. Mail volume took off, and so did profits, because the increased loads that resulted never substantially increased the carriers' costs.

Thanks to Congress, the well-being of Boeing Air Transport assured considerable business for the Boeing Airplane Co. And each of these Seattle-based operations furnished large orders to Pratt & Whitney Aircraft, which already had more business than Rentschler had anticipated even in his wildest 1925 dreams. The Navy alone promised over $4 million in 1928 business (53 percent of the final total); the Army had ordered another half-million dollars' worth of engines; and, flying on Lindbergh's exhaust, commercial customers such as Sikorsky had signed contracts for more than $3 million worth of George Mead's power plants. This added up to nearly one thousand engines as 1928's total production— even a conservative estimate of net profit came to over $2 million.[42]

Big money led Rentschler and Boeing to form a big idea. Profits on so many separate fronts could be boosted even further if the parts formed a new whole under the umbrella of a giant holding company. The two were consistent in their cooperation anyway, and with Gordon Rentschler's connections could combine their operations with the stock-market savvy of the best bankers in America.

To any rational businessperson, that sounded great; but in the irrational, merger-crazed twenties, it bordered on perfection. For any number of reasons— profits, power, efficiency, unified financing, a willing government, pure speculation— the business community saw advantages in linking companies at different stages of production and distribution. Whereas turn-of-the-century mergers such as American Tobacco tended to be horizontal, twenties mergers more often were vertical: a holding company controlled subsidiaries at every stage of the business process, ideally enlarged its share of the market while reducing costs. At giant Westinghouse, for example, one division made radios, another serviced them, and yet another owned the stations that broadcast programs. This was business at its profitable best, and many investors eagerly sought to build their own pyramid of profit in any appealing industry. After Lindbergh, few industries held more appeal than aviation.[43]

In fact, Rentschler and Boeing already had a vertically integrated operation— a plane factory, a huge engine business, and the basis for a transcontinental mail and passenger service— by July of 1928. Acquiring the companies of associates such as Thomas Hamilton and Chance Vought would strengthen a new holding company. As a by-product, the combination would yield the largest aviation business in America.

This prospect was so appealing to Frederick Rentschler and William Boeing that they gave National City Bank the go-ahead in September of 1928. Within four months, Rentschler and Boeing— in fact and in law— controlled the largest, and by far the most profitable, aviation company in the world.

3

THE UNITED AIRCRAFT AND TRANSPORT CORPORATION

"Giving is the vital impulse and moral center of capitalism."

George Gilder, *Wealth and Poverty*

Birth of a Giant

As of October 1928, Frederick Rentschler and William Boeing had relinquished their involvement in everyday aviation affairs to concentrate on establishing their giant corporation. For nearly a year they focused on acquiring companies, maneuvering in the stock market, settling into posh Park Avenue offices, and increasing their personal fortunes by many millions of dollars.

Throughout the first half of 1929, Rentschler and Boeing were to look up, not at planes in the sky, but at stocks on the big board. They merged their companies in two separate steps because, with the stock market booming and investors clamoring for aviation issues, one procedure couldn't fully exploit the market's potential. Instead, they determined that Boeing Airplane would go public first and then, when buyers went bullish on Boeing, Pratt & Whitney would follow. For insiders, the profits could be extraordinary, even during the Great Bull Market of early 1929.

National City Bank in New York handled the stock offerings. At that point, Rentschler's brother Gordon was a vice president; Edward Deeds held a position on the board of directors; and Joseph Ripley, who had assisted Rentschler and Boeing on a number of previous occasions and initiated the first phase of the merger negotiations in Seattle, was also a vice president.

It had been decided that "a few particular friends" of the National City Bank would purchase all shares of Boeing stock before it came on the market. The general public was excluded in an effort to limit the heavy speculation sure to follow any public offering and, more important, to expedite further mergers. With only insiders holding the stock, National City could merge and earn at will.[1]

Inside offerings of stock were commonplace in 1928. Investors wanted to make money, but rather than admit the obvious, they often justified private offerings as a public service. For example, J.P. Morgan and Co. maintained five lists of preferred investors to whom they sold stock deemed too speculative for the average customer. Presumably, wealthier investors could afford the loss and, following the logic of the brokerage house's argument, would remain loyal to Morgan because their preferred listing entitled them to lose extra money.[2] Similarly, Joseph Ripley explained National City's private sale of Boeing stock as a means of protecting the public. "The real reason," he said, "was the National City Company had not at that time come to the point where it felt justified in sponsoring the aviation industry to the investing public of this country."[3]

The brand new corporation, Boeing Airplane and Transport Company, was formed on October 30, 1928, as a holding company for the three businesses principally owned by William Boeing: the Boeing Airplane Company and the two mail lines, the Boeing Air Transport Company, and Pacific Air Transport. National City offered ninety thousand shares of the preferred stock and twenty-seven thousand shares of the common stock in units of ten preferred (at $50 each) and three common (at $30); one unit cost $590. The "particular friends" to whom shares were offered learned in a letter dated October 31 that National City had "obtained a 'toehold' in the business of airplane construction and air transportation." The Boeing Airplane and Transport Company "lent itself to expansion," the letter continued. "While the earnings of the company, as shown in the circular, quite definitely justified an investment rating for the preferred shares, the recent earnings were substantially greater and made very attractive the offering when it is rated as an investment in preferred stock, with an added substantial speculation in bonus common stock and stock purchase warrants."[4]

Within twenty-four hours all Boeing stock was sold. From a November 1 advertisement in a number of prominent newspapers, the public learned exactly what it had missed. According to the text, Boeing profits for 1928 "amounted to an annual rate over three times the dividend requirement of this issue of Preferred Stock. . . .

Considering the increasing demand for airplanes and parts, it was entirely reasonable to expect the combined enterprise to show substantially greater profit next year." At the top of the ad and in smaller print, the reader found another message:"These units have been sold privately. This advertisement appears as a matter of record only."[5]

Although on November 1 brokers had no shares to sell, by November 2 they had easily satisfied the demand the ad had created. The reason was that on October 31, the day the private-sale letter was mailed, National City submitted an application to list the Boeing stock on the New York Stock Exchange. Before selling it privately, in other words, the bank had already planned to offer it publicly. If this seems an odd way to protect the investing public, Ripley maintained it was done because "Mr. Boeing wanted to 'see his stock' on the big board."[6]

Sold privately at $590 per unit, the issue opened publicly at $771. Over the next week, the common stock bought by insiders at $30 ranged from a low of $55 to a high of $75; the $50 preferred moved between $57 and $70. Within the next five weeks, concern for the public's welfare disappeared entirely. Ripley sold his own 175 units of Boeing stock for a profit of over $67,000, and National City profited by nearly $1.7 million on the sales of its shares. Among the bank's "particular friends" who also benefited from such transactions were Gordon Rentschler, Edward Deeds, Percy Rockefeller, Bernard Baruch, and Deed's World War I associate Charles Kettering.[7]

While phase one of the merger process was getting under way Rentschler was occupied with similar preparations in Hartford. As of October 25, 1928, only five thousand shares of Pratt & Whitney Aircraft stock existed. The tool company held twenty-five hundred shares, and Rentschler, Mead, and Charles Deeds, the colonel's son, owned the rest.

Charles had joined the firm in May of 1926. In December of 1926 he bought 90 shares of Pratt & Whitney Aircraft stock from Mead and another 100 from Rentschler. While this purchase took place after the Wasp had proven itself, and after the large Navy order was in hand, Deeds still paid only twenty cents a share for his stock. This proved to be a great investment because, just before the company went public, Rentschler declared a stock split of seventy-nine to one. The result was that Rentschler now owned 99,935 shares of Pratt & Whitney (1265 × 79) supposedly worth twenty cents each. To pay for the stock, Rentschler simply transferred company funds from the surplus to the capital account. He issued a stock dividend and paid for it from the last three years' earnings.[8]

With one dividend in hand, Rentschler reached for the next. On December 15, he and the other owners of Pratt & Whitney Aircraft agreed to form a new corporation; at a rate of better than two to one, they exchanged their Pratt & Whitney stock for that of the Boeing Airplane and Transport Co. Rentschler's original 1,265 shares in Pratt & Whitney had now expanded to over 219,000 in the new corporation (which might still use the Boeing name), and Mead's 1,035 shares had become 179,767. Boeing was then selling for sixty dollars per share, so this multiplication of stock turned Rentschler and Mead into instant millionaires.

Of course, these were paper transactions. To ensure that the paper could be exchanged for cash, Rentschler and Boeing decided to include other companies in their new organization. To round out the holding company's operations, they invited Chance Vought to join them for a simple swap of stock and then wooed the Hamilton Aero Manufacturing Co. Owned and operated by the flamboyant Charles Hamilton, this Milwaukee-based business lost money on planes but did well with propellers. More importantly, it promised significant engineering advances. At the time pilots were demanding adjustable propellers that, like the gears of a car, adapt to a variety of conditions, and it appeared that Hamilton would soon satisfy them. He joined the Boeing company for another exchange of stock.[9]

Actually, after December 15 it no longer was the Boeing company— neither Rentschler nor Vought appreciated working for a corporation with only Boeing's name on the letterhead and were adamant about a neutral new name for *their* business. Rentschler's Pratt & Whitney now owned 50 percent of the new corporation's shares; with Vought's interest added, the reluctant Boeing was outnumbered. The United Aircraft and Transport Corporation was formally incorporated in Delaware on January 19, 1929.

With the name change and stock multiplications settled, Rentschler and Mead still had one other arrangement to attend to. National City Bank, the underwriter of the merger, insisted that Pratt & Whitney's founders remain with the firm. As Rentschler later explained, the bank "required George Mead and myself to execute a three-year service contract of their preparation. The contract bound us to the new United Aircraft and Transport Corporation at substantial salaries, with provision for additional compensation from the operations of Pratt & Whitney Aircraft."[10]

This mandatory contract linked Rentschler's and Mead's extra compensation to the number of engines sold. Rentschler correctly stated that such an arrangement was not unusual; he and Mead already had a similar contract with Niles Bement Pond. Since they alone had created such an extraordinarily successful operation, why shouldn't the holding company reward them for their achievement? But when he later described the contract that resulted in bonuses of more than $300,000 in a single year, he maintained there was a built-in gamble: had he and Mead "failed entirely," the extra-compensation provision "would have meant exactly nothing."[11]

In January of 1929, however, the bonus provision meant everything. Orders for large quantities of engines were on hand; the economy was booming; and Rentschler had just merged his operation with transport lines committed to using only his products. If that implied a gamble, Rentschler's definition of a sure thing would be interesting to see.

The New Year: 1929

United intended to offer its stock publicly at the end of January, but a number of private transactions occurred beforehand. Rentschler sold National City over sixty-five thousand shares of his own common stock at $70 each, yielding a profit of over $4.5 million. This sale came with a proviso: without the bank's consent neither Rentschler, Mead, nor Chance Vought could thereafter sell any of their common stock for less than $90 per share. Joseph Ripley explained this pool arrangement, which was to last for ninety days after Rentschler turned over the stock as a means of "protecting" the United Aircraft Corp.[12]

Ripley had already committed Rentschler and Mead to the three-year bonus arrangement, but nevertheless asked them to join the pool because he "was really scared to death that these gentlemen... might step out and lose their interest in the undertaking." National City owned United Aircraft stock, which like the Boeing Airplane and Transport Corporation's, had been first offered to its particular friends. Without a pool arrangement, Ripley could assure neither the bank's, his own, nor his customers' profits. In 1929, pools were a common means of protecting one set of investors from another set of investors and ensuring that no shares were dumped on the free market.

National City decided to open United's stock on the New York Curb Exchange, which specialized in new issues and was to change its name to the American Stock Exchange in 1953. Until United's application for a listing on the Big Board was approved, the Curb promised quick profits for an attractive issue. On January 29, insiders bought the common stock for eight dollars per share and the preferred for nearly fifty-nine dollars. Two days later, the preferred opened on the curb exchange at seventy-seven dollars per share, the common at ninety-seven. This was only the beginning, of course; as Joseph Ripley testified before a 1934 Senate Air Mail Committee investigating United's stock transactions, the market raised the price of the company's stock "so rapidly we could hardly keep track of it."[13]

If Ripley had trouble following United's takeoff, William Boeing did not. He tracked the stock from day to day and sold it whenever the price seemed right. During February he sold 9,400 shares at an average of $92, slowed down in March and, when United hit the big board in early April, resumed selling large blocks on a daily basis— 15,400 shares at $95 on April 20; 8,600 at $110 on the 23rd; 5,000 at $114 on the 27th; and 2,500 at close to $160 on May 11. Within three months, he had traded nearly 40,000 shares— the same shares he'd purchased in October of 1927 for six cents each— at an average price of $105.[14]

During the frenetic January-to-June period, United's common stock hit a high of $162 per share. William Boeing's total profits never appeared in the public record, but some of his colleagues reluctantly informed Congress what they had netted from their rapid sales. National City, for example, chalked up almost $6 million of profit, and Fred Rentschler earned more than $9.5 million from the sale of over 159,000 shares of his private holdings.[15]

With his personal fortune secure, Frederick Rentschler seemed more eager than ever to traffic in aviation. The sale of nearly two million shares of United's stock to the public had enriched the company treasury by over $14 million. Rentschler immediately committed significant sums to the purchase of other companies and the latest machine tools; at the same time, he expanded the industrial capacity of United's original holdings. In the process, he made his first serious mistakes.

Success was Rentschler's Achilles' heel, dulling his normally acute business sense and his tendency toward caution. He never saw the crash coming or, if he did, nevertheless created an empire through 1929 that, like the Pratt & Whitney tool company, soon was burdened with acres of excess industrial capacity in the face of a world depression.

While the stock market gobbled up United's shares, Fred Rentschler painted his company into a corner. To extricate themselves, he and his colleagues would be forced to make many unpleasant compromises, indiscriminately peddling weapons to customers that included a moustachioed German corporal whom company executives called "the evil genius of Europe."

Rentschler's Buying Spree

Rentschler had a grand scheme. With so much capital in hand, he envisioned establishing a transcontinental corporation that would control leading companies in virtually every aspect of aviation. United could manufacture a wide variety of planes, to be flown by pilots trained at its own school of aeronautics along its own passenger routes and, ultimately, landed at its own airports.

If economists termed this vertical integration, to Rentschler it demonstrated the corporation's ability "to concentrate and coordinate its engineering efforts by reason of the close affiliation of its manufacturing and transport activities."[16]

To realize his dream, he intended to use air mail revenues to fund transport lines, which in turn would furnish substantial business to his manufacturing subsidiaries. While the air mails and military paid the overhead, United could develop passenger ships to attract sufficient customers to cut his reliance on the federal government. With the resources of so many different components, the corporation's engineers could test their designs against performance, then study the performance in pursuit of further progress and, not incidentally, profits. The possibilities inherent in a truly integrated operation seemed endless.

First stop on Rentschler's buying spree was Detroit, home to

Henry Ford's trimotor planes as well as to Stout Air Services. Boeing's contracts covered the route from San Francisco to Chicago; from Chicago, National Air Transport carried the mail to New York. Unfortunately for Rentschler, NAT was controlled by Clement Keys, his archenemy and president of another aviation holding company, the Curtiss Airplane and Motor Co. Keys meant to fight for NAT rather than see the company sold to a man whose ambition matched his own.[17] Until he could get his hands on NAT, therefore, Rentschler would settle for Stout, which carried passengers from Chicago to Detroit to Cleveland— one step closer to the East Coast. Far more important, Stout held a permit to extend its service to Buffalo. Because this roundabout route might provide United's only entry into New York, Rentschler bought Stout in June of 1929 for an exchange of stock.

Rentschler next concentrated on the manufacturing end in the hope of producing better, more efficient planes. His first target was Northrop Aircraft of Los Angeles, California, a company with a solid reputation for the design and manufacture of high-speed airplanes. Through 1928 Northrop had experimented with an "allwing," all-metal plane that Rentschler hoped would be suitable for mail service. In exchange for complete ownership, United built Northrop a new plant on land owned by United Airports of Los Angeles, a new Rentschler creation.

Another summer 1929 purchase involved a man already famous on two continents. Igor Sikorsky, who had left Russia in 1919, quickly won a reputation in the United States as both an engineering genius and a financial risk. Although none of his early planes earned money, no one doubted his talents. The successful introduction of his S-38 amphibian plane induced investors to back him with $5 million. Incorporated in Delaware in October of 1928, the Sikorsky Aviation Corp. built a huge plant in Bridgeport, Connecticut, and accumulated orders from the Navy and from Pan American Airways.

Along with his "great belief in the engineering ability of Igor Sikorsky," Rentschler also perceived great possibilities for a well-managed, financially accountable Sikorsky Aviation Corp. In April of 1929, he had bought fifty thousand shares of the Aviation Corporation of America, the parent company of Pan American Airways. Rentschler knew that Pan Am soon would expand its service throughout Latin America, where landings occurred on water, and Sikorsky's superior amphibian planes would find a ready market. For another exchange of stock, Sikorsky became a United subsidiary on August 31.[18]

To round out his purchases, Rentschler picked up the Stearman Aircraft Company of Wichita, Kansas, a manufacturer of planes for "sport and transport" purposes. Despite his apprehensions about the future of private planes, Rentschler was pressured by United's largest investors. In a shotgun marriage in September, he traded 1 share of United's stock for every 3.75 shares of Stearman's[19]

That month also marked the creation of the Hamilton-Standard Propeller Company, another marriage of reluctant partners that occurred for legal reasons. Patents for the lightweight metal propellers manufactured by Milwaukee's Hamilton, a United subsidiary and by Standard in Pittsburgh were owned by the Reed Propeller Company. Throughout the twenties, Hamilton and Standard ignored Reed's vehement complaints about patent infringement, arguing that the patents were invalid; both companies felt secure that Reed could not afford a court battle. But in 1929, when Reed was purchased by Curtiss-Wright, itself the result of a recent merger between Curtiss and Wright Aero, the resources of a multimillion-dollar corporation supported its previously idle threats. Hamilton continued to make propellers without paying royalties. Standard, however, agreed to pay Curtiss for use of Reed's patents if Curtiss agreed to sue any violator— especially Hamilton.

In retaliation, Fred Rentschler promptly acquired Standard and combined it with Hamilton's operation in October of 1929. The new Hamilton-Standard Propeller Co. assumed the licensing agreements that permitted Standard to use Reed's patent. Now Rentschler not only owned the two largest propeller manufacturers in the United States; he also became the lucky employer of a new engineering whiz. Before working for Standard, Frank Caldwell had served as the Army's civilian propeller expert. Like George Mead with engines, Caldwell had original ideas for propellers— ideas that by 1934 would make the combined company the most prominent in the industry.[20]

With this latest acquisition, Rentschler controlled a corporation that by late 1929 included the following sixteen operations, six of which had been purchased within the previous twelve months:

United Equipment Companies
Boeing Airplane Company
   Boeing Aircraft of Canada, Limited
The Hamilton: Standard Propeller Corporation
Northrop Aircraft Corporation Limited
The Pratt & Whitney Aircraft Company
   Canadian Pratt & Whitney Aircraft Company Limited
Sikorsky Aviation Corporation
The Stearman Aircraft Company
Chance Vought Corporation

United Transport Companies
Boeing Air Transport, Inc.
Pacific Air Transport
Stout Air Services, Inc.

Other United Operations
Boeing School of Aeronautics
United Aircraft Exports, Incorporated
United Airports Company of California, Limited
The United Airports of Connecticut, Incorporated

Problems and Prospects

Now that United was the largest, most powerful, most profit-able aviation company in America, Frederick Rentschler sought a president to guide Hamilton-Standard through the depression. Because after so many years of fierce competition, Thomas Hamilton and Harry Kraeling, president of Standard, got along as well as the Army and Navy, a neutral new executive was the pro-peller manufacturer's best bet.

Rentschler decided upon Commander Eugene Wilson, an able administrator who knew everyone worth knowing in military avia-tion and who, at age forty-two, faced a dead end in his military career. After his stint as head of the Engine Section in the Navy's Bureau of Aeronautics, the Annapolis graduate had served with the fleet. But high commands went to sailors, not aviators, so Wilson either went to sea or idled on land. In December of 1929 he made his choice, resigned his commission, and took command of the Hamilton-Standard Propeller Corporation. His job was to make peace between two factories separated by hundreds of miles and to make money despite the consequences of the economic crash. What's more, Wilson had the anchor of overcapacity hanging from his neck even before he assumed his first civilian command.

His first move, after soliciting Rentschler's approval, was to close one factory. With the military's five-year program still underway, Hamilton-Standard had enough assured business to remain profitable only if the propeller operations were consolidated. Wilson carefully inspected both plants and was impressed by Hamilton's layout, but selected Standard's smog-covered Pittsburgh facilities because Milwaukee lay off the main East-West rail line and, more importantly, Wisconsin's heavy corporate income tax had to be figured into costs. Hamilton-Standard, newly headquartered in Pittsburgh, became the first of Rentschler's purchases to feel the sting of the crash.[21] It would not be the last.

Soon, all United's manufacturing operations would share the problem of overcapacity. Even at Pratt & Whitney, the Depression caused a sharp decline in commercial business. But as a result of decisions Rentschler made in mid-1929, he often was able to find foreign markets for at least some of his company's excess production.

Rentschler's export subsidiary, United Aircraft Exports, was organized in July of 1929 to handle foreign sales of the holding company's many manufacturing units. Although it sold to anyone with the wherewithal to buy, it concentrated its efforts on what we today call "developing nations." In China and Colombia, Argentina and Peru, conflict created a market that, for lack of domestic industrialization, could only be supplied from abroad. A Mexican general in search of the latest equipment or a Chinese warlord in need of a private bomber (an order that United later filled) had limited sources of supply, and United Aircraft Exports intended to be one of them.

According to the corporation's first annual report, "the excellence of United products may well be judged by their export record." Following Germany's lead, Japan, which already owned Wasp-powered Boeing fighters and Vought Corsairs, purchased licensing rights to manufacture Pratt & Whitney engines. In Latin America, the military forces of Cuba, Argentina, Mexico, and Peru used the Wasp power plant. As of year's end, "almost 50% of the total volume of 1929 aeronautical exports from the United States consisted of products of United Aircraft."[22]

Like most of his competitors, Rentschler perceived few problems with the export market, which existed to be exploited. Moral issues complicated simple business transactions; if Americans refused to sell arms, moreover, another country would. And if United charged underdeveloped nations more than other customers and sold to both sides in a war, well, its customers knew it. Warring parties demanded only that no favoritism be shown in matters of price and delivery. As Donald Brown— who became president of United in 1934— noted, suppressing United's sales abroad would only lead to "an increase in the volume of exportation from competitive producing countries at the expense of our own national military foundations and economic welfare."[23]

By the middle of 1929, Rentschler had lost his skepticism about aviation's future markets. He still avoided any involvement with the market for small planes, and he continued to subcontract 50 percent of United's work. Nevertheless, each of the corporation's manufacturing subsidiaries substantially increased their capacity that year, and two Canadian branch operations— Boeing's plant for planes in Vancouver and Pratt & Whitney's engine facility in Montreal— were established. United's mainstay, Pratt & Whitney Aircraft, built a factory that doubled yet again the floor space that had already been doubled the previous year.

Fred Rentschler's wife, Faye, dressed in white and standing in a field of weeds and farm buildings, broke ground for the $2 million new factory, "the most completely equipped aircraft engine manufacturing plant in the world," on July 16, 1929.

The efficient new East Hartford factory contained 400,000 square feet, making it more than three football fields long. Set up for mass production, it was crossed by twelve- and fifteen-foot aisles for transporting materials and subcontracted finished parts from the railway siding at one end.[24]

And just to increase the pressure for more business, Rentschler built another plant, the new home of the Chance Vought Corporation, next door. Specializing in military observation and fighter planes, Vought had sold 112 planes in 1929 at a profit of nearly $600,000. But to break even in the 175,000-square-foot factory, Vought was obliged to sell close to 100 planes.[25] Unless Congress funded more aircraft in 1932, the end of the first five-year building program, Vought might own a very modern facility in a great deal of trouble.

Still, as 1930 approached, United's worries lay in the future. Rentschler's bottom line showed $9 million profit— a figure that discouraged pessimism about the corporation's short- or long-term financial prospects.

In comparison, another of America's aviation giants, the Curtiss-Wright Corporation, had bet on the private flier; its far-flung string of aviation schools and airports resulted in losses of nearly a million dollars in 1929.[26] Even after Rentschler's enormous expansion program, United entered the thirties better prepared than its competitors. It had a backlog of at least two years of military business, and as long as Congress continued to generously fund the air mails, the transport operation could easily carry troubled subsidiaries.

Rentschler's only concern was the federal government. Although he had been correct in relying on its subsidies as the axis of United's profits, he was aware that all his diversified holdings were dependent on the attitudes and actions of the president, the Senate and the House of Representatives. In 1929, over 95 percent of transport industry revenues came from air-mail postage. Pratt & Whitney did 47 percent of its business with the military; Hamilton-Standard thanked the military for 75 percent of its revenues; and Chance Vought derived over 96 percent of its sales from the Navy.[27]

The relationship between United and Washington was dialectical, with each affecting the other. A single government action could threaten disaster. For the United Aircraft and Transport Corporation, it was Washington or bust.

Dividing the Sky

Frederick Rentschler began the new year with an old battle. He needed National Air Transport to fulfill his dream of a transcontinental airline, especially now that one of his competitors, Transcontinental Air Transport, seemed about to initiate cross-country service via Texas, Kansas, and Ohio. Rentschler feared that if Boeing's routes continued to end at Chicago it would eventually be rendered obselete by other carriers. Why bother changing planes at Chicago if another line offered service all the way to New York? Because it made little economic sense to share the skies, Rentschler attempted to outflank Clement Keys, his enemy at NAT. As he told a *New York Times* reporter, "The air between the coasts is not big enough to be divided."[28]

Three groups of investors owned the bulk of NAT's stock. Keys controlled the New York contingent; Howard Coffin, who had headed aircraft production in World War I, held power in Detroit; and Earle H. Reynolds, NAT's president and largest individual stockholder, was the most influential figure in Chicago. Reynolds, who with his colleagues owned nearly a third of the company's outstanding shares, was a banker. Rentschler arranged for agents of his brother Gordon, by then president of National City Bank, to approach Reynolds on his own bankerly terms. By the end of March, United owned nearly a third of NAT's outstanding shares. As *The New York Times* observed, "this interest was believed on Wall Street to be close to constituting working control of NAT."

Close, but not enough. The adamant Keys convinced NAT's board of directors to resist a takeover, whereupon Rentschler went over the board's head and, on April 4, 1930, submitted a public offer. At an exchange rate of one United share, worth ninety dollars, for every 3½ shares of the twenty-five dollar NAT, stockholders were invited to turn in their certificates as fast as they could. Rentschler's offering letter indicated that United sought proxies for use at the annual meeting of NAT's stockholders on April 10.[29]

Keys fought back by applying what today is called "shark repellent." Three days before the meeting, the NAT board adopted new by-laws that enabled the Keys group to retain control of the airline. Instead of a simple majority, it now took two-thirds of the voting stock to remove board members or to change any by-laws, but a majority of the existing board could change the rules whenever they saw fit. And, conversely, instead of a majority, a quorum of stockholders and a quorum of the board existed if one-third of either was present.[30] So that a simple majority of the stock could forestall action neither by the board nor the stockholders.

At the stockholders' meeting, Rentschler learned that his takeover efforts had been neutralized. He had planned to gain more time for stock purchases by holding back the voting power of his shares. The meeting would have been postponed if no quorum existed, but Keys had eliminated that maneuver by lowering to one-third the number of shares needed for a quorum. On April 9, the board of directors had authorized the issue of 300,000 new shares of NAT stock. Coincidentally, these shares would be bought in a private offering by North American Aviation, a company controlled by Keys, who now held a majority of the voting stock and then some. It looked as if Fred Rentschler had been outsmarted, not to mention publicly throttled, by none other than Clement Keys.

United's lawyers immediately challenged the legality of the changes in the by-laws, and the Delaware Chancery Court issued an injunction restraining the NAT directors from issuing the new shares. Meanwhile, Joseph Ripley— working for both Frederick and Gordon Rentschler— was busily accumulating more NAT shares. By April 17, Rentschler announced control of over 57 percent of NAT's stock.[31]

Keys refused to give in. Because the new rules specified control of two-thirds of the stock in order to change directors, he defied United's call for a new board. Rentschler thereupon sued to have the April 10 meeting voided because of the quorum changes. On April 22, Rentschler stunned Keys with one of NAT's old corporate rules: an overlooked provision of the by-laws maintaining that anyone holding one fifth of the outstanding shares could call a stockholders' meeting. Rentschler exercised this option and announced a meeting at which the main order of business would be the removal of Keys. On May 7 the assembled stockholders would rewrite the rewritten NAT by-laws.

Back on Wall Street, Joseph Ripley was busier than ever. He boosted NAT shareholders' rate of exchange for United stock from one to three to one to 3½ and persuaded Earle Reynolds to advise them to accept United's latest bid, whereupon Keys gave in.

On April 23, a group of United and NAT officers assembled in Key's office in his absense. United agreed to drop its suit if a majority of the NAT board resigned. When they obliged, Frederick Rentschler became chairman and president of National Air Transport and finally acquired his transcontinental airline. And just to ensure that everyone knew who was boss, he published a new edition of NAT's monthly newspaper. The cover of the first April issue had featured a picture of the new company president, Clement Keys; the second April issue depicted president Rentschler alongside a story explaining that NAT had become a subsidiary of United Aircraft, the first coast-to-coast airline.[32]

Rentschler closed the NAT deal at a crucial time in the development of American aviation. Since September of 1929, airline representatives had been negotiating new contracts with

Postmaster General Walter Brown, who abruptly decided to transform the air mail system with the assistance of the carriers. In his opinion, the existing system was a mess. On some low-traffic routes, two lines competed for passengers; on other, heavily traveled routes, the carrier had made no provision for passengers in purchasing or designing equipment. Airmail rates, too, were arbitrary, ranging from nine cents to three dollars per pound. And as the system stood in January of 1930, contracts with one line simply passed to the new owner— all terms intact. So, when holding companies like United absorbed smaller lines, the government failed to benefit from any reduction of overhead and increased efficiency made possible by the larger operation.

Rentschler tried his best to prevent the changes mandated by Postmaster Brown. Having the only transcontinental route, no serious competition, and only 2 percent of its 1929 revenues garnered from passengers, United carried people where it thought best. Now Brown intended to create a second transcontinental line, to demand passenger service on every existing route and, most frightening of all, to significantly reduce a carrier's mail payments as passengers took up the slack. Because Brown was adamant, United grudgingly helped write the McNary-Watres bill, which received congressional approval on April 29, 1930. According to the new law, carriers were paid on the basis of cargo space alloted for the mails; even with no letters aboard, a carrier received up to $1.25 per mile simply for flying a ship.

The bill also specified that as of May 1, 1930, all carriers were obliged to provide seats for passengers; if they flew mail, they also flew people; and they did so with the clear understanding that the Postmaster General meant to reduce mail payments "from time to time" but "without material loss to the operators." Any carrier that failed to cooperate with Brown risked losing postal certification.

To add more incentives for better service, the new law raised a carrier's postal pay on the basis of several variables besides available space for mail: if carriers flew at night or carried more than ten passengers, for example, or if the plane boasted two-way radios or more than one engine. Brown wanted the best system possible and he was willing to subsidize it— for the short run.[33] Once again, the government was underwriting aviation by providing airlines with an incentive for manufacturing larger planes.

United's potential transcontinental profits were threatened on several fronts, but there were few alternatives to working within the system. Besides, by negotiating the best deals, Rentschler won some of the highest rates in the nation. Under the new law, United's Boeing subsidiary provided the best passenger service in America, and was thus entitled to mail pay near the post office's upper limits. Since early 1929 the line had been using the twelve-passenger "Model-80" plane, which featured hot and cold running water, upholstered seats, individual reading lamps, the first stewardesses in the United States, and three very capable Wasp engines. By the time McNary-Watres passed Congress, an improved Model-80A was equipped with three Hornet engines, carried sixteen passengers, and reached then-impressive speeds of 125mph.[34]

On the newly acquired Chicago to New York run, however, NAT had no planes suitable for passenger service. Rentschler deftly handled the problem by eliminating one United subsidiary— Stout Air Lines— and selling its Ford trimotor to another— NAT. Because the three-motor Ford planes carried twelve to fourteen passengers, United cashed in on the Post Office's variables, beginning transcontinental service with pay rates very close to the $1.25 per mile limit, whereas Boeing's initial agreement called for $1.18 and NAT's for $1.15.[35]

But despite these advantages, after May of 1930 United had to carry equal or even greater amounts of mail for less money. Rentschler adapted to Postmaster Brown's forced changes by making some of his own. For an exchange of stock he bought Varney Air Lines, which complemented Boeing's routes in the Northwest, and for no expenditure whatever he created United Air Lines. This holding company within a holding company, established in July of 1931, was designed to achieve economy and efficiency by supervising the current service of forty-one cities in fifteen states by Boeing, Varney, NAT, and Pacific Air Transport. Fred Rentschler became chairman of United Air Lines; Phillip Johnson of Boeing was its first president; and "old-timers" like William Boeing and Edward Deeds sat on its board of directors.

United Air Lines existed solely for the benefit of its operating companies, which paid its expenses. The new holding company managed plane traffic; adjusted schedules, fares and regulations; bought insurance; procured new equipment; and, alone among the competition, advertised the existence of "the first form of transportation to take people off the ground." Although Americans still shuddered at the thought of planes, Rentschler predicted they would feel reassured by a huge national organization. Advertising that stressed the size of the United family, the vast experience of its thousand employees and the on-time reliability of its 120 planes might influence the public to fly United and, as Johnson wrote, "recommend our services to those who are not riding on airplanes today but whom we must interest in doing so."[36]

Rentschler next dreamed of outclassing the competition with a revolutionary transport plane. Then, while the others were catching up, United could use its profits to fund research to produce yet another plane years ahead of the aviation pack. With its vertically integrated manufacturing companies, after all, it had the expertise with which to design the plane that would make United the dominant force in air passenger travel, compensating for its losses on the federal government's mail by capturing a larger share of the passenger market from its competitors.

The Boeing 247 did, in fact, initiate a revolution. The problem was that, while others reaped the benefits of United's audacious strategy, the new plane tore United apart. Not only did George Mead threaten to quit Pratt & Whitney, but Donald Douglas, a primary competitor, produced his own revolutionary plane. United Air Lines not only lost the lead in passenger travel, but the United Aircraft and Transportation Company lost its commercial manufacturing business at the very time the Depression was eroding the military budget. As it happened, the 247 was probably the biggest business mistake Fred Rentschler ever made.

The B-247 vs. the DC-2

Back in the spring of 1930, while Fred Rentschler fought with Clement Keys for control of National Air Transport, workers were hauling the wings and fuselage of a peculiar new plane called the Monomail from the Boeing factory to Seattle's King Country Airport. With its long fat cigar-shaped fuselage and two all-metal wings, the Monomail had been designed to maximize the propulsion provided by George Mead's 560-horsepower Hornet engine. Company publicists boasted that this new ship would fly four thousand pounds of mail at speeds approaching 160 miles per hour.

On the ground the plane did look odd, especially since the

fuselage was painted green, the tail gray, and the wings orange. In the air, it delivered on all its designers' promises and quickly passed qualification tests on May 6, 1930. Only a week before, unfortunately, the McNary-Watres bill had rendered it useless as, designed to transport mail, the Monomail was unfit to carry passengers.

When Boeing staffers "stretched" the fuselage to accommodate six and then eight passengers, comfort was sacrificed and amenities were impossible. The obvious solution was to provide a new transport plane that employed the Monomail's innovations without eliminating the luxury demanded by air travelers. In Seattle, Boeing designers went to work on a large, sleek twelve-passenger monoplane weighing sixteen thousand pounds and propelled by two of George Mead's most powerful Hornet engines.[37]

When United's pilots were confronted with plans for the new ship, however, they immediately compiled a list of its major faults. No field in existence, they claimed, could safely take an eight-ton plane. Pilots accustomed to Wasps, moreover, would find Hornets overpowering. Though the designers were willing to return to the drawing board, George Mead and his Hartford colleagues were appalled at the notion of compromising quality because of the pilots' timidity. The power plant, they argued, was the heart of any plane; a splended craft with the wrong engine might perform like the lethal Liberty-powered de Havilands. Who wanted to transport passengers in flying coffins?

As head of all the United companies, Frederick Rentschler was responsible for the final decision. In Seattle for consultations, he confirmed that "to a man, the United Air Lines pilots insisted they could not safely fly or land any airplane of greater than 12,000 gross pounds on the existing and available regular and emergency airports."[38]

George Mead, who emphatically disagreed, cabled Rentschler in Seattle: "I urge you to use Hornets for these planes, as I do not believe the Wasp can provide sufficient margin of safety, even for the scaled-down model."[39]

When Rentschler stood by the pilots, Mead took the decision personally. He was, after all, engineering head of the United companies and one of the ablest men in American aviation. If he let Rentschler run United's business side with a free hand, he expected similar leeway in his area of expertise. He agreed to try to develop a Wasp cable of powering the smaller version of his transport plane, but he never forgot the insult. He knew he was right, and within a year so did the rest of the United States.

If Rentschler hedged on developing the newest possible plane, he displayed his normally acute business acumen by boldly opting to re-equip United Air Lines with sixty planes at a cost of sixty-eight thousand dollars each. Boeing at the same time turned down an order to similarly supply Transcontinental and Western Airlines, a cross-country carrier created by Postmaster Brown under the auspices of the McNary-Watres Bill. Not until United had its sixty new planes aloft would Boeing consider a competitor's business. After all the idea was to eliminate other airlines, not to help them fly.[40]

But there was a rub in the vertical integration that permitted United to lock out its competition. If TWA found another source for a new airliner, and if that other plane proved superior to the 247, United itself could be locked out of the "fastest plane" market. To Rentschler, however, this seemed at best a long shot. Despite the compromises that enraged Mead, the 247 promised to be the best transport ship in the air.

In August of 1932, TWA responded to Boeing's turndown by sending confidential letters to every conceivable manufacturer of large transport planes offering to buy ten or more trimotored transport ships from anyone who could better the Boeing 247. Cost was of such little concern that there was no mention even of a ball-park price. On the stationery a prominent streamer was printed: Save Time—Use the Air Mail.[41]

In Santa Monica, Donald Douglas was intrigued by TWA's request. Until 1932 he had neglected the uncertain commercial market; the military furnished nearly 90 percent of his business. Now, however, the letter had been followed by a visit from Harold Talbott, Jr., a TWA director and, as chairman of North American Aviation, the holder of 89,000 shares of Douglas stock (an intimate associate of Colonel Deeds during World War I, he was to become Secretary of the Air Force in 1953) Talbott stressed that Ford seemed ready to abandon its aviation interests, that the new air mail law assured a market for passenger planes, and that, if Douglas could out-engineer the Boeing 247, he had a clear shot at all the orders that Boeing rejected. It was time for Douglas to build TWA a plane that would enable it to eliminate the competition.[42]

Douglas accepted the challenge. Within a week he had submitted preliminary designs, and within ten months the Douglas DC-2 was up and flying— better than anything else in the sky.

Douglas had built the plane United's pilots refused to consider. Powered by two 710-horsepower Curtiss-Wright engines, the Douglas monoplane flew faster and carried more cargo than the 247. If Boeing's plane cruised at 170 mph, Douglas's reached 191. If Boeing's plane carried four hundred pounds of mail, the DC-2 carried close to five hundred. And if Boeing's plane flew ten passengers with a great deal of noise, Douglas flew fourteen in the quietest passenger ship yet. The DC-2, moreover, had the corner on comfort. Whereas the 247 had one narrow aisle bisected by the main wing spar eighteen inches above the floor, the DC-2 offered wide aisles with no obstructions. Finally, because the DC-2 had wider and higher windows than the 247, the cabin seemed much larger and brighter.

The 247 lost out in everything but timing: United had a year's head start. When the first 247 was launched on the transcontinental run in May of 1933, passenger revenues immediately soared. Until Douglas's plane began its TWA service in July, 1934, the 247 enjoyed a brief supremacy in air-passenger travel. Not surprisingly, as soon as the carriers could appreciate the performance and appointments of the DC-2, they quickly placed their orders. Boeing's first production run of sixty ships was its only one. Although orders for fifteen additional planes, including "a special militarized 247 for a private owner in China," trickled in, Douglas had effectively eliminated its competitor from the commercial transport market. Boeing didn't make a comeback until after World War II.[43]

At Pratt & Whitney, the long-term commercial situation looked just as bad. Losing the DC-2 business to the Curtiss-Wright Cyclone, the Hornet's equal in every way, marked the engine-maker's first major business defeat since the advent of the Wasp and Hornet. Now, thanks to Boeing's failure, Pratt & Whitney found itself shut out of an already shrinking market. In 1933 there were perhaps five hundred transport planes in the world. The 247 had initiated a revolution that *reduced* the number of transports made; as planes got bigger, airlines needed fewer of them. Large profits from passenger travel might have been a lifesaver, if large profits existed. But the McNary-Watres Bill specified that, as carriers increase the space devoted to passengers, mail revenues drop. United grossed over $8 million on the mails in 1931, but only $5

million in 1933. Although passenger revenues did increase
dramatically— from $1.4 million in 1931 to $3.9 million in 1933—
passengers never produced profits; and they also demanded
fashionable airports as well as fashionable (and expensive) planes.[44]

On the bottom line, the bad news was that United Aircraft's
net gains from air transport operations totaled $1.8 million in 1931,
$1.2 million in 1932, and a mere $179,578 in 1933.[45] At the height of
the Depession any profits looked good, but the decision to build the
247 had boomeranged in so many ways that the company's long-
term prospects appeared dim at best. The situation was equally
gloomy at Hamilton-Standard, Vought, and especially Sikorsky.
United's first real losses were flying in from every direction.

Russian Relief, Controllable Propellers, and Idle Machines

Aside from substantial losses due to the Depression, Sikorsky
Aviation was plagued by guarantees it had given to Juan Trippe,
the head of Pan American Airways and, according to Eugene
Wilson, a predator. At the height of the 1929 boom, Pan Am
solicited bids on large amphibian planes to carry passengers and
cargo along its Caribean and South American routes. Igor Sikorsky
won the competition with the S-40 American Clipper, which was as
sleek as a dolphin, as graceful as a sailing ship— and an unmitigated
financial disaster. Sikorsky's original price was $125,000 for each
Clipper. But as the work failed to progress, Sikorsky's costs
mounted to the tune of well over $100,000 for initial engineering
development alone. When a satisfactory design was finally achieved,
Pan American insisted on enforcing Sikorsky's guarantees. As
Eugene Wilson later put it, "When the specifications for the first
Pan American Clippers had been reviewed by Colonel Charles A.
Lindbergh, Pan American's advisor, and incorporated into the con-
tract, they didn't mean a thing." Sikorsky never imagined the plane
would be hard to produce, and Rentschler never imagined Juan
Trippe would hold him to the letter of their contract.[46]

As Trippe demanded that each feature he'd been promised be
delivered, even such luxurious amenities as swivel-handled toilets
and back-lighted card tables, Sikorsky watched helplessly as costs
rose and losses mounted. By the end of 1931, when the first Clipper

ships were flying, Igor Sikorsky had lost over $600,000 and, in the hope of recouping some of that money, signed yet another contract with Pan Am for an improved version. However, the second time around, he had to do better for United. As Rentschler told his colleagues, "there was a limit to the contribution United Aircraft could make to Russian relief."

As for Hamilton-Standard, earnings were in a decline because of the military's concern about the company's monopoly of the propeller market. By law, procurement officers were obliged to seek competing sources of supply; otherwise, the government would find itself at the mercy of manufacturers' arbitrary pricing policies. To placate Congress, as Eugene Wilson explained, the services solicited bids "from any little shop on the corner who could grind a blade or any little fly-by-night machine shop that could turn a rotor hub." Without the burden of research costs and unused capacity, these small firms easily outbid Hamilton-Standard, and the military happily distributed its propeller business. For Hamilton-Standard, any new orders depended on new developments, without; as Wilson angrily stressed, "any production to write it off on."[47]

Between March 1929 and August 1930, the propeller manufacturer saw sales of nearly $3.5 million and profits of $485,000. Between January 1931 and May 1932, sales totaled $1.7 million, profits $224,397. But between June 1932 and April 1933, when sales sank to $664,000, profits were a paltry $38,500.[48]

Long before that low, Rentschler took a drastic step. Because propeller revenues "could no longer support the separate establishment in Pittsburgh on the reduced amount of business available," he moved Hamilton-Standard into the unused portion of Pratt & Whitney's Hartford plant. Less than a year later, he consolidated both manufacturing operations; the small staff imported from Pittsburgh confined its work to sales, services, and engineering while Pratt & Whitney workers made the propellers.

Hamilton-Standard's situation looked dismal until its super-engineer Frank Caldwell, inspired by Rentschler's insistence that aviation products lasted too long, perfected the controllable in-flight pitch propeller that finally allowed pilots to "shift gears" while flying. Working in a wooden test house "just large enough to hold the propeller and a low-powered electric motor to whirl it," Caldwell gave Hamilton-Standard the means to survive. Even the military could safely buy from a monopoly that owned the patent rights to a device that significantly improved flying performance, in the crucial areas of climb, cruising economy, and single engine performance.[49]

Although Caldwell's invention brought large profits only after 1933, Rentschler gladly carried the subsidiary until it could win over the industry. In the meantime, he was delighted to employ the increasingly idle machinery at United's most profitable company, Pratt & Whitney Aircraft.

Pratt & Whitney's best year so far had been 1929, when it accounted for over 55 percent of United's $9 million profit. On sales of 2,017 engines, Pratt & Whitney made a $5.2 million profit, 33 percent on sales alone. Although engines sales dropped to 1,589 units in 1930 and 1,286 in 1931, profits were over $2 million. The company would continue to be successful— if, that is, the military kept buying engines.

In 1930, Army and Navy purchases constituted 65 percent of Pratt & Whitney sales; in 1931 the figure climbed to 75 percent. But because 1932 marked the end of the military's five-year building program, and because Congress had no intention of funding weaponry instead of food at the height of the Depression, military budgets were reduced. In 1932 Pratt & Whitney sold only 805 engines. Despite a million dollars' profit on these sales, Rentschler had clear cause for concern. At each of United's subsidiaries sales and profits had dropped, and new military policies threatened to make them drop even further.[50]

As a result of the Depression and an unstable world situation exemplified by Japan's 1931 invasion of Manchuria, Congress once again was focusing its attention on munitions manufacturers. In 1932, for example, a joint executive and Congressional committee recommended a constitutional amendment to prevent profiteering by taxing "95% of all income above the previous three-years' average."[51] Though Secretary of the Treasury William Wooden rejected this suggestion, the military and the manufacturers alike anticipated continuing Congressional scutiny.

The result for Pratt & Whitney was that the military held the company's profits to a much tighter margin. Between 1927 and 1931 Pratt & Whitney averaged 26 percent profit on its Navy contracts and 27 percent on its Army contracts. By 1932 Navy profits fell to 9.3 percent and by 1933 to 5.5 percent. Army profits came to a respectable 12.8 percent in 1932, but plummeted to 0.2 percent a year later. With $3,754 profit on Army sales of $1.8 million, yet another of Rentschler's companies was walking a tightrope between red and black ink.[52]

His solution was to exploit the markets abroad but, unlike in 1928 or 1929, with a decided sense of urgency.[53]

United Aircraft Exports

During 1932 and 1933, United's export sales accounted for 10 percent of the company's total business but easily 20 percent of its net profits,[54] thanks in part to the special salesmen who exploited the foreign markets. These men were fluent in many languages, skilled at entertaining clients, and adept at stroking government officials, and none embodied those skills more successfully than Thomas Foster Hamilton.

Born on the wrong side of Seattle's tracks in 1894, Tom Hamilton had entertained on all-American ambition— to be fabulously rich— since childhood. He began his career by trying to "match Bill Boeing dollar for dollar," using his envy of Boeing's inherited wealth as a plane uses a propeller. And though he never matched his rival's fortune, he did become a rich man when United Aircraft acquired his propeller company. But Hamilton lived in such splendid style that by 1931 his hard-earned wealth had evaporated. Unless he could accept a more ordinary existence, he required another fortune.

Hamilton visited his friend Eugene Wilson at Sikorsky to nominate himself as United's European sales representative. After Rentschler endorsed this idea, Hamilton immediately left for Paris, where, in Wilson's words, he set up shop in a suite at the posh George V Hotel and proceeded, in Wilson's words, to "entertain the deadheads and crownheads of Europe."[55]

Anything was grist for Hamilton's mill. When he "smelled out" a need for engines in an impoverished Arab state, he agreed to accept one-third of the purchase price in the form of oriental rugs. The rugs were shipped to a dealer in New York, who sold them at inflated prices. United emerged with greater profits than if Hamilton had held out for cash.[56]

In another Mideast deal, Hamilton had arranged for a Pratt & Whitney mechanic to install its engines in British-made planes. A Mr. L.G. True was dispatched from Hartford to London, where he tried to back out of the assignment upon learning that he was expected to enlist in the Turkish army. From Berlin, Hamilton insisted that service in the Turkish army was the accepted practice for airplane representatives; along with the repair and maintenance of engines, True also would promote United's products to the Turkish armed forces. What better way to achieve this goal than by becoming a true comrade of his Turkish brothers?

If the Turkish and other Arab deals involved everything from carpeting to foreign intrigue, United's German sales, on the other hand, were straightforward business transactions, at least initially. In January of 1933 the Bavarian Motor Works requested licensing rights on the Hornet D engine. Hamilton's job was to ensure greater profits than those resulting from the German Wasp licenses of 1929.

On February 6 Rentschler wrote to Francis Love, president of United Aircraft Exports, that "it seemed pretty clear that Germany was about to insist upon a reasonable armament program. . ." Thus, it was probable "that royalties in the next five years might amount to a reasonable sum." He agreed to grant the licenses on the condition that prices for engines produced by BMW would equal, but never undercut, the cost of Hartford-made engines; that the royalty rate should be at least $200 per unit; and that there should be some guaranteed minimum royalty."[57]

Hamilton saw no cause for concern. As he informed his boss, "The German government was so anxious to obtain a reliable high-horsepower air-cooled engine that a satisfactory agreement would be quickly signed. My conversations with the various departments indicate that their interests extend far beyond matters of traffic."[58]

By the end of March the transaction was concluded, and a new relationship between Germany and United began. Germany's purchases totaled $8,000 in 1931 and 1932 and climbed to $234,000 by 1933. The following year, Germany— able to produce all the weapons it wanted— bought $1.5 million worth of engines and planes. A hefty 78 percent of Hitler's 1934 aviation orders went to the United Aircraft and Transport Corporation. Later, Eugene Wilson was to complain that America complacently watched Germany rearm. "Hitler made no bones about it," he recalled. "Such Nazis as Goering, Milch and Udet bragged about their prowess to every American who visited Germany." But despite Wilson's critical comments about America's stance, he and his business colleagues knowingly helped the Nazis turn their desire for a mighty war machine into a ghastly reality.[59]

Meanwhile, civil war had transformed China into a series of armed camps. United, with the assistance of the United States government, furnished weapons to several of the combatants. Through its Bureau of Foreign Trade, the Department of Commerce supplied aviators to teach the Chinese how to fly and what to buy. In early 1933, the Department sought United's approval of the men it intended to send to Canton. United was delighted to acquaint American pilots with Boeing's and Chance Vought's line of goods—especially after they had prompted the sale of more than forty Vought Corsairs within the next year for over one million dollars. Perhaps not incidentally, Leighton W. Rogers, the federal official who dispatched the pilots, soon afterward resigned his government job for a post in private life. He became a vice president of the industry-funded Aeronautical Chamber of Commerce.[60].

United's South American business was handled by its export division president Francis Love. Involved in the export trade for over thirty years, Love had worked for the Crane Company selling toilet seats and wash bowls and somehow acquired contacts in the right circles. He exploited ongoing conflicts throughout Latin America and considered supplying both sides in the potential war an accepted and acceptable business practice. He insisted, however, that United play no favorites; each party paid the same price for its weapons, and, if possible, deliveries were simultaneous. Although United was similarly scrupulous elsewhere, extra care was required in this part of the world, where Curtiss-Wright was better known. In every country Love visited there was at least one army or navy pilot who had been trained at the Curtiss School and therefore was partial to this competitor's products. To boost United's recognition in pilot's minds, Love conceived of a series of aviation "scholarships"; United would bring pilots to the States, train them in Boeing or Vought planes, and send them home as United's arms ambassadors. This "capital idea," he maintained, "might be worked out in such a way as to be a tremendous help in getting future business in South America."

However capital an idea it was, United never offered scholarships because wars proved to be a far less expensive sales tool. Colombia bought thirty planes in 1933 for over $650,000. Her enemy, Peru, which then purchased mostly Curtiss-Wright equipment, nevertheless spent over $135,000 for three Vought Corsairs and miscellaneous aviation equipment. Even before these deals were completed, Brazil had ordered fourteen Boeing pursuit planes plus forty-five Corsairs. With a conflict between Paraguay and Bolivia also boiling, United's share of the South American market seemed secure.[61]

Getting paid for the goods shipped, however, presented problems. The Peruvian government owed United over $750,000 in 1932. When Peruvian officials pleaded poverty, United seemed likely to suffer a very substantial loss until Love proposed a solution. On islands off the Peruvian coast lay hundred-foot mountains of bird droppings. This "guano" served as a great natural fertilizer. As Love explained to Congress in 1934, "I worked out a scheme whereby I agreed to charter the ships, to pay the cost of weighing and sampling and testing, and to pay the freight and advance." Peru was expected to meet the terms of its long contract with United. For example, the notarized agreement stipulated "pure and unadulturated" guano, free of stone and feathers.

For the Peruvians, the guano deal was quite profitable. They kept fifty percent of the sale proceeds, and 25 percent went toward United's old debt. With the remaining funds, Peru agreed to buy new weapons from the United Aircraft and Transport Corporation.[62]

As a result of the guano transaction and other deals, the company's 1933 annual report boasted that, with $2.5 million in revenues, United Aircraft Exports had enjoyed its best year. And with another $2.2 million in unfilled orders, the export backlog exceeded the 1932 figure by over 300 percent. What's more, "intensive effort has been and is still being made to increase the volume of export business."[63]

However, in 1934 United was a corporation desperate for revenues. A letter accompanying the annual report explained why: without warning and "wholly without justification," the Federal government had cancelled all United's airmail contracts. Through the first quarter of 1934, losses came to a quarter of a million dollars per month, and executives had no idea of when matters would be settled. They did know that the company was in serious trouble. As the letter stated, even if "no permanent air-mail legislation had yet taken final form in Congress, it was highly probable. . . that the complete separation of transport companies from manufacturing companies would be stipulated as a condition to the reletting of air-mail contracts on any other than a temporary basis."[64]

Washington threatened to break United apart, and the most galling aspect to men like Frederick Rentschler and William Boeing was the government's explanation. Senator Hugo Black of Alabama actually said that "the control of American aviation had been ruthlessly taken away from the men who could fly and bestowed upon bankers, promotors and politicians, sitting in their inner offices, alloting among themselves the taxpayer's money."[65]

And for taking the taxpayer's money, ruthless men like Rent-schler and Boeing would be forced in 1934 to pay any penalty imposed by the taxpayer's purchasing agent— even if the penalty was the destruction of the United Aircraft and Transport Corporation.

4

INVESTIGATIONS:
THE BLACK, DELANEY,
AND NYE COMMITTEES

SENATOR BLACK: "Do you believe that it was fair
to the people of the United States to make such
mail business that in one year a company will
make a million dollars profit of a $750 investment?"

PAUL HENDERSON (Vice President, United Air
Lines): "There is only one answer to that, sir. It
is no; it is no, of course not."

The Black Committee

The Depression hit most Americans in 1929. Five years later, when it reached United Aircraft, it impacted full force through a combination of declining sales, unused capacity, and Senator Hugo Black's political exploitation of the startling facts that accidentally came his way.

Black's "Deep Throat" was a Hearst newspaper reporter named Fulton Lewis, who learned in the summer of 1931 that Luddington Air Lines had lost its bid for the New York-to-Washington, D.C., route to Eastern Air Transport. Although the law mandated awarding a contract to the lowest bidder, Luddington had bid twenty-five cents per mile compared with Eastern's eighty-nine. Like any good reporter, Lewis sought scandal and promptly began rummaging through the Post Office's files to determine why it was paying sixty-four cents more per mile than necessary. As he burrowed deeper into the public record, he had a hard time containing his excitement. This story— comprised of Frederick Rentschler's immense personal earnings, stock speculation, the avoidance of competitive bidding and an invitation-only "spoils conference" in the Postmaster General's own office— was a political keg of dynamite that the Hearst organization would relish.

Or so Fulton Lewis thought. He wanted to break his expose in early 1932, but his cautious superiors instructed him to send the material to Mr. Hearst himself. He quickly did so. And then he waited. And waited. And waited.

Hearst never replied. Apparently reluctant to embarrass the

Hoover administration, Hearst sat on Lewis's story in hopes that his silence would kill it.[1]

Hearst would have had his way if Senator Black, a Democrat from Alabama who was chairing the special Senate Committee investigating ocean mail contracts, hadn't heard about Lewis's work. Once Black examined the material and obtained William Randolph Hearst's reluctant consent, he made the air mail contracts the basis for an extraordinary series of hearings. And if Lewis never had the satisfaction of scooping his peers, he did sit at Senator Black's side, coaching the chairman throughout his interrogation of the many executives testifying about the intimate workings of the air mails and the aviation industry.

To substantiate Lewis' charges, Black's committee stationed about a hundred Interstate Commerce Commission investigators at the main offices of America's large and small aviation companies. At precisely 9:13 A.M. on October 15, 1933, flashing I.D. cards and search warrants, the I.C.C. squads seized a mountain of air mail correspondence.[2]

Senator Black had caught the industry with its filing cabinets open. He had no compunctions about revealing the private enterprise side of public policy, starting with the controversial issue of subsidy. For delivering the mail, Washington paid carriers far more than the cost of postage; in 1932 alone, the government's shortfall totaled nearly $18 million. Under the circumstances, Senator Black considered the $1.2 million profit of a company like United Aircraft to be unconscionable. Without public funding United could never survive, much less profit, from the transport of letters and people.[3]

On the subject of survival, Senator Black was correct. But when it came to subsidies, he totally ignored the stated purpose of the air mail legislation. From the first Kelly Act in 1925, which turned the air mail over to private carriers, to the McNary-Watres Bill five years later, the government had deliberately and openly used the public's money to stimulate the growth and development of American aviation in order to provide the industrial base necessary for quick mobilization in the event of war.

In 1934, in an America full of hungry children and unemployed workers, private profits extracted from public funds seemed like dirty money. More accurately, however, carriers that pioneered the air mail routes simply made the most of a good thing. They benefited quite legally from a policy designed to indirectly assist the military forces of the United States. Unless the government nationalized air mail service, private citizens were bound to profit; United's only sin in this regard was that it had taken too much—and much too readily.

Senator Black's committee concentrated on salaries, bonuses, stock manipulation and "proper" profits. In examining the earnings of United associates Rentschler, Mead, Boeing, Ripley, and Charles Deeds, the chairman tirelessly questioned the morality of their making so much money so fast. When George Mead admitted that he had earned almost $8 million from the sales of his Pratt & Whitney stock, purchased for twenty cents per share in 1925, Black asked if Mead considered his profits "a logical growth in this business as set up."

"I did not set the market price," Mead replied. "I do not know what is logical. That is what the market was at that date and what we got for it."[4]

Because George Mead refused to declare that he had made too much money, Black rested content with public disclosure of the profits accumulated by United's officers and bankers. In 1934, after all, these men would surely be judged in the harshest possible terms— especially Rentschler, given stock manipulations for which he was personally responsible. Four doors from the Black committee's hearing room, Senator Duncan Fletcher's Banking and Currency Subcommittee was conducting an open investigation of stock exchange practices. To satisfy public curiosity about the cause of the great crash, reporters had been disclosing the financial shenanigans throughout 1933 of witnesses such as Gordon Rentschler and Joseph Ripley of the National City Bank. In Ripley's case, Senator Fletcher, a Democrat from Florida, instructed his investigative staff to focus on profits on the sale of the Boeing and United stock offerings. The forthcoming revelations became the impetus for rules governing a new financial watchdog, the Securities and Exchange Commission, which was established in 1934.

By the time Black initiated his hearings in late 1933, therefore, many Americans already were eager to oust the "money changers" and slick Wall Street brokers who had fleeced the people and left the country in ruins. As United's men testified, the senator appeared most upset at profits that resulted, not from hard work, but from clever investments and the veil called a "holding company." When Charles Deeds took the stand, Black asked, "Did you ever make any invention of any kind of an airplane improvement?"

"No, sir."

"You have nothing whatever to do with any invention that had been made to improve aircraft in America?" the chairman repeated, and again Deeds answered, "No, sir." Black then asked yet another question containing a subtle insinuation: "Did you ever risk your life flying over the country?"[5]

Black was aware, of course, of the history of each of the witnesses. He wanted to dramatize that men like Deeds, Ripley, and Rentschler had profited from other people's sweat. Criticism of the speculator, the investor, the profit-taker struck a responsive chord in the minds of many Americans, who believed that one should struggle to succeed. As long as good times prevailed, few cared enough to attack such capitalists, but in 1934 latent venom against the smart operator manifested itself in a variety of ways. The Fletcher hearings on stock-exchange practices provided a satisfying forum in which to examine the ethics of investors, and Senator Black was expressing the popular resentment when he lambasted William Boeing.

> BLACK: What is the United Aircraft and Transport
> Corporation of Connecticut?
> BOEING: A holding company.
> BLACK: What is the object of it?
> BOEING: To hold.
> BLACK: The object is to hold your surplus money and
> surplus property, isn't it, and to use it as a
> repository for profits, isn't that it?
> BOEING: Possibly.[6]

In the end, Senator Black let Boeing off the hook, but he never let the American public forget the obscene armchair profits amassed by companies like United Aircraft. Although he never contended that Rentschler or Boeing or Deeds had committed illegal acts, his moral judgments had a devastating effect on United Aircraft. After publicly humiliating its major executives, the senator documented backstage collusion in the awarding of air mail contracts.

As America soon learned, Hoover's Postmaster General, Walter

Brown, called the first "spoils conference" on May 19, 1930, inviting a select group of airline operators to discuss rewriting the aviation map of the United States. Using his own interpretation of the authority granted to the postmaster general by the McNary-Watres Law of April 1930, Brown intended to establish new transcontinental routes, consolidate smaller lines with larger ones whether they liked it or not, and extend many routes in order to furnish nationwide passenger service at a reasonable profit.

When William McCracken, the representative of Western Air Express, accidentally learned of the conclave and tried to sit in, Brown's assistants made it clear he was unwelcome. Once the invited guests had completed their work, McCracken would be permitted to see the results.

One of United Aircraft's representatives was colonel Paul Henderson, who opposed the creation of new competing lines and openly questioned the legality of such a gathering— Brown's actions made a mockery of the spirit of the air mail law. Understandably, Henderson sought to protect his and his company's livelihood.

Chester W. Cuthill, the counselor for North American Aviation, quickly eliminated Henderson's fears. "I quite agree with you," he said. "If we were holding this meeting across the street in the Raleigh Hotel, it would be an improper meeting; but because we are holding it at the invitation of a member of the cabinet, and in the office of the Post Office Department, it is perfectly all right."

In any case, the operators had no choice. Walter Brown had made it quite clear that, if they failed to do the job themselves, he would redraw America's aviation map alone.

When the smoke from this and other meetings cleared, aviation's Big Three— United Aircraft, the Aviation Corporation of America (now American Airways), and North American Aviation (now TWA)— had walked off with all but two of the twenty airmail contracts to be awarded. To avoid any form of competitive bidding, Brown and the operators rewrote the guidelines to effectively eliminate any carriers of whom Brown disapproved. Before long the postmaster general had his two new transcontinental airlines. He also had granted twenty-five route extensions to his approved carriers and added nearly six thousand miles to the American aviation system.[7]

When Brown himself later testified before the Black committee, he declared that the government had never tried "to transport the mails at the lowest possible cost." Rather, the purpose of bills such as McNary-Watres was "to foster the maritime and aeronautical industries." Brown, who administered the government's open subsidy, "had exerted every proper influence to consolidate the short, detached and failing lines into well-managed and well-financed systems." If the carriers had continued to operate without the benefit of organized competition, they would have undermined one another's financial well-being, required increased subsidies, and failed to achieve the aeronautical progress so vital to national security. As a result of the favor he had done for America, Brown continued, the carriers now earned less than ever before; passenger ships such as the DC-2 were ready for takeoff, and no objective analyst doubted the country's worldwide lead in the aeronautical arts. What more could Senator Black or anyone else demand from legislation that was less than four years old?[8]

To such a pointed question, Hugo Black had a ready answer: different means. No matter what Brown had accomplished, he had used corrupt methods— collusion, forced mergers, unfair regulations, elimination of the small guy— to achieve his aims. The carriers had carved up the nation's sky as if it were a pie, and Senator Black meant to make each and every one of them pay for his un-American appetites.

His opportunity came at a January luncheon at the White House. The senator used this private time with President Roosevelt to lobby for immediate cancellation of all air mail contracts. By law the postmaster general could invalidate all routes obtained by fraud or conspiracy. Black assured the president that the aviation industry was guilty on both counts; if Roosevelt really meant to give America a New Deal, he had to wrest control of aviation from the bankers, brokers, and promotors who had ruthlessly usurped the nation's airlines.

Roosevelt apparently knew little about the aviation situation, but the passion and bitterness of Black's presentation impressed him so much he agreed to act at once if the charges were sustained by a report currently under preparation by Post Office Solicitor Carl Crowley.

Two weeks later, when the completed report confirmed Black's charges, Roosevelt wanted to cancel the air mail contracts immediately. His own Postmaster General, James Farley, objected. If the president waited until June of 1934, Farley argued, the Post

Office would have time to find new carriers and Americans would suffer no interruption in their air mail service.

Roosevelt nevertheless decided to act at once. After assurances from Brigadier General Benjamin Foulois, Chief of the Army Air Services, that his pilots could handle the mail, Roosevelt "annulled" all domestic air mail contracts on February 9, with no warning to any of the affected companies. The private carriers were to complete their last runs on February 19. If that left United Air Lines with few sources of income, too bad; by engaging in conspiracy and fraud, the carriers had violated a public trust and would pay an economic penalty for their unethical business practices.[9]

William Boeing's anger knew no bounds. Laughed at in 1927 for his ridiculously low air mail bid, he was now criticized for profiting on his own stupidity. A proud and private man, he vowed to avoid any further dealings with either the federal government or the aviation industry. If Washington wanted to treat him like a scoundrel, he simply refused to take it. William Boeing severed all his ties with United Air Lines and turned his back completely on the aviation industry.

Frederick Rentschler, who felt that United's "only crime was earning a reasonable profit in a field where most others had lost their shirt," contained his anger. Despite the public flogging administered by Senator Black, he had no desire to abandon the company he had created. As a colleague later suggested, Rentschler measured himself by the value of United's stock; in a period that saw a 40 percent drop in the price of a common share, he either continued doing business or relinquished his self-esteem.[10]

While United executives were maintaining a low profile, the angry Democratic Congress began discussing new ground rules for commercial aviation. Although the company stood to lose $300,000 every month that Congress deliberated, in the highly charged atmosphere generated by Black's revelations and Roosevelt's actions it seemed best to let the furor die down. Rentschler might try ever so discreetly to influence legislation, but he would never substantiate Black's accusations by offering once again to assist the legislators in writing the nation's aviation laws as he had for the McNary-Watres Act.

Beginning on February 19, 1934, United patiently and generously helped inexperienced Army crews take over the mail routes in the middle of winter. Even the best fliers were endangered by snow and ice; General Foulois's task was made even more difficult by the virtual absence of experienced commercial crews. Offering wages only half those paid by the private carriers, the government got few takers when it tried to hire the airlines' pilots. As Will Rogers warned the nation, "You are going to lose some fine boys in these army fliers who are marvelously trained in their line, but not in the cross country flying in rain and snow."[11]

During the first week of Army mail service, gale-force winds and blinding snowstorms should have grounded all fliers. But because the Air Force was determined to prove its worth, pilots took off in weather that guaranteed disaster. Within seven days, five pilots were dead and six were hospitalized with serious injuries. A damning newspaper cartoon, in which Roosevelt and Postmaster General Farley were shown leading a procession of skeletons wearing Army caps and goggles, summed up popular reaction to the tragedies. The caption read: "Roosevelt's forgotten men. The dead air-mail pilots."[12]

So much needless death put Franklin Roosevelt on the defensive, especially after the aviation industry tried to underline the president's error by using Charles Lindbergh, the second most popular man in America, as its spokesman. The famous aviator, now employed by Pan American Airways, openly accused Roosevelt of behaving "contrary to American principles." By cancelling the air mail contracts "without just trial," the president "placed no premium on honest business." In Lindbergh's eyes, the New Deal was a raw deal for aviation.[13]

Only sixteen days after the Army's takeover, Roosevelt tried to save face by reducing the number of mail flights until the weather improved. He also sent Congress a letter recommending legislation to "establish a sound, stable and permanent air-mail policy" and, on March 7, announced his decision to turn over the mail routes to private companies. Although citizens could profit once again from air mail business, the new law would prohibit the award of *any* contract to *any* company having *any* connections "with subsidiaries, affiliates, associates, or holding competitive routes *or in the manufacturer of aircraft or other materials or accessories used generally in the aviation industry."*

This, of course, dictated the breakup of companies like United. Only two days after receipt of the president's letter, Senator Black introduced a bill that eagerly seconded Roosevelt's views. After December 31, 1934, it stipulated, no manufacturer of aviation products could have anything to do with authorized mail carriers. Other provisions were directly based on the revelations of Rentschler and his colleagues. Firms holding air mail contracts, for example, must limit executive salaries to $17,500 per year; holding companies were not permitted to own any interest in the carriers; and any participant in the spoils conference of 1930 was banned for five years from any position with any company holding an air mail contract. During processing of the Black-McKellar bill, which was approved by Congress on June 12, 1934, the private carriers could resume business at sharply reduced rates of pay by bidding on temporary contracts first advertised on March 30.[14]

Back at United's headquarters in Hartford, Rentschler told stockholders on March 28 that "in order that the United Air Lines system may be in a position to participate in bidding for air-mail contracts in the future," United Air Lines must be established immediately as an independent group. The sooner the transport side of the business was free from ties to infamous men like Rentschler, in other words, the better its chances of regaining at least some of the contracts lost in February.

Without a transport operation to link them, Rentschler continued, "there would be left two widely separated groups of manufacturing companies." Although this was not illegal even under the Black bill, United's directors decided "to segregate the western group of companies from the eastern." A committee already had been appointed to submit a detailed plan of divorce and reorganization. Stockholders could expect to receive copies within a matter of weeks, whereupon it would be their responsibility to approve or disapprove the voluntary dissolution of the United Aircraft and Transport Corporation.[15]

One Becomes Three

Accompanying the reorganization plan submitted to United's Board of Directors on May 14 was a neat little chart illustrating the dissolution of the holding company into three new corporations, each of which received its own assets and liabilities.

Boeing Airplane Company
Boeing Aircraft Company
Stearman Aircraft Company

United Air Lines Transport Corportation
Boeing Air Transport
Pacific Air Transport
National Air Transport
Varney Air Lines
United Air Lines
United Airports of California

United Aircraft Corporation
Pratt & Whitney
Hamilton-Standard
Chance Vought
Sikorsky Aviation Corporation
    United Aircraft Exports
    United Airports of Connecticut
    Northrop Aircraft Corporation*

Everything looked letter perfect except that the box on the chart labeled "Boeing" was virtually empty. The air transport group contained six subsidiaries and the eastern manufacturing group seven. In the west, however, Boeing encompassed nothing more than its own airplane company and the Stearman private plane operation in Kansas.

The new law— signed by Roosevelt— mandated a separation of carrier and manufacturing operations; United Air Lines clearly had to receive all the transport companies. But when it came to splitting the manufacturing groups, Boeing was being penalized for its lack of profitability. Since 1929, the eastern group, principally Pratt & Whitney and Hamilton-Standard, had netted ten times as much as Boeing's manufacturing plant. During the first quarter of 1934, while the East had netted over $400,000, Boeing had lost more than $200,000. Now it had to take what it was dealt.

Although the eastern and western groups had successfully bridged the continent for over five years and could have continued to do so, there really was no reason to keep Boeing on the team.

---

* United liquidated *this* Northrop Corporation in 1934. It had been located at United Airports of California.

Besides, all United's moneymakers— Pratt & Whitney, Hamilton-Standard, and Chance Vought— shared the same East Hartford facilities. Unless United sold off each firm's capital stock separately, there was no way to break them up. Boeing stood essentially alone.

The board quickly accepted this plan and, in a May 22 letter, urged stockholders to do the same. Although no one applauded the forced dissolution of the United family, at least this way the new corporations had a head start in their struggle to survive the economic depression and the Roosevelt administration.[16] Stockholders formally aproved the three-way split on July 11, 1934.

The new United Aircraft Corporation began business with a bill of sale for the valuable patent rights and license agreements signed by its subsidiaries. And, as a vivid way of emphasizing the eastern group's importance, $34\frac{1}{2}$ percent of the assets went to the United Airlines Transport corporation, $14\frac{1}{2}$ percent to the Boeing Airplane Company, and 51 percent to the new United Aircraft Corporation which began its new lease on life bereft of many of its former directors. William Boeing, Edward Deeds, and Joseph Ripley held no positions in the new company. Donald Brown, the factory manager from the early days in Hartford, became United's new president. Despite his title of chairman, Frederick Rentschler willingly let other executives take charge of "his" corporation. He did this because he intended to focus exclusively on corporate policy; because he had been deeply humiliated by the congressional investigations; and, perhaps most important, because the United Aircraft Corporation stood a much better chance of success if he stayed in the background. All of Fred Rentschler's companies were burdened with a national reputation for profiteering. By mid-1934, procurement officers were avoiding United because of the scandalous revelations of the air mail hearings— and because of the concurrent, and equally shocking, findings of the Delaney Committee.

The Delaney Committee

At a January 2, 1934, appropriations hearing, the passing reference to United Aircraft's 43 percent profit on a particular Navy contract might have passed unnoticed. But now that Hugo Black had splashed the aviation industry across the nation's headlines, Congress authorized Representative John Delaney of New York,

Chairman of the Subcommittee on Aeronautics of the Naval Affairs Committee, to investigate the possibility of profiteering on Navy contracts.

After extensive and detailed hearings, the Delaney committee found no evidence of illegal activities or of complicity in the awarding of contracts. But as they examined Army and Navy procurement records, the congressmen soon reached the same conclusion drawn by Senator Black: "The aviation industry is really a single company." With so many interlocking directorates and so much joint ownership of stock, it proved difficult to separate one company from another.

For United, this independent confirmation of Black's accusation was damning enough. But to add to United's public relations problems, the Delaney Committee singled out Pratt & Whitney for special attention. Ignoring the small profits in 1932 and 1933, the congressman emphasized Pratt & Whitney's overall rate of profit— 23 percent since 1926— insinuating that the big earnings resulted from the company's "virtual monopoly" of the engine market. Pratt & Whitney, after all, had manufactured 56 percent of all the Army's engines and 68 percent of the Navy's since 1926. After calculating the sales of the Curtiss-Wright Company, the committee discovered that of the 7,403 engines purchased by the military services over eight years, only 49 engines— less than 1 percent— came from a manufacturer other than Pratt & Whitney or Curtiss-Wright.[17]

In February of 1934, it was hard to imagine a more controversial conclusion. Anger, legitimate concern, and self-righteousness filled the halls of Congress. If justice demanded that legislators consider the basis of Pratt & Whitney's market share (the Wasp and Hornet engines) plus the stated intention of the Morrow Board to award production orders only to companies with large and active design staffs, justice got few seats in congressional hearing rooms. Besides, even if the inflated market share could be explained, what about the rate of return? If Rentschler had returned excess profits in 1927, why not in 1928 through 1930?

Coinciding with the Black and Delaney hearings, and at the worst possible time for United Aircraft, came the publication of *The Merchants of Death*. This widely publicized book, written by H.C. Englebrecht and F.C. Hanighen, suggested that munitions manufacturers not only made unconscionable profits, but that they had helped start World War I. *Fortune* magazine, no radical publication, wrote that arms makers had supplied everything from "cannons to a cause belli" in their selfish pursuit of profits. Compared to that of many of the nation's dailies, *Fortune's* treatment was gentle. Many Americans promptly assumed that blood dripped from every figure in the arms industry's balance sheets.

Congress acted quickly, attaching a flat limitation on all arms manufacturer's profits to the same bill that authorized a larger Navy. If any company earned more than 10 percent on any particular contract the Vinson-Trammel Act of March 7, 1934, stipulated that excess earnings were to be returned to Washington; companies that refused to relinquish the money voluntarily would have it added to their income taxes. Considering the Navy's right to inspect and audit all account books, a contractor seemingly had little chance to escape the sharp limits imposed by the widely applauded new legislation.[18]

But even with a semiretired Fred Rentschler basking innocuously in the Florida sun, Washington wasn't through with the United Aircraft and Transport Corporation. Not content with the military and air mail investigations, Congress authorized Senator Gerald Nye of North Dakota to chair a special investigating committee with a mandate to examine the export policies of many arms merchants. United's men, scheduled to testify in September of 1934, were anticipating the final nail in the company's coffin. Even after all the federal scrutiny, export sales looked better than ever. Germany had already placed large orders for 1934, and in a new licensing agreement Pratt & Whitney had permitted BMW to build 250 or more engines per year for an annual minimum royalty of fifty thousand dollars. Senator Nye was threatening United's last source of unchecked profits.

Arms Are Immoral

Today we call it the "devil theory of war." But in late 1934, as a result of countless sensational news stories, it was considered a fact of American political life that arms merchants cause wars. It was truth, not fiction, that amoral capitalists thrived on bloodshed by roaming the world selling what was needed to whomever had the money (or rugs) with which to pay. *The Merchants of Death* detailed enough corruption to suggest that profit-hungry devils such as Basil

Zaharoff and Alfred Krupp bore responsibility for World War I. If the book had stopped with them, Senator Nye might have ignored United Aircraft. But a short discussion of contemporary practices (such as Curtiss-Wright's sales in China) in its final pages prompted the senator to examine the present as well as the past, United and Curtiss along with Krupp and Armstrong-Vickers.[20]

Called to testify in late September of 1934, the statements of United's men fill one complete volume of the seven published on the Nye hearings in 1934 and 1936. Americans learned of the guano deals in Peru, the scholarships for pilots, the selling to both sides, the enthusiasm for increased purchases by Hitler's Germany, and enough other revelations to confirm the worst conclusions drawn in *The Merchants of Death.* It was one thing to read about the past, but when United and Curtiss explained their recent operations to Congress, it seemed apparent that manufacturers seeking to profit from any war had to be controlled, then and there. Senator Nye told anyone willing to listen that arms merchants, who engaged in "highly unethical practices" to sow the seeds of disturbance the world over, were "a discredit to American business." It was also evident that, unless the federal government controlled weapon exports, these "selfishly interested organizations" would continue "to goad and frighten nations into military activity."[21]

At United, the senator's strong language constituted yet more abuse from the same old source: its best customer, Washington, which was disgracing the company through the use of its own records. On a personal level, too, United's executives deeply resented the charges: thirty years later, Eugene Wilson still bridled and said as much in an interview for Columbia University's Oral History Project. As late as 1962, Wilson remained convinced that the long series of accusations was part of a New Deal effort to take over the aviation industry. To Fred Rentschler, listening from the background, nothing stung worse than the "terrible term of 'profiteer.'"[22]

Donald Brown, president of the new United Aircraft Corporation, also understood the threat posed by Senator Nye's recommendations for munitions control to the company's "absolutely indispensible" export orders. In two separate responses to Nye's suggestions— essentially pleas for a hands-off export policy—he argued that the extraordinary success of American aviation rested on three "interlocking factors": the air mails, military procurement policies, and exports. This harmonious trio had been woven into a "carefully planned governmental policy" that, up until 1934, had "balanced proper governmental assistance with individual freedom of competitive development and operation in such a manner as to provide the best possible conditions for the operation of private initiative." Only privately owned firms, in other words, could provide the technical progress America needed. In the event of a federal takeover of the aviation industry, the dead hand of Washington would quickly produce "the rapid atrophy of aviation and ultimately the end of successful development in this country."

Unlike Congress, Brown continued, the military knew the score. The military understood that the reason for the booming export market was "the quality and price of our products," and that export profits helped fund the research that made us preeminent in military aviation. Any "prohibition on the export of aircraft and kindred products at the present time," moreover, probably would increase the likelihood of war, prompting the very conflicts it was designed to avoid. An American refusal to sell aircraft to a friendly nation might provoke "reprisals" harmful to trade and foreign relations; in any case, other nations would rush to fill those orders, leaving us trailing behind in the race for military superiority. And a nation that failed to buy from us or, in the event of an international embargo, from anyone else might build their own factories. That in turn "would stimulate new sources of manufacture and new races for sales volume." In sum, manufacturers would readily agree "to conduct their export business on the highest ethical plane." But for America's sake, Congress must never prohibit the exports indispensible to the one industry "upon whose prompt convertibility into the manufacture of military material in wartime the nation must depend for its security."[23]

Brown's comprehensive defense had everything, except the support of the American people. After the Nye hearings, many citizens applauded the "isolationists" who aimed to keep the country out of the next world conflict. Along with a neutrality law, the nation required regulation of the aircraft industry and the export of arms. After all, if greedy capitalists caused wars, then curbing their greed meant a better chance of preserving world peace.

Congress passed the first neutrality act on August 31, 1935, imposing arms embargoes whenever the president declared that a state of war existed between two or more nations. Any manufacturer intent on shipping weapons must register with the Secretary of

State as an arms-maker or dealer and comply with the permanent
licensing regulations mandated by the act. Licenses could be obtained only by letters of application indicating the type of goods,
the final destination, the foreign purchaser, and the foreign con-
signee. Thus, Congress and the people could examine the amount
and type of weapons exported by particular companies.[24]

To United's officers, the Neutrality Act seemed like another of
Roosevelt's attacks on the company treasury. For the last four months of 1934, United had recorded an overall loss of $20,000; in 1935,
it lost over $480,000 on Navy business alone. Only the small profits
on domestic commercial business and the large profits on exports
(18 percent in 1935) kept the company in the black, yet here was
Washington threatening its very survival— 1935 exports equalled 12
percent of United's overall sales but 56 percent of its half million
dollars of net profit.[25] Men like Brown and Wilson could only hope
that Roosevelt would never proclaim a state of war between nations
vital to the company's well-being. If the president announced that
Japan and China were at war, for example, the immediate embargo
imposed would end United's lucrative sales to both sides. Short of
that, however, the United Aircraft Corporation would continue to
expand its export operations to compensate abroad for losses at
home and the chaos at— of all places— that dependable old profit-
maker, Pratt & Whitney Aircraft.

Troubles and More Troubles

In 1935, Pratt & Whitney was in a state of turmoil for which
Washington bore only partial responsibility. One major problem
was the hostility between Donald Brown and Pratt & Whitney's
head of engineering, George Mead, who had taken less interest in
the company since the bitter dispute over the Boeing 247. When
Frederick Rentschler decided to resign his position as president of
Pratt & Whitney after the reorganization of 1934, he narrowed his
choice of successor down to Mead and Brown. Mead, whose talents
lay in technical matters, was not interested in the top job and, Rentschler reported, "just doggedly took the point of view that willy-nilly
I had to remain as president and that he and Don would function
under me."[26]

Although Mead liked and respected Brown, with whom he had

worked since their days at Wright Aeronautical years before, he felt that Brown's skills lay in production. As head of the factory, Brown had no equal; as head of Pratt & Whitney, he had no experience. When Rentschler nevertheless offered the position to Brown, Mead simply refused to cooperate with the new president of Pratt & Whitney and, later, of all United Aircraft.

As the company's own history — *The Pratt & Whitney Aircraft Story*— notes, the result of Mead's disenchantment was "badly frayed teamwork." Not only did the company's vice president for engineering fail to oversee the progress of several different power plants at various stages of development, but he actually built separate design facilities at his West Hartford home and was occasionally unavailable when colleagues required guidance.

In an attempt to restore a semblance of order, Brown appointed Leonard Hobbs, with the company since 1927, as Pratt & Whitney's engineering manager. While Hobbs (with Mead's assistance) tried to put the design program back on track, Curtiss-Wright threatened to replace Pratt & Whitney as the nation's premier manufacturer of large airplane engines. The Curtiss Cyclone had won the competition to power the Douglas DC-2 two years before and, by early 1936, was used in the popular DC-3 as well. Now that Douglas held a virtual monopoly on the construction of new commercial aircraft (of the 109 planes ordered by the airlines for 1937 delivery, 85 were made by Douglas), Pratt & Whitney was struggling desperately for the remaining commercial business. Pratt & Whitney's loss made the entire United organization more dependent than ever on an administration that promised to minutely monitor the business practices of the military services, especially the Army Air Corps.

The military had itself to blame. In yet another 1934 aviation scandal Congress had discovered that, despite a law designed to encourage competitive bidding, clever aviators had been circumventing the intent (if not the letter) of the law. In 1932, none of the 413 planes put out for contract was advertised competitively; between 1926 and 1934, fewer than 1 percent of military aircraft orders were submitted to official competitive procedures.

The Air Corps' excuse was that manufacturers' competitive bids were submitted in the form of paper proposals. If the service made selections based only on such untested designs, the resulting planes might prove to be disasters or the price might skyrocket. Remember, too, that because the military held builders to their paper bids, aviation manufacturers generally lost money on ships developed from design competitions. To avoid such losses to the industry, procurement officers began to negotiate the costs of experimental planes, bargaining for the finished craft they wanted. Unfortunately, ambitious manufacturers bid so far below cost that the negotiated awards, too, led to substantial losses. There was no guarantee, moreover, that a production order would result; other builders might underbid the company that produced the experimental plane. If that happened, the military was legally obliged to accept the low bid.

To bypass the law, procurement chiefs ignored the Air Corps Act and turned to general Army regulations, where they found a rule permitting noncompetitive awarding of contracts "if the manufacturer of the article was the sole source and no similar or suitable item could be procured elsewhere." Because the manufacturer of an experimental plane undoubtedly was the sole source of that particular craft, Air Corps officials were home free to negotiate an experimental contract and subsequent production contracts. Without a speck of open competition, the Army had its planes and the manufacturer had its order.

Although such artful evasion was not illegal, it did contradict that stated intent of the Air Corps Act, and thus resulted in no less than three separate Congressional investigations beginning in January of 1934. By June, the Rogers Committee had concluded that "the various subterfuges used by the Air Corps added up to a pernicious, unlawful system of procurement" and that the chief of the Air Corps, General Foulois, was guilty of "deliberate, willful, and intentional violations of the law."[27]

To at least reduce the impact of the scandal on the long-range prospects of the Air Corps, officers determined to clean up their act. By early 1935, a new procuremeent system was in place, obliging manufacturers to provide samples of their wares at their own expense. Only after pilots flew a plane would the Air Corps consider a production contract; even then, an order might now be large enough to cover the costs of development and tooling up. As the Charles Barney investment house informed customers considering aviation stocks, "The hazards to manufacturers arising from such a policy will be evident."[28]

In other words, a company could lose money. And that is exactly what happened shortly thereafter at the Chance Vought division of

United Aircraft. In 1936, Vought entered an Army competition with a plane developed by Jack Northrop. Northrop had abandoned his attempt at securing this contract when his craft disappeared over the Pacific but agreed to prepare a new model within sixty days for Eugene Wilson, now senior vice president of United Aircraft. With Northrop's help, Vought easily had its ship ready for testing at Dayton's Wilbur Wright field. Instead of a careful assessment of each plane, however, the competition turned into a "promising contest." Army officers "played us one against the other," Wilson recalled in his memoirs. Soon he "had reached the point where I'd promised about ten miles more per hour than I knew the airplane could possibly make." But because "there were penalties if you failed to meet that guarantee, and serious ones," he dropped out of competition, $100,000 poorer because of the expenses involved in producing a sample plane.

The Navy, not surprisingly, refused to consider "any part of an airplane that had been rejected by the Army, even if it was suited to their needs." Nor did the export market look promising until Tom Hamilton, United's top export salesman, told Wilson "we've got a customer." Mitsu, a Japanese trading company with offices in New York, had purchased a number of Hamilton-Standard propellers in 1935. Upon learning from Tom Hamilton of the new fighter plane, Mitsu sent a small contingent, including a pilot, to Rentschler Field in East Hartford for a test flight. According to Wilson, the pilot "put on the most beautiful demonstration that you ever saw— put the airplane through its paces— came back and landed— walked out of the airplane, nodded his head to the businessmen and disappeared."

Eugene Wilson considered the ensuing sale a lucky break for Vought, which shipped the craft to Tokyo in the summer of 1937. Six years later, visiting Admiral Nimitz in San Diego, Wilson was shown one of the captured Japanese Zero's then killing so many young Americans in the Pacific. "There on the floor was the Vought V 142 or just the spitting image of it, Japanese-made," he reported. Though the Zero seemed larger than the original Vought plane and incorporated features from other Japanese purchases, the "power-plant installation was distinctly Chance Vought, the wheel stowage into the wing roots came from Northrop, and the Japanese designers had even copied the Navy inspection stamp from Pratt & Whitney type parts."

When an interviewer later solicited Wilson's reactions to the Zero, United's man responded with a rationalization underlining the inherent problems of exporting arms: "The moral of all this is. . . that you never know whom you're going to fight in the next war. These countries that go to war, they are allies one time and enemies the next, and you don't know where you're going to fight or who you're going to fight or how you're going to fight."[30]

Thus, United sold to anyone and hoped that today's customer was not tomorrow's enemy— (Iran is probably the most conspicuous contemporary example of friend turning into foe. United's philosophy, nevertheless, appears not to have changed. As United vice president Clark MacGregor told a House subcommittee on trade in 1978, "Gentlemen, all exports are in the national interest."[31]) No one at United wanted to help Japanese kill Americans, but the federal government did approve all export sales. It was naive to assume that, under the new Neutrality Act, manufacturers would settle for lower profits rather than accepting customers such as Japan. If Washington intended to maintain an industrial base without a liberal export policy, the only choice was to provide the funds needed by companies like United Aircraft. Otherwise, most manufacturers would do whatever was necessary to stay aloft. In Chance Vought's case, that included signing a contract that Washington refused to approve.

Buenos Aires Bound

Vought was by far the biggest drain on United's resources. For the last four months of 1934, the division's losses totaled over $240,000; in 1935 the red ink added up to more than $400,000; and projected losses for 1936 loomed so large that Eugene Wilson determined to forget profits. "The problem now with Chance Vought was purely survival," he notes in his memoirs.[32]

Help came from the Argentine Navy, which wanted twenty Vought Corsairs, machine guns and all, if they could be delivered by early 1937. Not only did this order mean about a million dollars in gross business for Vought but, more important, it meant at least one year's more work for the staff. Without the Argentine business, Wilson announced, "I had to shut Chance Vought down, and not just shut it down but actually to disperse that great collection of specialists and trained people that represented the heart and soul of the place."[61]

Unfortunately, the almost-obsolete Corsairs still were modern enough to require a special export imprimatur from the American Navy plus, because of the new neutrality legislation, the approval of the State Department. United's representatives quickly obtained the Navy's informal okay if the planes left America without two or three devices considered too secret for export. Admiral E.J. King, head of the Navy's Bureau of Aeronautics, would not grant a unconditional release because these components remained too technically advanced for other nations to inspect and perhaps imitate.

Wilson, who had no problem with a special versus an unconditional release of the fighter planes, next visited Joseph Green, chief of the State Department's Office of Arms and Munitions Control, accompanied by Thomas Hewes. A former Assistant Secretary of State, a "college pal" of Joe Green's and (at least temporarily) a Chance Vought representative, Hewes allegedly was sufficiently sophisticated to negotiate any potential roadblocks. Greene politely explained that, under the new laws, a plane could be exported only if the Navy granted a universal release by declaring that the plane was no longer of secret military interest. Otherwise, the State Department had no choice but to refuse Vought's request.

On April 3, 1936, Green received a call from Fred Rentschler, then in Florida. Rentschler, "remembering their boyhood friendship," was determined, "in the interests of his company," to urge Green to expedite action in regard to the Argentine dive bombers.

Green considered the call amusing. He apparently never considered United's Chairman whom he hadn't seen in thirty years, a boyhood chum. Advising patience, he told Rentschler that "as soon as the questions at issue had been decided," he would tell Mr. Hewes, United's representative.

On April 17, Hewes was informed that the license would be granted. It looked like clear flying, except that the Navy broke its word on the same day. Admiral King reversed his reversal and refused to grant the universal release, leaving Vought back at square one and much the worse for the wear.

Rejecting the idea of meeting with the admiral because King was "a cold fish that you could never appeal to on the basis of how many people were thrown out of work,"[63] Wilson decided to go to the top. With help from Tom Hewes he obtained an appointment with Secretary of State Cordell Hull, to whom he announced that "this wasn't a question of selling munitions, this was a question of selling an obsolete plane, and the issue lay as to whether or not we are going to throw 800 more people on relief, and at the same time destroy one of the assets of the defense effort."[33] Wilson's plea was clearly ineffective, because Hull abruptly broke off the interview. Still without the license, Wilson had gained the enmity of the Secretary of State.

Wilson then turned to the chief of Naval Operations, Admiral N. H. Standley, whom he knew from his Navy days. Sailor to sailor, Wilson implored the admiral to overrule King and grant the universal release of the planes. Announcing that Wilson's suggestion was "preposterous," Standley brusquely ended the meeting.

Despite some progress during June and July, Wilson never obtained his license, and the Vought factory was closed. With nothing to lose, he decided to force Washington's hand. Wilson simply flew to Buenos Aires, signed the contracts, and set his staff to work upon his return to Hartford.[34]

Wilson won his bet. Under overwhelming political pressure to keep workers employed, Washington authorized the sale; the Argentinians got all the dive bombers they wanted; and Chance Vought managed to stumble along another year. Although losses in 1936 increased to nearly one million dollars, slightly increased military expenditures at home plus conflicts throughout the world promised the opportunity to once again make money— if, of course, Washington permitted. The company had taken a loss of nearly 40 percent on its 1936 Navy business. Unless the government took a more liberal attitude toward export sales or rethought the tight-fisted policies established by the Vinson-Trammel Act, Vought's future rested on the ability of Pratt & Whitney and Hamilton-Standard to carry it.[35]

Laws of Supply and Demand

Everyone wanted what Hamilton-Standard had to offer: the best propellers in the world. After 1934, Frank Caldwell's easily adjustable blades became the industry standard, earning a very high rate of return on all business— even that conducted with the Navy. Because manufacturers were losing enormous amounts of money as a result of the flat 10 percent limitation on any individual contract, a mid-1936 change in the Vinson-Trammel Act provided that the limit now applied, not to any one contract, but to the bottom line on all of a company's Navy business. For United, this meant that losses on some orders (such as those at Vought) could be offset by profits on others (such as those at Hamilton).

From 1936 through 1938, the Hamilton-Standard subsidiary's application of the new law produced about 20 percent net profit on all its Navy business; but potential earnings in this area were limited by the military's moderate budgets for increasingly expensive equipment. Navy transactions averaged a mere million dollars annually in 1936 through 1938, and Army orders exceeded those of the Navy only slightly.

Prospects elsewhere were far brighter. From 1936 to 1938, Hamilton-Standard averaged about $2 million per year in commercial business, with average profits of 23 percent. During the same period, the propeller company enjoyed a nearly 800 percent increase— from $536,085 in 1936 to $4,222,715 in 1938— in export business. Average net profits during those years totaled 51 percent, yet even this enormous gain fails to illustrate adequately the contribution exports made to the company's financial well-being. In 1937, for example, exports came to 27 percent of sales and 49 percent of profits, but in 1938— the $4 million year— exports equalled 45 percent of sales and a whopping 64 percent of profits. Fully 51 percent of United Aircraft's total net profits in 1937 ($3.8 million) and 58 percent in 1938 ($5.4 million) were contributed by Hamilton-Standard, which netted $3.1 million in 1938 on only 29 percent of United's total business.[36] At Chance Vought, too, the profit prospects steadily improved. At Sikorsky, however, it was time to end United's contribution to what Rentschler called "Russian relief." On the famous Flying Clippers made for Pan American Sikorsky had turned no profit at all, and on the Flying Aces built for American Export Airlines, the company (as in 1932) once again lost a substantial amount of money.

Eugene Wilson reluctantly broke the news to Igor Sikorsky: "I'm sorry to have to tell you, but the decision is taken, and we're just going to have to close the company. We can't carry the burden any longer." Sikorsky understood. He agreed to join forces with Vought —United formally created the Vought-Sikorsky subsidiary in 1939— and United agreed to fund development of Sikorsky's fondest dream. He would be given a corner of the Vought factory in which to develop his helicopter.[31]

At Pratt & Whitney the ongoing problem was the military, which accounted for over 60 percent of the firm's business in 1936 through 1938, yet refused to permit a reasonable profit. For example, on the $7 million worth of engines the Navy purchased in 1937, Pratt & Whitney's rate of return came to 1 percent. In 1938, on $6.8 million of Navy orders, the company made 0.89 percent profit— slightly more than $60,000 after taxes.

On commercial orders, Pratt & Whitney's greatly improved engines regained some of the ground lost to Curtiss-Wright. Airlines only accounted for 17 percent of the enginemaker's business, however, and even a high profit margin (about 19 percent in 1936 through 1938) never compensated for the dismal military outlook. Neither did the approximately $3.5 million that the company annually earned abroad, although the 25 percent net profit from customers such as Germany, Russia, China, and South Africa did keep it solidly in the black. In 1937, exports equalled 19 percent of Pratt & Whitney's business but 41 percent of its profits; in 1938, the figures were respectively, 21 percent and 60 percent.[35]

To keep its huge factory running at somewhere near capacity, Pratt & Whitney needed even marginally profitable military orders. In 1937, Congress had already reduced procurement by halving the number of spare engines purchased. If the military ever cut back on its primary orders, Pratt & Whitney might face the same prospect as Vought in 1936: the most celebrated enginemaker in the world might have to close up shop.

But with the threat of war looming large in Europe, Pratt & Whitney's procurement prospects appeared quite positive. In such an ominous atmosphere, no sane official would dare threaten the survival of an essential source of American military engines. Although the company might have to settle once again for nominal profits, its stature certainly guaranteed enough orders to keep the factory in operation— or so thought the executives at Pratt & Whitney Aircraft.

Poker at Wright Field

In mid-1938, appropriations problems had stalled the military procurement process. With orders in hand only through May of 1939, Pratt & Whitney saw its backlog dwindling. When the appropriations bill finally passed in midyear, General Hap Arnold, head of the Army Air Corps, summoned Don Brown to Washington, where they settled on an engine order that allowed Pratt & Whitney a measure of security; and the general informally annouced that Pratt & Whitney had beaten General Motors' Allison division for a $15 million contract.[39]

In his rush to start production, the confident Brown never bothered to sign a contract. On Hap Arnold's word, which had been an ironclad one in the past, Pratt & Whitney placed numerous orders with its subcontractors and began manufacturing the Army's engines. Disaster struck at the turn of the new year. Without warning and some months into the verbal contract, Louis Johnson, the Assistant Secretary of War, gave the Corps order to Allison, which had no production facilities, for its liquid-cooled engine.

Brown immediately took the company plane to Washington. According to a confused Hap Arnold, "Somebody at Wright Field in the materiel division had become concerned that the liquid-cooled engine was about to go out of general use." This individual had written Johnson a "strong letter" proposing that Allison get the order because "if liquid-cooled engines were needed, only they could provide them." If Pratt & Whitney wanted any more Army business, Arnold concluded, it had better quickly develop a liquid-cooled engine of its own.

Industry rumors attributed the reversal to a "procurement man who had never lost a game of poker to a General Motors representative."[40]

This bribery charge was never substantiated, but in any case it made little difference to Pratt & Whitney executives, who had laid off 20 percent of the work force and were seriously considering closing down the entire operation. If that happened, the entire United Aircraft Corporation was threatened with its second breakup in less than five years.

Things looked miserable. And then they got worse.

Don't Sell to Japan

Although China and Japan had been at war for years, President Roosevelt refrained, in a decidely un-neutral way, from using the neutrality laws. Because Japan manufactured many of its own weapons and he wanted to support China with American arms, he never declared a state of war.

At that time, world leaders were still horrified when civilians were the deliberate target of air bombardment. For years, military officers such as General Billy Mitchell and British Air Marshall Hugh Trenchard had advocated the use of indiscriminate bombing to undermine morale, but Japanese employment of these strategies was deemed "barbaric." During the wanton air bombardment label- ed the "Rape of Nanking" in December of 1937, Japanese warplanes killed thousands of civilians. Perhaps more important to America, the Japanese not only attacked the American ship Panay, but they actually strafed survivors trying to escape in lifeboats.[41]

In June of 1938, an appalled Franklin Roosevelt called this kind of war "immoral" and requested that the State Department declare a moral embargo on the shipment of arms to Japan. By July 1, aircraft manufacturers received a letter announcing that the United States government "strongly opposed" the sale of airplanes or aeronautical equipment that would "materially aid or encourage the practice of civilian bombings." It would "with great regret issue any licenses authorizing exportation, direct or indirect, of any air- craft, aircraft armament, aircraft engines, aircraft parts, aircraft ac- cessories, aerial bombs or torpedoes to countries the armed forces of which are making use of airplanes for attack upon civilian populations."[42]

Whether in moral agreement with Roosevelt or in fear of government retaliation through decreased military orders, virtually every aircraft manufacturer in the United States refrained from requesting Japanese export licenses. There was, however, one exception.

On May 3, United Aircraft had agreed to sell Mitsu 450 Hamilton-Standard propellers. When the State Department received the application for an export license for this enormous order, officials called in United vice president J. Reed Miller to discuss the new policy regarding sales to Japan. During the July 8 meeting, the State Department attempted to determine whether United intended to press the letter of the law despite the government's strong opposition. Would the company demand an export license that could not be refused because Roosevelt had refrained from declaring China and Japan formally at war?

Miller repeated that he wanted the license. He agreed to keep the department informed of further Japanese deals but, in the meantime, United expected to ship the propellers.

On August 12 Miller kept his word, informing the State Department that the license request had expanded to encompass eight hundred propellers. The department repeated its moral embargo policy. If United refused to follow the president's lead, it should at least understand "the danger of drastic mandatory action against such exportation by the next Congress if shipments of this character continue in the volume which they have maintained during recent months."[43]

By September 16 the State Department could no longer stall on United's export license. But before complying with the law, the department summoned United executives in order to explain "the ill repute which the corporation was reflecting on the entire industry." The hope was that United "might be persuaded to observe in the future the department's policy in regard to Japanese arms sales."

On November 8, when United submitted a request for yet more licenses for yet more propellers, the State Department responded with a threat. Unless United stopped shipping armaments to Japan, the government "would be constrained to make available to the public the facts in regard to this most recent sale."[44]

On December 16, United requested a license to send "600 propeller blade forgings and accessories to Mitsu and Company, Ltd." As Charles Yost wrote in a State Department memo, "It was clear that the United Aircraft Corporation had decided to disregard the Department's urgings in regard to aeronautical exports to Japan and that the Japanese were therefore likely to take advantage of the corporation's attitude by placing with it large orders which have been refused by other American aircraft manufacturers."[45]

On January 12, 1939, the State Department attached the following announcement to its regular monthly press release relating to arms exports: "With only one outstanding exception, American manufacturers of aircraft and aircraft parts have complied with the President's moral embargo on arms shipments to

Japan. This exception is the United Aircraft Corporation of East Hartford, Connecticut. The above tabulation in regard to arms export licenses issued during the month of December includes the most recent license issued to this corporation for an exportation of this kind, specifically 600 propeller blade forgings valued at $102,000."

Reporters immediately publicized United's exceptional attitude. *The New York Times* headlined its story "Hull Plea Ignored by United Aircraft." The *Hartford Courant* bannered "United silent in Airplane Sales to Japs" on page one, noting that United was "the sole American airplane manufacturer not cooperating in the government's unofficial ban on the sale of airplanes and parts to Japan." The *Courant* ended its piece with a statement by United's president, Donald Brown: "No comment."

In private, however, Don Brown was overwhelmed. He had been seriously ill for months; Pratt & Whitney was in horrible shape without the promised Army Air Corps order: and release of the Japanese sales information proved devastating to the company's public image. As Eugene Wilson said, "United was once again in a position of munitions racketeers and war mongerers who were deliberately selling American secrets to a potential enemy."[47]

But this time United and its men had no excuse— except the need of money— for their actions. Government officials had warned the company for months, yet new order was piled on new order. Incredibly, despite the State Department's repeated threats, no one at United linked the sales to Japan with the mysterious (and never explained) cancellation of the huge Army order. Even Wilson, so insightful in other instances, never suggested that Pratt & Whitney lost the Army's business because of the Roosevelt administration's vengeance for United's flagrant disregard of the president's moral embargo.

To smooth things over, Don Brown went to Washington. There, an "absolutely brutal" Cordell Hull listened to Brown's profuse apologies and his assertion of United's newfound willingness to comply with government export policies. Unfortunately, despite the apology, there seemed to be no way for the company to cut its losses. United entered the new year labeled as a war profiteer but, due to Pratt & Whitney's desperate situation, there were no profits.

Finally, the public and private turmoil prompted United's

executives to seek outside assistance. As Wilson put it, "They invited Fred Rentschler back into the company" because, if anyone could restore order and profits, Frederick Brant Rentschler was the man.[48]

5

THE FORTUNATE CIRCUMSTANCE: WORLD WAR II

"The French had deteriorated to almost nothing in aviation following World War I and with the emergency looming up ahead there was nothing left for them to do except turn to this country for help. This fortunate circumstance at least partially provided for what otherwise might have been a complete drying off of orders from any other source. . . ."

Frederick Rentschler
An Account of the Pratt & Whitney Aircraft Company

To United Aircraft, the new year promised nothing but disaster. Its reputation for profiteering had been resurrected by arms sales to Japan; there was no serious business on the order books; and the Army and Navy would not be resuming procurement until after mid-1939.

In this time of desperation, Eugene Wilson recalled in *Slipstream*: "United had but a single remaining hope: Tom Hamilton in Paris."[1] For over five years the ever-eager salesman had been pursuing French orders for United's products, and for over five years the French, committed to domestic armaments, had refused him. But as the threat of war with Germany drew closer, pragmatism superseded nationalism. The French ordered $2 million worth of Pratt & Whitney engines in 1938 and, not incidentally, finally opened the door for Hamilton.

When Hitler threatened to annex the rest of Czechoslovakia in early 1939, Hamilton immediately resumed his hard sell, both to assist the foundering United and to earn a small fortune in commissions on any prospective purchases; he would receive over $760,000 on France's 1939 orders. Although Rentschler, who toiled to keep the company afloat while Hamilton lived lavishly in Paris, resented the commission, he never quarreled with the profitable results of Hamilton's aggressive salesmanship.

After all, Tom Hamilton (and France and World War II) saved United Aircraft. On February 14 France ordered over $25 million worth of Pratt & Whitney engines, $10 million more than the mammoth Army contract the company had lost. Instead of closing up shop, Pratt & Whitney actually began to increase engine production capacity in anticipation of further demands from France.[2]

With a full year's business in hand and the likelihood of more to come, Pratt & Whitney appropriated 115,000 square feet that Hamilton-Standard had been occupying in its factory. The propeller subsidiary moved into the adjacent Chance Vought plant while Vought, completing plans made in 1938, moved down to Stratford, taking over most of the floor space formerly used by Sikorsky.

Ultimately, United was able to fulfill the French orders without adding to its existing industrial capacity. As Eugene Wilson explained, "The last thing we wanted was more factories. We had. . . plenty of factories for any ordinary requirements. Not only that, but for years we'd been overburdened with excess facilities. . . All those factories did was to sit there and eat their heads off, because you had to charge depreciation against them, and you didn't get any production out of them, and no matter how great a job you did over here, you had a great burden of losses there. We'd had a terrific time trying to liquidate those excess war facilities of the previous war. So we were gun-shy. . ."[3]

Although United's executives sympathized with the Allied cause, their single overriding concern was the profitable survival of the company; they had no intention of being burdened with the excess capacity that had proved so costly in the past. In midsummer, when France tried to place an order that could be filled only by building another factory, United's terms amounted to extortion.

In early October of 1939, United agreed to construct a 300,000 square-foot addition to its Pratt & Whitney plant and strive for a production level of 265 engines monthly, resulting in as many as 3,000 by March of 1941. This was one of the largest orders the engine company had obtained to date, and it also was one of the most profitable. The French agreed to pay the entire cost of the new factory — eight million dollars — through the addition of an 8 1/3 percent surcharge on each and every engine. This bonus came about because, in the language of the October 2 contract, the company deserved "an inducement for providing such expanded facilities to meet such accelerated delivery requirements." United was expanding "its manufacturing and processing facilities to an extent not justified by its present or anticipated volume of business exclusive of this contract."

The French, moreover, were obliged to pay in advance. An immediate $1.7 million covered the initial outlay for plant expansion; within ninety days, United's customer disbursed 60 percent of the price of the engines— in cash. Surcharges, such as when an engine required "overseas packing," added still more to the tab. United's job was to make the engines; France's was to pick up its purchases at the gate of the factory it had paid the costs of building.

France, which had been at war with Hitler since September 3, had no choice but to accept these terms. In fact, the beleagured nation was risking its money even by signing its October contract with United; at the time, it was illegal for American firms to export armaments to any nation at war. Fortunately, France won its gamble when Congress repealed the Arms Embargo Act on November 7, 1939.

On November 13, less than a week after the act was repealed, L. Wilmot Johnson of United Aircraft's export operations sent the following letter to the Department of State's office of Arms and Munitions Control: "There is attached hereto our application to export to Germany 3 Pratt & Whitney SIE 3 G Hornet engines. An early issuance of the corresponding export permit will be much appreciated."[5]

Had the request been for five hundred or a thousand engines, United's desire to ship arms to Hitler might have made financial sense. But *three* engines? And at a time when France, the company's saviour, was formally at war with Germany? To men like Fred Rentschler and Eugene Wilson, however, the war presented a business opportunity for executives who could exploit an unpredictable situation. No one knew when the fighting would end, so a good executive ignored his biases and accepted all the orders, large and small, that came his way. Otherwise, a competitor would; and an opportunity lost, even in a seller's market, was lost forever. Thus, United did not terminate a propeller licensing agreement with Italy's Fiat until December 15, 1941. It only cancelled another agreement with Mitsubishi in February of 1940, when the Japanese firm decided not to exercise its option; and as late as June 7, 1940, United Aircraft was sending Mitsubishi the latest propeller data released for export by the United States government.

Nothing symbolized United's dispassionate approach to World War II better than the efficient French addition to Pratt & Whitney's facilities, which was designed "as a complete manufacturing unit. . . producing exclusively engines of the 1200hp twin Wasp type." If France's needs changed, the new wing "could be shut down later without disturbing the even production flow of the old plant."[6] With the flick of a switch and the slam of the specially constructed doors separating one factory from another, United could simply shut out the war.

More Requests, More Demands

Like the French, the English desperately needed weapons. But in early 1940, United faced the British negotiators after one of the best years in its history. On sales of over $51 million, the company netted 18 percent profit— $9.4 million, more than $4 million over the year before.

United's 1940 annual report explained that the "abnormally sharp increase in the business of the Corporation" was largely due to "transitory conditions." "Without discounting the stimulating effects of current military demands," the text continued, "management felt justified in believing that the increase in the Corporation's shipments in 1939 and the unprecedented volume of its unfilled orders (already over $127,000,000) at the end of the period evidenced the high reputation for excellence which your Corporation's products enjoyed both at home and abroad."[7]

Stockholders could rest assured, the report suggested, that United's prudent management would adamantly refuse certain types of business— even if the customer was the British government sponsored by America's secretary of the Treasury, Henry Morgenthau, who was also chairman of the president's Liaison Committee. Because President Roosevelt wanted to assist the French and British war effort dispite the isolationist sentiments of the War Department, he established the committee in December of 1939 to coordinate procurement of domestic and foreign arms. Morgenthau, who shared Roosevelt's beliefs, ostensibly was instructed "to prevent conflicts over materials and facilities." In reality, he spent most of his time assuring adequate military supplies to the allies.

Morgenthau entered the scene during deadlocks in United's negotiations with England caused by the condescending attitude of the chief British representative and by the fact that United, which already had all the business it could handle, refused to lower its prices.

Talks were finally suspended when Eugene Wilson, United's senior vice president, announced that after careful deliberation, "United Aircraft had reached the decision that it was not interested in expanding its operations under any circumstances." If Washington altered its tax laws, of course, the company might reconsider. Until then, negotiations would not be resumed.[8]

Considering the isolationism then prevalent across the country, the Treasury secretary was virtually helpless. To supply England with arms, it seemed that both the British and American governments had no choice but to accept the terms dictated by the management of United Aircraft. In desperation, Morgenthau appeared at Pratt & Whitney's factory door in the middle of a winter's night and instructed a night watchman to telephone Eugene Wilson at home. The message: The Secretary of the Treasury had just walked in and wanted to see Wilson as soon as possible.

When Wilson arrived shortly thereafter, he took Morgenthau on a tour of the new French wing, still under construction, to impress the secretary with what the company could do under the right business conditions. As soon as they sat down to talk, Morgenthau urged that United take the British contract without delay.

"I'm awfully sorry," Wilson replied. "We are. . . already operating far beyond any capabilities of ours, with respect to working capital, with respect to facilities. . . and we do have a sense of responsibility to our stockholders and to our country. We are utterly unwilling to take this contract unless you can arrange to alter the provisions in such a way that we could write this facility off the books over the shipments comprising the first contract."[9]

Morgenthau surrendered. He agreed to push Congress for changes in the tax laws, and United Aircraft agreed to build an $8 million British addition right beside the French addition. Once again the customer would pay up front for a plant that became United's property. Along with the tax breaks, United Aircraft now had signed contracts for another $60 million worth of engine business. As for Tom Hamilton, his commissions for 1940 on the French and British orders came to $1,466,619.22.[10]

In less than a year, Europe's war had tripled the United Aircraft Corporation's sales, doubled its net profits, and tripled its work force from fifty-two hundred at the beginning of 1939 to about fifteen thousand by the middle of 1940. Its crucial manufacturing role lent it sufficient confidence that, directly after its defeat of Secretary Morgenthau and the British, United took on Franklin Roosevelt and the American Congress.

Fifty Thousand Planes

On May 16, 1940, the president startled the nation by issuing a call for an aircraft industry capable of producing fifty thousand planes per year to stock the Army Air Force. Since the entire 1938 production totaled eighteen hundred, and since an industry-wide study set five thousand planes as the 1940 maximum,[11] Roosevelt's goal seemed fantastic. Who would build the plants required to even remotely approach such huge numbers? What about financing? And profits? And accelerated amortization? Most important, what had prompted the president to scrap years of careful military planning for the sake of an untested subdivision of the Army?

The 1940 military budget provided a clue to Roosevelt's reasoning. While he was demanding 50,000 planes, the War Department was requesting that Congress authorize 166. Congress, unconcerned that the air arm's available strength totaled 2,760 planes, approved an order for 57. The previous year, after all, they had authorized 5,500, by far the largest air force in American history. In 1938 the staff of General Hap Arnold, Commander of the Army Air Forces, had submitted a recommendation for 7,500 planes— at the general's prompting, an inflated number— to meet American requirements the world over.

Throughout the 1930's, in fact, conservatism had dominated military procurement policies. Congress did slowly increase expenditures as the European and Pacific situations worsened— boosting aircraft spending from $29 million in 1932 to $45 million in 1936 and to $70 million by 1939— but military leaders continued to think small. Even if they had conceived of a mighty air force, the unending animosity between the Army and Navy would have precluded cooperation; each sought to usurp the other's rightful role in American military aviation. And with no agreement between the services on strategy and tactics, it was impossible to accurately compute their quantitative or qualitative requirements.[12]

Because Roosevelt thoroughly understood the gross inade-
quacies of the nation's aviation planning, he pushed for radical
change to help America as well as the Allies, whose orders exemplified the enormous amount of equipment necessary to fight a total
war. The president's request for fifty thousand planes was intended
to shock the military, the aviation industry, and the public into a
reevaluation of national air strategy— and to demonstrate the need
to build the largest air force in the world.

Aside from massive industrial production, America needed to
develop strategic and tactical doctrine to guide the military in the
proper use of aircraft. The country could follow Germany's example
and use planes primarily in support of Army and Navy operations
or, like the English, strive to create a strategic force able to win the
war single-handedly. The English, who had established the first
independent air force in 1918, had recognized the crusing effect of
aerial bombardment on civilian morale as early as 1919, when Hugh
Trenchard, the first head of the British Air Forces, said, "At present
the moral effect of bombing stands undoubtedly to the material
effect in a proportion of twenty to one."[13]

In considering a moral and military policy for the use of planes
in time of war, in other words, Roosevelt could either limit the effects
of air power or sanction the indiscriminate bombing favored by so
many progressive flyers. Until May of 1940 he had come down emphatically on the side of restraint, as he demonstrated with his
harsh criticisms of United Aircraft for selling weapons to a Japan
that was wantonly bombing any moving target. And on the first day
of World War II, Franklin Roosevelt had told the world, "The bombing of helpless and unprotected civilians is a tragedy which has
aroused the horror of all mankind. I recall with pride that the
United States has consistently taken the lead in urging that this in-
human practice be prohibited."[14]

The president's demand for fifty thousand planes on May 16
was not intended to endorse the deliberate slaughter of civilians,
but rather to legitimize air power and, in fact, make the Air Corps
the equal of the Army and the Navy. Once America entered the
war, however, the temptation to exploit those planes would prove
hard to resist, especially when they promised a quicker end to the
war. After all, only five days before Roosevelt's call to aerial arms,
Winston Chruchill had announced that "the bombers alone provided

the means of victory," and sanctioned the strategic bombing of
Germany.[15]

Arguably, Roosevelt's decision to establish a huge air force was
a necessary and important step toward American's ultimate victory
in World War II; but, however inadvertently, the fifty-thousand-
plane program started the nation down a road that made terror
bombing moral and the air force the procurement equal of the
other services. Seemingly overnight, civilians became the principal
target of air strategy, cars took a back seat to planes, and a mammoth
aviation industry was an institutionalized component of American
life, eventually becoming the largest employer in manufacturing.
The moral situation was so confused that United Aircraft, condemned in 1938 for selling Japan the equipment needed for terror
bombing, was blamed in 1943 for not producing enough of the
equipment America needed for terror bombing.

Building the Planes

To oversee the nation's supply of planes (and ships and rifles
and tanks), President Roosevelt created the National Defense
Advisory Commission in May of 1940. Headed by William Knudsen,
president of General Motors, the commission had no authority to
coerce industry, yet was expected to convince reluctant manufacturers to expand capacity in preparation for total war, or partial war,
or perhaps just large-scale support of the European allies. To assist
him in this unenviable job, Knudsen appointed nationally recognized
captains of industry to manage programs for ships, munitions, and
aircraft. Although these men brought with them obvious conflicts
of interest— an executive experienced in aviation, for example,
could hardly be objective about awarding plane contracts or formulating policies affecting his former employer— in 1940, nobody had
time to care. These businessmen could talk to executives like Fred
Rentschler knowing exactly what he was (and was not) up against.
They spoke the same language, and America simply made a bet that
the language of big business included words such as "unselfishness"
and concepts such as country before company.

To head the aeronautical section of the National Defense
Advisory Commission, Knudsen advised Rossevelt to name George

Mead, who had severed his links with United Aircraft the previous year. Despite his strong personal attachment to the company he had helped establish, Mead's bitterness over the B-247 decision in 1932 never disappeared. He and Fred Rentschler never reestablished the intimacy and confidence that characterized their relationship in 1925; their policy disagreements eventually became so heated that, in 1939, Mead had declined reelection to United's board of directors. He did not, however, quit aviation. In October of 1939, he had become president of the National Advisory Committee for Aeronautics. In January of 1940 he received the Reed award for outstanding achievement in aviation, and in May his national efforts earned him a telephone call from Washington. President Roosevelt asked George Mead to serve as an advisor for the procurement of material for national defense— specifically, fifty thousand planes.[16]

After selling his United Aircraft stock to avoid potential conflict of interest, Mead went to Washington to set about determining how much industrial capacity the aviation industry needed and when the factories had to be in operation to produce the requisite number of planes. On June 1, 1940, he was given four years to procure the fifty thousand planes; by June 15 the deadline had been shortened to April 1, 1942, twenty-one months away.

Mead requested more time in which to deal with a series of human roadblocks. First, it was necessary for the Army and Navy to cooperate in delineating their requirements. Then, once Mead knew how many of what type of aircraft to produce, he needed an official decision on who got what when. At United Aircraft, for example, the British had appropriated the French engine orders after France fell to Hitler, leaving England with the majority of the company's production precisely when America wanted engines of its own. The final and most important obstructions concerned money. Who would pay for plant expansions or new factories? What, if any, financial incentives would be offered to the manufacturers, all of whom were reluctant to expand capacity? Bargaining chips were essential to convince companies like United that patriotism was good business.

Mead expressed his doubts to Knudsen in a series of memoranda, and got results. By July 10, the Army and Navy, at the commission's request, agreed on an initial allotment of planes— 36,500 for the Army, 13,500 for the Navy— and established a joint procurement program under which each service would assume total responsibility for the equipment it needed. This way, the services would avoid each other, and administration of contracts would be simplified. Each service would control the companies with which it had experience and current contracts. The initial division of the aviation industry was as follows:[17]

Army		Navy	
Planes	Engines	Planes	Engines
Beech	Allison	Brewster	Pratt & Whitney
Bell	Continental	Grumman	Ranger
Boeing	Jacobs	Spartan	
Cessna	Lycoming	Vought	
Curtiss	Menasco	Consolidated	
Douglas	Wright		
Fairchild			
Lockheed			
Martin			
North American			
Republic			
Ryan			

United's Chance Vought operation naturally went to the Navy, which had provided over half of its 1940 business. For many years, in fact, Vought was as much a subsidiary of the Navy as of the United Aircraft Corporation. In Pratt & Whitney's case, about two-thirds of its 1940 business came from Britain and, before Hitler's victory, France. The Navy purchased only slightly more than the Army; it was, rather, years of experience working together that prompted the Navy to link up with Pratt & Whitney.

After the National Defense Advisory Commission had allotted each manufacturer to a particular service, the problem of who got what portion of each year's production remained. British purchasing agents were crossing the country buying up equipment, and the commission was informed only after contracts were signed. At Pratt & Whitney, the services received only two of every ten engines produced in 1940. "It was essential that some definition of the United States government's policy in this field be obtained at an early date as a first step toward obtaining control of the situation," Mead insisted in a July memorandum.[18]

In response, Knudsen met with the Army, Navy, and British personnel on July 23 to establish the definite distribution of future production. Despite the necessity for constant revisions of the initial agreement at least each part now would know which planes it could have, from whom they would come, and approximately when they would be delivered.

Next on Mead's agenda was the sensitive issue of industrial expansion. A July 30 conference of advisory commission members and aircraft manufacturers first addressed the issue of profits. Limitations imposed by the Vinson-Trammel Act had been increased on June 28, when Congress reduced the maximum profit margin from 12 to 8 percent. This move, prompted by memories of the abuses perpetrated by Colonel Deeds in World War I, incensed the industry and, according to the War Production Board's history, "was perhaps the most important obstacle to the speedy procurement of aircraft during the hectic summer of 1940."[19]

This was 1940, not 1917, argued the aircraft executives, protesting that their industry had been unfairly singled out. Besides, because of the Vinson-Trammel restrictions, the subcontractors they needed were turning to the more profitable business available in other manufacturing sectors.

Knudsen, driven by the need to get the program moving, agreed to push for new legislation. On July 30, he told industry representatives that Vinson-Trammel would be repealed within two weeks to two months. While manufacturers waited for a more liberal law to appear, Knudsen suggested a compromise: contracts signed now would be on a cost- plus fixed-fee basis. The government would underwrite manufacturers' legitimate expenses. Even if the maximum profit remained at 8 percent, the companies would be insured against loss.

The thorniest question of all, who would pay for the essential plant additions, had yet to be tacked. The surcharge United had added to the unit cost of a plane or engine on the French and British contracts was rejected as a complete giveway to the manufacturers. With the country not yet at war, it was unthinkable to donate factories to those companies fortunate enough to be producing armaments. Aviation, moreover, was already concentrated enough; bonuses to existing firms would discourage postwar competition.

The next suggestion on the table involved Emergency Plant Facility (EPF) contracts, whereby manufacturers would build whatever factories the government needed— without regard to postwar market conditions— by borrowing money from a bank. The War Department would repay the bank in sixty monthly install- ments, thus causing no immediate drain on its severely limited 1940 appropriations. Aside from easing the government's burden, EPF arrangements assisted the banking community, which for months had "anxiously clamoured for an opportunity to participate in the expansion about to be launched" across America and actively op- posed any form of financing that eliminated banks as middlemen.[20]

Knudsen accepted the EPF idea but, despite active opposition from the banks, also recommended direct government financing of new factories with funds from the Depression-born Reconstruction Finance Corp; an RFC subsidiary, a Defense Plant Corp., could ap- prove construction of a factory that the manufacturer would then rent from Washington. Instead of taking sixty months to repay the banks, the government would own title to the factory from start to finish.

Because the Commission's plan insured them against loss, the aircraft industry willingly endorsed it. But Knudsen and Mead demanded immediate action, and both funding plans required months of effort before they could yield the signed contracts without which the manufacturers were reluctant to move. To quiet their fears, Knudsen offered a letter of intent: each manufacturer would receive the government's written authorization to proceed with the purchase of jigs, dies, tools, fixtures, and other equipment that took longest to produce. When the facilities contracts were finally signed, manufacturers already would have on hand the tools needed to begin mass production of planes, engines, and other avia- tion equipment.

One last stumbling block remained. The aviation industry, led by Eugene Wilson, now president of United Aircraft, insisted on major changes in the tax laws. As Wilson explained, manufacturers traditionally had refrained from installing the equipment required for mass production because their orders had been relatively small. Now that vast numbers of planes were needed, the best way to reduce overall production costs and, therefore, unit prices to Washington, was to install the tools to allow a company like United to produce more goods more cheaply and more quickly. If the manufacturers were permitted to write off equipment costs over five years, with a provision for quicker writeoffs in case of peace, they would not suffer financially because of excess capacity even if the war ended in under five years.[21]

To the staff of the National Defense Advisory Commission, Wilson's plea made sense. After obtaining the approval of President Roosevelt and Secretary of the Treasury Morgenthau, Knudsen assured industry representatives that the tax laws would be changed within a matter of months. All plant modernizations could begin at once because Washington would permit the industry to deduct from its wartime profits the costs of its wartime tooling-up. Or, as economist Eliot Janeway later put it, "The difference between the earnings artifically depressed for tax purposes and the real earnings accruing to the stockholders' equity was a bonanza for business."[22]

Even before America entered the war, the aviation industry had won its battle. After July of 1940, despite Congress and the memory of Colonel Deeds, the manufacturers' legal gains would far exceed anything ever acquired through dubious means by the colonel and his colleagues. Without any significant increase in their corporate liabilities and without the sale of even one share of new stock, United Aircraft and its competitors were guaranteed an extraordinary, yet risk-free, increase in their net worth— and, when the war ended, they would be in a far better financial position to face an uncertain future.

Too Much of a Good Thing

United Aircraft's sales had increased 250 percent — from $51 million in 1939 to $126 million in 1940— within one year. Profits, too, increased dramatically. In 1939 the company netted a $9 million profit, which was 28 percent on net worth; in 1940 the figure reached $13 million, close to 36 percent net profit on its capital investment.[23]

To complement these rosy financial statements, United received government orders that promised growth for years to come. To fill Washington's demand for thirty-five thousand engines to be delivered by June 30, 1942, Pratt & Whitney would use its original factory, the French addition (which began operation in June of 1940), the British addition (scheduled to be in operation by early

1941), and the American addition. This latter $18-million annex, completely financed by Emergency Plant Facilities contracts, was begun in September of 1940. As Rentschler told stockholders in the 1940 annual report, "All the French and British contracts provide for advanced and partial payments, as manufacture progresses, so as to be practically self-financing."[24]

Hamilton-Standard's near-monopoly on propellers translated into a substantial increase in business and, to a lesser extent, in industrial capacity. To produce the sixty thousand propellers the government wanted by June 30, 1943, the subsidiary enlarged its East Hartford facility and leased a plant at Pawcatuck, Connecticut. As usual, Rentschler tried to cut his long-term risks by limiting expenditures. Hamilton-Standard had netted over $4.8 million — an 18 percent net profit— on sales of $26.8 million. With that kind of return, there was no need to be greedy. Let others share the wealth and, if cutbacks came, feel the pain.

In Stratford, Vought-Sikorsky had been awarded a contract for over a thousand Scout-Observation planes— a huge order by anyone's standards, but incredible to old-timers who remembered company parties for any order of more than twenty-five. Now a major operation in its own right yet United's only weak link, Vought might use the Scout order to do something different: make money. On its 1940 Navy business, the subsidiary had lost 50 percent; its total 1940 losses approached one million dollars. When Vought shaped up, United Aircraft would be in the strongest financial position in its history.[25]

This strength would come from the profitable handling of war orders, but Rentschler and Wilson also had made some rewarding arrangements with the automobile industry. In essence, they had deftly managed to take the business they wanted and give companies like Ford and Buick the business they rejected.

In his memoirs, Eugene Wilson explained how United helped the car makers join the wartime aviation industry. Along with Guy Vaughn, head of Curtiss-Wright, Wilson had been invited to Sunday dinner at the home of Treasury Secretary Morgenthau, who requested that the enginemakers share their business with the auto companies by accepting licensing agreements for their products.

"We won't license," stated Vaughn. "We'll fight you."

Wilson, in contrast, surprised the secretary by announcing that

United would readily grant a license to any company that cared to do the job. What's more, he assured the dubious Morgenthau, who had not overestimated Wilson's patriotism since their altercations over the British contracts, there was no catch. For one dollar per engine, United would permit the automobile industry to manufacture all the extra engines the government needed. The secretary, he added, need not suspect his or United Aircraft's motives.

"The truth of the matter was that under the contracts we had with the War and Navy Departments, they had the perfect right to license," Wilson later bragged. "All they had to do was exercise that particular option and they could have anybody build the dog-gone things, but they didn't know that."[26]

Wilson had agreed to do the licensing because he had no choice. He had previously cleared the matter with Fred Rentschler, who maintained that too much business was bad business. United's rapidly expanded operations were already spreading management resources too thin. Just doing a good job in East Hartford, where Pratt & Whitney was producing one million horsepower per month in December of 1940 compared with 120,000 horsepower in July of 1938, was backbreaking. To protect the integrity of the main operation, Rentschler was more than willing to relegate to the automobile industry complete responsibility for the government's overflow engine orders.

After Wilson accepted the licensing proposal, Rentschler went to Washington in July to confer with Knudsen and Mead and to suggest that Ford manufacture Pratt & Whitney engines. Knudsen, himself an automative executive, endorsed the idea— if, of course, Henry Ford could be convinced to take the job. The previous month, Ford had contracted to manufacturer Rolls Royce engines for the British, but cancelled the order when a public announcement by Lord Beaver Brook suggested that Henry Ford supported England. Ford wanted nothing to do with the British or with the dreadful American president who favored entering the war. Knudsen was certain of Ford's refusal to help Franklin Roosevelt, but if Mead or Rentschler wanted to try, they had his blessing— and his sympathy.

Mead went to Detroit, where he succeeded simply because Henry Ford admired his engineering ability. In August of 1940, a team of fifteen Ford engineers arrived for an eye-opening two-week examination of Pratt & Whitney's factories. The key to successful production of an airplane engine is a precision unknown in the automobile industry. A Twin Wasp twelve hundred horsepower engine, for example, was composed of eight thousand parts, all of which had to be as clean and smooth as mechanically possible. Ford's engineers saw nothing wrong with the parts that Pratt & Whitney rejected, but eye inspection rarely sufficed for aeronautic power plants; parts were submitted to a chemical bath that often showed minute flaws.

Ford's men ultimately recommended the construction of new facilities. The easiest way to start production within the shortest time, they noted, was to duplicate Pratt & Whitney's factories.

Fred Rentschler agreed to let Ford build a Pratt & Whitney replica in Michigan, whereupon the automobile manufacturer signed a contract on November 5, 1940, to produce over twelve hundred of Pratt & Whitney's R 2800 engines, which powered the Vought Corsair among other planes. Ford would receive a 5 percent fee on the $122 million order, and United would be content with one dollar per engine.

When Mead, hungry for yet more engines, suggested bringing in the Buick division of General Motors, Rentschler willingly agreed to give Buick the same deal he gave Ford. In early January of 1941, Buick signed on for two thousand Pratt & Whitney engines; by late February, another five thousand were in the works. "The licenses were for military purposes only and for the period of the emergency," Rentschler informed stockholders. But at least the long-term pressures had been relieved on United's, and especially on Pratt & Whitney's, already overexpanded facilities.

Even with a high-priority rating for tools and supplies Ford and Buick, to Detroit's embarrassment, would need at least eighteen months to prepare for airplane engine production. In the meantime, Pratt & Whitney once again doubled production quotas. In 1940 and 1941, Pratt & Whitney manufactured half the large airplane engines in America.

With such unprecedented sums going to defense contractors, Fred Rentschler was growing nervous. In 1941, he was determined "not only that United would render the best account possible but on a basis where during the war or later we could not be accused of the terrible term of 'profiteer.'"[27]

Keeping the Company

Throughout 1940, Fred Rentschler and Eugene Wilson lived in fear that Franklin Roosevelt wanted to take over the United Aircraft Corporation. They believed that the president had intended to nationalize United in 1934 but had been prevented by his own mistakes with the air mails. Now, with war almost certain, he had a reasonable pretext readily available. If United played into Roosevelt's hands by making a serious error of its own, the president would seize the opportunity like a true New Dealer, stamping out monopolies. United Aircraft would be a publicly owned company, in the very worst sense.

No taint of scandal could ever again touch United's corporate name, even if that meant rewriting the corporation's history. When interviewed on August 9, 1940 for "Airways" by Henry Ladd Smith, Rentschler denied Colonel Deed's involvement in the founding of Pratt & Whitney Aircraft; and, to avoid any harsh political consequences from United's increasingly profitable operation, Rentschler decided to convince the skeptical American public that United Aircraft was a patriotic member of the country's defense team.[28]

Rentschler explained the corporation's situation in the spring of 1941 as having successfully avoided the inefficiency and expense involved in cost-plus contracts. As orders streamed in for more and more engines and propellers and planes, he was able to increase production dramatically. In essence, while costs for capital, equipment, supplies, and labor remained relatively stable, the know-how acquired through experience translated into much higher profits at the back end of a fixed-price contract.

To avoid any potential charges of war-profiteering and, not incidentally, to improve its corporate image, United volunteered to reduce its prices to what Rentschler called "a percentage point which was obviously conscionable." If it seemed that too much money was forthcoming on a particular contract, prices were reduced before the government completed payment. As Wilson noted, "When we introduced the technique of renegotiation, we renegotiated ourselves in advance of the shipments, so that we didn't receive any money we'd have to give back. We just never took it. That was all thought out from the very beginning."[29]

United's executives also anticipated the effect of voluntary renegotiation on the Navy personnel who audited its books and decided what constituted a fair profit. When the price-reduction plan was ready for implementation, Rentschler presented it to Secretary of the Navy James Forrestal, who commended him and Wilson for the "fundamental soundness" of their approach. Like Rentschler, Forrestal believed that the readjustment of prices offered both the manufacturers and the Navy means to avoid public castigation for their methods and motives; on the contrary, by voluntarily returning profits, the industry would win high praise for its patriotic assistance to the war effort.

United succeeded easily in accomplishing its goal of netting a profit lower than the fees earned on cost-plus contracts. In 1941, overall profits on sales were no more than 5.4 percent; profits on Navy business were held to a "completely conscionable" 4.87 percent. This rate applied to all three subsidiaries, with Vought's 2.38 percent the lowest. Five percent was less than any of the fixed limits set by any of the Vinson-Trammel Acts. What's more, the company returned $10 million in 1941. United looked good, as long as no one peeped backstage at what Rentschler and Wilson had hidden behind the curtain and called "renegotiation."

If United's profits were calculated as a percentage of invested capital, the 1941 rate of return jumped to 42 percent. Because many of its factories had been built with other people's money, the company earned much of its profit without risking capital of its own. Equally as significant as risk-free profit was the gentleman's agreement with the Navy reached as a result of Rentschler's renegotiation efforts. "Under this profit control arrangement that we had set up," Wilson explained, the company agreed to stabilize its net profit based on the money "we had earned the year before we went into the big war effort, on the sale of aircraft to foreign countries, to France, and Great Britain."[30]

United and the Navy determined to use the company's 1940 net profit— over 13 million— as the basis for computing maximum net profits in future years. This stabilization agreement could not affect the money made in 1941, of course; with no law on the books, the Navy had no right to limit the year's net profits through renegotiation. But Rentschler and Wilson had seen the writing on the wall; realizing that legislation was imminent, they settled for a "guaranteed" net profit of $13 million beforehand— plus the assurance of no adverse publicity as a result of net profits that were 250 percent higher than those totaled in 1938, the last year before war demands materialized.

By taking the initiative on profits, Rentschler had kept Congress at bay. Nobody called him a profiteer, and nobody bothered to put renegotiation into effect until after December 7, thus rendering 1941 United's best year ever. Sales came to over $317 million, with 58 percent of the merchandise going to the United States government and most of the remainder shipped to Great Britain. Net profits climbed to a heady $16.7 million, but this figure excluded $5 million of profit reserved for a "going-out-of-war" account. In the annual report, Rentschler and Wilson noted the large expenses incurred to begin war production. In 1940; it would cost good money to reconvert the factories when peace was declared. So, as of December 31, 1941, United had set aside $5 million in a special reconversion account to current operation costs." However, "because of the serious doubt that any further substantial sums can be charged to operating costs in the period ahead, an additional $5 million had been transferred from earned surplus."[31]

Rentschler and Wilson knew what was coming. Japan's attack on Pearl Harbor had brought war, and war meant even tighter congressional control of the methods manufacturers used to compute profits. United therefore would take advantage of the existing tax laws by using $10 million of "excess" war business to reduce its taxes on regular war business: The same $10 million would help the company prepare for peace with the extra money earned from war. If the government later financed the aviation industry's reconversion, the special fund could turn into a savings account that earned interest while it reduced the company's taxes.

But in early 1942, when war held more interest than peace, United Aircraft assured the nation of its patriotism with the following pledge in its 1941 Annual Report:

A Statement of Principles

We dedicate ourselves to the great Task of presenting the goods and rendering the services required by the war effort at the maximum rate and the lowest cost consistent with the required quality.

In the execution of the foregoing, we pledge ourselves:

1) to limit profit to that necessary to maintain the business in the sound financial position to execute the Task;

2) to stimulate output and reduce costs by rewarding individual initiative and performance with adequate compensation and to provide the best possible working conditions;

3) to take all measures consistent with accomplishment of the Task to the end that after the war we can help restore peace and stabilization in the shortest possible time.[32]

That United had a right to profit from the production of its and the government's factories seemed obvious and fair. What was devious and arguably unfair was the definition of a fair net profit with which Rentschler and Wilson entered 1942. Because they had agreed with the Navy on guaranteed profits at the 1940 level— $13 million— any further computations were academic. As Wilson was to explain in later years, "When we worked out our cash requirements and our forecast, we started off with that. Well, if labor moved in and, under government support, raised the wages all over the country, that didn't make any difference. That just increased the costs. If they put 50%, 75% excess profits tax on that, that was alright, that just had to be added into the price. Every one of those punitive measures they took against us ended up only increasing the price. The result was that when we got through, that just meant that that much money went through our hands long enough to give it back to the Treasury Department, and it just inflated the whole financial operation without changing anything."[33]

United, in other words, emerged with the same bottom line, yet was protected from reproach for accumulating excess profits. Although sales were sure to rise as the war progressed, the stability of profits assured a lower rate of return calculated on the basis of sales. United thus could earn exactly what it wanted, yet maintain that its profits declined as war progressed; it was adhering to the principles it set forth and clearly doing its part— and more— to execute the Task.

This deliberate and successful strategy on profits was complemented by the cautious attitude toward the postwar situation manifested in the $10 million first installment on United's insurance policy against a World War I-type demobilization; it was possible, if unlikely, that Roosevelt would follow Wilson's horrible example and leave aviation to fend for itself. Frederick Rentschler, determined to weather whatever storms peace might bring, demonstrated his resolve in two separate yet related ways: he requested that United play a part in the government's jet engine program; and he decided to resurrect the Sikorsky Aviation Corporation.

From Jets to Helicopters

United had been funding a small jet research program that Wilson later called the "Glastonbury Project" as early as 1940. But the handful of engineers charged with investigating the possibilities of their vibration-free PT-1 engine were in no hurry— a flight engine was too far in the future as well as contrary to the explicit orders of the federal government. In 1941, Army officials with orders from Hap Arnold instructed United to "devote no— repeat, no— engineering talent to the design of new engines." Victory in World War II demanded total concentration on the task at hand; besides, United's future markets were of little concern to America's policymakers.

Although Wilson and Rentschler essentially followed orders, they soon learned of government-sponsored research programs underway at General Electric, Westinghouse, and Allis Chalmers. General Electric engineers had actually gone to England, analyzed the Whittle jet engine, and returned with a license to manufacture it in the United States. Not surprisingly, United's executives were outraged at the thought of postwar markets in another company's pocket; General Electric's edge would make it that much harder, perhaps even impossible, for Pratt & Whitney to catch up. So in early 1942, Rentschler and Wilson hopped into the company plane and flew down to Washington to enlist the aid of Robert Lovett, then Assistant Secretary of War for Air.

Lovett affirmed that, under orders from General Arnold, Pratt & Whitney and Curtiss-Wright were excluded from participation in the government's jet-engine programs. United was to focus on conventional engines because the Army needed them and because the British had agreed to license the Whittle only if it was manufactured by companies unlikely to offer their domestic firms postwar competition; following America's lead, England had seconded Pratt & Whitney's exclusion from jet-engine research. Lovett was sorry, but he could only maintain the status quo.

When Rentschler and Wilson informed him that they would continue the Glastonbury Project in order to keep up with companies such as General Electric, Lovett angrily ended the meeting, also ending any chance that Washington would help United Aircraft into the jet-engine market.[34]

On jets, United was grounded. On helicopters, however, the company was set for takeoff.

Immediately after Eugene Wilson had forced him out of the airplane business, Igor Sikorsky had turned his attention to the design of a single-rotor helicopter. Reasoning that one twirling blade was difficult enough to control, he gladly let the competition (which in America constituted the Kellett Company) deal with the burden of two.

On September 14, 1939, the VS-300 helicopter (VS for Vought-Sikorsky) was if not up and flying, at least off the ground. Photographs show a mass of exposed tubes and struts tied to four stakes in the ground to eliminate the possibility of the craft taking off for parts unknown.

In the pilot's seat was Igor Sikorsky, wearing a suit, a white shirt, a tie, a dark overcoat, and a fedora with the brim turned up. Although he never dressed like a pilot, he certainly had what contemporary aviators call "the right stuff." When he started the 75 horsepower engine, the VS-300 vibrated and the controls shook in his hand; one observer maintained that it "rocked like an angry elephant at his pickets." In response to the violent shaking, Sikorsky increased power. Despite even more rocking from the tied-down machine, first one wheel, then two, and finally all four were off the ground. As a matter of record, the ship "flew" for no more than ten seconds.

Sikorsky returned to the factory, made change after tiresome change and, within a matter of months, sent photography buff Eugene Wilson motion pictures of his new flying machine moving through the air with grace and speed.

The VS-300 looked quite promising, Wilson told Sikorsky over the telephone, but "your helicopter goes up and down. Your helicopter she goes right and left. Your helicopter she goes back. But she never moves forward."

A laughing Sikorsky admitted that forward motion "was one of the minor engineering problems we have not yet solved."

By early 1941 the VS-300 flew well in every direction. It so impressed the Army that Sikorsky was commissioned to build a more powerful experimental ship for possible military use, with an enclosed cabin and the capacity to carry at least one passenger. The Army wanted its helicopter in the air as soon as humanly possible.

To a company with only one experimental ship to its credit, the Army's demands presented an enormous challenge that Igor Sikorsky met. By January of 1942, the 175 horsepower XR-4 was ready for preliminary testing and spent two hours in the air. (X stood for experimental model, R for rotary wing, and 4 for the fourth Army contract; the first had gone to Platt-Le Page and the second and third to Kellett. Sikorsky's was the first single-rotor configuration.) After extensive further changes, the XR-4 was scheduled for a demonstration before a number of "less-than-enthusiastic Army officials on April 20. After all, the XR-4 displayed none of the spit and polish of a finished craft; according to Charles Morris, Sikorsky's pilot, it looked like a do-it-yourself model with an Army decal pasted on the side.

Whatever its appearance, the ship's performance created in others the enthusiasm Sikorsky had always felt. The XR-4 climbed all the way up to five thousand feet and demonstrated agility flying in every direction. Once it completed one hundred additional hours of mandated Army exams in July of 1942, this second Sikorsky ship became the first production helicopter in American history. The Army placed an order for fifteen, and also asked Sikorsky to build two more experimental helicopters with increased speed and load capacity.

The Army order represented the first real business in three years from the lesser half of United's least profitable subsidiary. Sikorsky and his staff had had to build their experimental ships in a corner of the Vought factory. Now, to build the Army's ships, United Aircraft leased a vacant plant in Bridgeport. And to underline the significance of Sikorsky's achievement, Vought and Sikorsky were to be separated as of January 1, 1943.[35]

Sikorsky's monopoly on capable helicopters seemed to assure

the new company's future. Unfortunately, just like the older parts of United, Sikorsky was basing its short-term prospects on World War II and its long-term prospects on the attitude and actions of the federal government.

Igor Sikorsky took justifiable pride in his helicopter's life-saving potential. Through its ability to hover, it could save lives that otherwise would be lost at sea; through its efficiency, it could travel easily to remote spots inaccessible to a vehicle unable to fly straight up and straight down. And, indeed, his helicopters have saved thousands of lives. But to sell them, Sikorsky Aviation was forced to build to its only customer's specifications and plan for the customer's long-term needs. Because the military demanded a combat vehicle, Sikorsky helicopters were adapted from the first to combat needs; bombs racks, for example, were installed, and Army trainees eventually became reasonably accurate in heaving twenty-pound dummy bombs over the side of the XR-4. Unless Sikorsky, like every United Aircraft company, found commercial markets for its products, it either made weapons or went out of business.

America's War: More Capacity, More Fears

United Aircraft entered 1943 looking back at a year of incredible technical and financial accomplishments. Although Sikorsky's creation of a unique aircraft may have received the most attention, Pratt & Whitney had doubled its production every nine months; Pratt & Whitney engines powered everything from Douglas transports to Grumman fighters, Lockheed's medium bombers to the Goodyear blimp. Using three goverment-financed "feeder plants" within a twenty-five radius of Hartford, the engine subsidiary was shipping nearly 4 million horsepower per month— 25 percent of the horsepower delivered by all the major manufacturers combined, not counting licensees. When the military exerted pressure for even more, Pratt & Whitney agreed to accept another factory (groundbreaking occurred in July of 1942 in Kansas City, Missouri) and to train over four hundred mid-Westerners in the art and science of aviation engines in order to meet the government's 1943 production schedule.[36]

Hamilton-Standard, which as of January 1, 1943, had produced

75 percent of all combat and advanced training propellers delivered to the Army and Navy, had accelerated production from about 260 propellers per month in 1939 to 4,000 by the end of 1942. Now that Nash-Kelvinator, Frigidaire, and Remington Rand had taken out licenses from Hamilton-Standard, the nation's 1943 propeller output would be increased substantially at the same time that Hamilton-Standard's risks would be cut (just as Pratt & Whitney was protected by its licenses to Ford and Buick).

Chance Vought, meanwhile, had begun production of its Corsair fighter, the plane that soon shot down the superb Japanese Zero, which also traced its ancestory to Vought. Powered by a two-thousand horsepower Pratt & Whitney engine and reaching speeds exceeding four hundred miles per hour, the Corsair was the fastest shipboard military plane in the world, and the Navy wanted as many as Vought could deliver. By December of 1942, the company stood a chance of winning the Navy's E award for manufacturing excellence.

Given United Aircraft's many achievements in production, its 1942 balance sheets looked especially good. On sales of half a billion dollars, net profits came to over $17 million— only 3 percent as a percentage of sales but, figured on the $13 million minimum of 1940, a $4 million increase. And, according to plan, the company had neatly sidestepped the accusation of profiteering. But, though the bottom line pleased both the company and Congress, United's executives were haunted by the everpresent fear of overexpansion. As Eugene Wilson recalled in *Slipstream*, "In United Aircraft, we lived in mortal terror of a sudden cessation of hostilities which, like that following the Armistice, would lead to disorderly reconversion and the extinction of the private manufacturing industry."[37]

In 1942, the government had attempted to allay the aviation industry's fears with the Federal Revenue Act, which gave manufacturers a postwar credit representing 10 percent of excess profits taxes to help with reconversion expenses. United's credits totaled $3,897,270. Nevertheless, the 1942 annual report noted, "after careful consideration, United's directors believed that such sum was wholly inadequate, and they have accordingly transferred an additional sum of $10,000,000 from earned surplus to the transformation reserve, resulting in a total transformation reserve, to date, of $23,897,270."[38]

This, Rentschler and Wilson maintained, represented "prudent management." At the outset of 1943, after all, United was obligated to increase its already incredible output. United Aircraft, like a balloon, was inflated to the danger point by war. Peace, they feared, might be the pin that burst it.

One of the de Havilands powered by Colonel Deeds's Liberty engine. *Boeing Photo*

The Pratt & Whitney tool company in decay. These were the buildings in which Mead, Wilgoos, and Rentschler set up shop to build the Wasp. *The Hartford Courant*

The first Wasp to be built. This picture was taken on December 23, 1925. *Courtesy of Mrs. George J. Mead*

The Wasp as it looked on the test stand in the factory of the Pratt & Whitney tool company. *Courtesy of Mrs. George J. Mead*

The control room at the Pratt & Whitney tool company's factory. Notice the Wasp through the window. *Courtesy of Mrs. George J. Mead*

The Boeing mail plane with room for passengers. The adventuresome sat directly behind the engine (notice the windows).
Boeing photo

Frederick Rentschler in
February of 1941. *United
Press International*

George Mead, designer
of the Wasp and Hornet
engines that fueled
United Aircraft's early
success. *Courtesy of
Mrs. George J. Mead*

Colonel Deeds in late 1918. *United Press International*

Charles Deeds before the Black Committee in 1934. *United Press International*

Tom Hamilton, with the Countess Von
Blixen-Finecke. Taken in 1936, this
photograph shows Hamilton and the
countess disembarking from the dirigible
Hindenburg. United Press International

An S-40 flying into Pan Am's Miami base in or about 1931. *Pan
American World Airways Photo*

One reason Sikorsky lost so much money on the S-40 was the luxurious interiors demanded by Juan Trippe. *Pan American World Airways Photo*

Juan Trippe outlining his plans for Pan American and the aviation industry. *Pan American World Airways Photo*

The Boeing 247, the first real passenger ship. Notice the cramped quarters for passengers and the obstacle course which served as an aisle. This was the plane that drove a wedge between Mead and Rentschler. *Boeing Photo*

The Boeing 247. *Boeing Photo*

6

THE PAX AERONAUTICA

"In United Aircraft, we lived in mortal terror of a
sudden cessation of hostilities. . . ."

Eugene Wilson, President,
United Aircraft

"It was strongly in my mind at this period that we
must begin thinking in terms of postwar. . .I believed
that Wilson's ability could well be utilized in an attempt to revive interest in the Aeronautical Chamber
and get it going again as an active functioning body
at once, ready to be the industry's mouthpiece in
postwar."

Frederick Rentschler,
An Account of the Pratt &
Whitney Aircraft Company

Air Power for Peace

At the outset of World War II, airplanes remained a largely untried weapon. Questions abounded— Could air power single-handedly defeat Hitler? Would the Army and Navy be obsolete at war's end?— but answers were in short supply.

Air force advocates, capitalizing on the opportunity to prove their theories, were so successful that by mid-August 1945 many Americans believed air power was the winning weapon. Strategic bombing had proved so effective at leveling cities that the assumptions of a radical such as General Billy Mitchell, who had devised the mock bombing of New York City in 1921, were adopted by the entire nation.

But though air power helped win the war, the bombers' victory was United Aircraft's defeat. For three solid years, 1943 to 1945, United's men conducted a public relations campaign to stress the concept of air power for peace and thereby acquire commercial postwar customers. But despite a quarter of a million dollars spent to sponsor books, articles, public speakers, United Aircraft lost its battle to escape military domination.

One Terrific Prang

Writing about Hitler, Albert Speer, his minister for war production, maintained that "fire was his proper element. Though what he loved about fire was not its Promethean aspect, but its destructive force. . . I recall his ordering showings in the Chancellory of the films of burning London, of the sea of flames over Warsaw, of exploding convoys, and the rapture with which he watched those films."

Otherwise decent people, including America's Allies, also delighted in the devastation of their enemies. After the first "thousand-bomber" raid on Cologne on May 30, 1942, British Air Marshall Arthur Harris announced, "We are going to scourge the Third Reich from end to end. We are bombing Germany city by city and ever more terribly in order to make it impossible for her to go on with the war." And when British pilot Tolley Taylor returned from his grisly work in Cologne, his first response was, "Terrific prang. Weren't the fires great?"[1]

"Prang," British aviation slang for "destruction," was the consummation pursued by both sides in World War II through their strategic bombing policies. Through 1942 many American and British citizens delighted in the havoc caused by military aircraft. They saw nothing wrong in the terror bombing of civilians and their cities; on the contrary, some people wanted aviators to do more of the same.

The official culmination of the growing Allied support for obliteration bombing came on January 21, 1943. Meeting in Casablanca, the combined Chiefs of Staff issued a directive calling for pilots "to pursue the destruction and dislocation of the German military, industrial and economic system and the undermining of the morale of the German people to the point where their capacity for armed resistance is fatally weakened."[2]

With this policy, the Allies openly embraced what Churchill and Roosevelt once had labeled "odious" and "barbaric" forms of warfare. But even if subsequent air attacks failed to stop the German war machine, the public never stopped believing in the efficacy of air power as the decisive weapon. Although air power did not singlehandedly win World War II, the Allies' flamboyant displays of destruction ingrained themselves on the popular imagination to such an extent that the Army and Navy suffered a loss of public esteem as the air corps slowly moved to center stage.

The effect of this newfound faith in air power was a long-term *raison d'etre* for the industrial capacity created since May of 1940. Because bombers might mean the difference between victory and defeat, the air force and the aviation industry shared the public's loud applause.

Soon after the Casablanca Conference, General Hap Arnold begain lobbying to make an autonomous air force the largest and most important part of America's postwar military system. From April of 1943 on, air power advocates treated the other services as backups, while they made plans to capture the major portion of any postwar budget for the independent United States Air Force they were certain was forthcoming.[3]

To the air industry, and especially to Fred Rentschler and Eugene Wilson, huge postwar expenditures seemed uncertain. They never shared the air corp's optimism because a fickle Congress was, still, the final arbiter of aviation's future. After years of riding on the peacetime federal roller coaster, Rentschler and Wilson doubted Congress's willingness to fund a large air force once the fighting finally ended. Their concern was peace and its consequences. United's reserve fund for postwar reconversion continued to grow but, unlike air force supporters, United's men had no one plan in mind. They knew what they were up against —overcapacity and overdependence on the military— and to assure a profitable peace, Rentschler and Wilson decided to develop a proposal that would also protect aviation's future from these twin perils.

The trick was to find commercial markets other than the airlines. Neither passengers nor their air mail could possibly keep United's mass production factories humming. But no other non-military markets were apparent until Eugene Wilson hit upon an extraordinary scheme: the Pax Aeronautica.

The Pax Aeronautica

In August of 1943, Frederick Rentschler and Eugene Wilson went to Washington to present Secretary of the Navy James Forrestal with a preliminary survival plan for the entire aviation industry. If the Aeronautical Chamber of Commerce —the industry's moribund PR group— was resurrected with Wilson as its chairman, United Aircraft and its competitors could effectively lobby for postwar freedom from military domination.

As Wilson reported in his 1960 book *Kitty Hawk to Sputnik to*

Polaris, Forrestal opened the meeting by saying, "You fellows are swamping us with your production. You've got engines, propellers, and airplanes running out of our ears. In short, the time has come to cut back."[4]

Wilson laughed. That morning's *Washington Post* had charged the industry with treason for producing too little too late; now Forrestal was accusing them of too much too soon. Rentschler, who was known as a "sobersides," was not amused. He announced that he had been worried all along about a postwar surplus, but had kept silent in the face of newspaper stories chiding the manufacturers for production shortfalls. Now that the secretary had mentioned it, however, Rentschler noted that "our present output is all out of proportion to our own meager resources. If there should be a sudden cessation of hostilities, as in World War I, and if no more preparation has been made for such an event than now exists, the whole aircraft industry will be wiped out in a matter of days."

United had been "ultraconservative" in its precautions against sudden peace, Rentschler continued, but because all contracts legally must be terminated once the fighting stopped, the corporation would be unable even to meet its five thousand-plus payroll without liquidating its resources. If Forrestal wanted to help prevent the industrial chaos imminent at war's end, plans must be made today.

Although Forrestal agreed that a new national aviation policy was essential, he asserted that the aircraft industry contained "about the choicest collection of cutthroat competitors in my experience" and must learn "how to cooperate in the public interest as enthusiastically as they compete in their own self-interest."

Together, the three men quickly determined that the aviation companies first must stop fighting among themselves if they hoped to implement a satisfactory reconversion law; divided, they would struggle for their portions of any available pie and, in the process of destroying themselves, destroy the industry as well.

Second, government leaders must stay in the background; in the summer of 1943, public support of arms merchants was out of the question. Instead, the aircraft industry must mount a nationwide public relations campaign, spearheaded by Eugene Wilson, whose countless contacts and proven ability with words admirably suited him for the task. Besides, United Aircraft needed new blood at the top. If Wilson moved up to the vice chairman's position, the company could help itself to a new president while the old one developed an industrial program for postwar survival.

Formulation of a specific plan for profits in postwar America occurred soon afterward in the boardroom of United Aircraft's East Hartford headquarters. On the richly paneled walls hung portraits of the company's executives, with Rentschler's poised slightly higher than the others. When a key meeting came to order around the massive oak table, the ad hoc "war council" easily concurred on personnel changes at the top. Horace Horner, who had been with United since his graduation from Yale in 1926, had been groomed for its presidency since 1940. Rentschler would remain as chairman of the board. And Eugene Wilson, who was to assume the newly created position of vice chairman, would retain responsibility for general supervision of research and development but would devote the majority of his time to industry relations once the war council formulated its goals.

The winning idea came from Raycroft Walsh. A member of the United family since 1930 and currently a senior vice president, Walsh looked backward to move forward: he wanted another Morrow Board. Because Congress, the Army, the Navy, and the manufacturers had all benefited from the Morrow Board's support in 1925, he advised the same approach twenty years later. Nothing could focus national attention on an issue more effectively than a presidential commission, Walsh noted, especially if it involved matters of national security. And United's executives seemed uniquely suited to put this plan into action— Rentschler, after all, had served on the industry committee that lobbied Calvin Coolidge to establish the Morrow Board. Wilson had written the Navy's press releases, and Walsh had done the same for the Army. Between them, Rentschler, Wilson, and Walsh knew the system inside out. Now it was Wilson's job to use their combined experience as the basis for the new industry-schooled President's Advisory Commission on Aviation.[5]

Before leaving for California to feel out the nation's foremost aviation concerns, Wilson stopped in Washington to inform those aviation officials who mattered— Robert Lovett at the War Department, Hap Arnold at the Army Air Force, and John McCain at the Navy— of United Aircraft's intentions. All three expressed favor for the plan. Unfortunately, the response was less positive from Wilson's West Coast peers, who travelled in the same social circuit as their Eastern counterparts and attended the same parties. Wilson had hoped, through the friendships formed in this manner, to influence his competitors' ideas—he wanted someone else to suggest a new version of the Morrow Board so he could second the motion.

When no one did, he decided to seek an appraisal of prevailing opinion from the West Coast Aircraft Production Council which, with its East Coast namesake, had been established to coordinate the war program (Rentschler never joined because of fears generated by the Black Committee of the accusation of industrial collusion). The council's manager, John Lee, directed Wilson to the November 22, 1943, *Time* magazine cover story on aircraft manufacturer Donald Douglas, who had summarized his forecast for peacetime aviation in a few select words: "You just shut the damn job up."[6]

The remark may have been apocryphal, but it nonetheless reflected the West Coast's pessimism about postwar aviation; nobody knew how to cut the small postwar pie into pieces fit for giant companies. Unless he could add substance to his Morrow Board proposal, Lee added, Wilson might as well head back to Hartford. Even if he did, moreover, the approval of the enormously powerful Donald Douglas was necessary before the other manufacturers would listen.

With this pessimistic assessment in hand, Wilson retreated to Palm Springs where Russell Vought, Chance Vought's brother and United's West Coast representative, owned a bungalow that he could use as an office. There, he had a brainstorm: a memory pertaining to British seapower revealed to him exactly how the aviation industry could be saved.

Like any other Annapolis graduate, Wilson was aware that Britannia ruled the waves. What he had overlooked until then was the possibility that, just as Great Britain had used her ships to spread freedom over the world, America could do the same with planes. "Air transporation was unlikely to replace maritime transportation, but given an injection of technology, it might give it a run for its money," he recollected in each of his three books. "Remember those commercial air transports that hurdled the Seven Seas and leapfrogged the Himalayan Hump when the German subs threatened to sever our lines of communication? *Air Power for Peace!* How about that postwar objective?"[7]

To assure the future of the United Aircraft and every other

plane manufacturer, America had only to expand the use of airlines to transport anything and everything across the country and around the globe. Besides helping aviation, this concept also would help the world. As Wilson conceived it, the Pax Americana would be a Pax Aeronautica. The United States would carry its message of freedom and equality on the wings of companies like United. What better means of communication than a machine invented by two young men equipped with nothing more than perserverance and American ingenuity?

Stripped of its grandiose claims, Air Power for Peace was actually an original idea. If the hoped-for Air Policy Commission convinced the nation to base substantial portions of its commerce on planes, it would guarantee stability and profits for the industry. After the war, the government's task would be to help industry create the commerce that would end its reliance on the government.

Wilson took his proposal to Donald Douglas in the form of an "attractive pamphlet entitled merely 'Air Power.'" He stated his agruments succinctly, provided even shorter summaries in the margins, and added appealing illustrations to capture the attention of the man who allegedly wanted to "shut the damn job up."

Douglas's response was as concise as Wilson's pamphlet: "I'll buy this. What do you want me to do?" Wilson asked him to support the Pax Aeronautica at the April meeting of the National Aircraft War Production Council as well as at an earlier meeting of the Aeronautical Chamber of Commerce. If the board of governors approved his air transport scheme, the chamber could serve as a front for the public relations campaign he was planning.

Douglas refused to head the board of governors— that, he insisted, was Wilson's job— buy he agreed to lend all the support requested. The other manufacturers followed suit— in varying degrees. Traveling from Boeing in Seattle to Grumman in Long Island, Lockheed in Glendale to Curtiss-Wright in New York, Wilson discovered more ingrained pessimism than he had imagined. Said John H. Kindleberger, of North American Aviation in Los Angeles, "This industry reminds me of those toy rubber balloons you buy at the circus. Blow them up and they look like a fat pig. Release the pressure and they collapse with a plaintive dying sequel, a wrinkled remnant of overstressed rubber."[8]

He was determined to continue his efforts even if they became a one-man crusade. He would serve as an evangelist for the Pax

Aeronautica to save the aviation industry and, equally important, to avoid being remembered as nothing more than a war profiteer.[9]

War, Peace and Exports

As Wilson struggled for a profitable peace, United continued to perform its significant wartime role. In 1943 Army and Navy transport planes, 96 percent of which used Pratt & Whitney engines, flew more than a million miles every 24 hours. Chance Vought had increased production so efficiently, turning out 1,780 Corsairs in 1943, that, like Pratt & Whitney and Hamilton-Standard before it, it finally earned the government's coveted "E" for manufacturing excellence. Although Sikorsky was ineligible for an "E" until it reached full production, it completed the Army's initial R-4 order, received another contract for one hundred more R-4s, and also delivered the two experimental helicopters requested by the Army.

All in all, United had enjoyed a remarkably successful year. Total business climbed to over $733 million, with net profits adding up to more than $15 million, or 1.6 percent as a percentage of sales. Calculated as a percentage of invested capital, however, the return was 15 percent— lower than most of the aviation industry but still 1½ times the average rate of return— 9.9 percent— of all manufacturing industries in 1943.

By continuing his prudent management and keeping his eye on the postwar future, Rentschler added another $4 million to the reconversion account. This sum was charged to operations, along with another $2.2 million to write off a "large portion" of the tool and supply inventories United "deemed excess" based on its estimate of peacetime manufacturing requirements.[10] Such legitimate writeoffs saved the company millions of tax dollars but could hardly substitute for postwar customers. So while Eugene Wilson covered the home front his nephew, Joseph Barr, was instructed to reopen United's export operations.

Barr had been with United since 1932, first at Chance Vought and then, as of 1937, in exports. When war ended export activities he returned to Vought, presumably for the duration. Early in 1944, Barr was asked by Horace Horner, United's new president, to establish a new sales organization in South America so the company could compete as soon as the war was over. While the European competition was busy fighting the war, Bar could get a head start on accumulating the contacts necessary for sales.

As Barr recalled in his *The Time of My Corporate Life,* he found in South America a set of "ethics and procedures which were entirely different from any others in the world including the Far East." Bribes, for example were dispensed in the form of contributions to charitable institutions, usually with Christian-sounding names invented for that purpose. Barr, a realist, soon learned that unless one paid, a competitor got the business. By establishing and reestablishing United's contacts in country after country— Chile, Peru, Venezuela, Colombia, Mexico— he quickly laid the foundation for postwar business, commercial as well as military. "It had been a fabulous trip," he noted. "I had set up an organization that helped us to achieve a volume of sales in South America exceeding my predictions; by the middle 1950's it had created a market far beyond our fondest hopes."[11]

But Joe Barr's success notwithstanding, exports could not carry United unless his uncle convinced the federal government to adopt a new aviation policy. The situation looked promising. By May of 1944, Eugene Wilson was formally head of the board of governers of the Aeronautical Chamber of Commerce, which had appropriated $250,000 for his public relations campaign. More importantly, the Chamber had recommended the implementation of an American air power policy under the following general principles:

The United States should maintain an air power sufficient (in conjunction with other forces) not only to win this war, but also to keep the peace:

1. By maintaining adequate air forces at such strength and in such state of readiness as to preclude a successful assault upon our country or its possessions.
2. By acquiring and maintaining air bases essential to our security and that of overseas trade.
3. By facilitating the orderly and economic expansion of domestic and international air transport and of private flying.
4. By preserving a strong aircraft manufacturing industry.

By wrapping these recommendations in the flag, Wilson had successfully engineered the acceptance of his own aviation policy by the industry. Now he had only to convince the general public to support Air Power for Peace. He began with an essay in the June

1944 issue of *Aviation,* an industry magazine now called *Aviation Week and Space Technology,* stressing the airplane manufacturers' unique public position; because they were "almost wholly dependent on government policy," they required a government that understood aviation problems and a citizenry aware that "good business judgment demands no dumping." Once the war ended, Washington would own thousands of up-to-date airplanes in excellent condition. If the surplus was dumped on the market, it could destroy the aviation industry as easily as Colonel Deeds' planes did after World War I. To avoid such a catastrophe, Wilson argued, "the most modern surplus military aircraft should be stored in reserve." Until they were needed, the nation should "employ available excess facilities" for military work. Surplus planes capable of quick conversion to commercial use, on the other hand, should be sold in an orderly manner to "create demand for improved equipment" through increased passenger traffic and, especially, the air transport of merchandise.[12]

Wilson rarely missed a trick. Aware of the low circulation of a magazine like *Aviation,* he set up a series of "speaker teams" to evoke national attention to his program from service organizations across the country. Wilson and his assistants packaged their material on sixty-four cards so that any speaker "could shuffle those cards and the paragraphs would still tie together. You could take enough of them for the length of time you wanted to talk and work almost a complete speech out of that on air power."[13]

While his speakers, decks of cards in hand, fanned out across America, Wilson went to Washington to address the Senate's Committee on Military Affairs.

Speaking as vice chairman of United Aircraft and as chairman of the Aeronautical Chamber of Commerce's board of governors, Wilson responded to yet another charge of excess profits. Without mentioning United's profit agreement with the Navy or his own reservations about unconscionable profits, he cited a recent study by Gordon Rentschler's National City Bank indicating that the rate of return figured on sales for the twenty-four major aircraft and parts manufacturers was a tiny 1.8 percent— hardly excess profits. He continued that United Aircraft's profits were actually "a temporary bookkeeping entry." Because the cost of postwar reconversion was unknown, the industry could conceivably wind up with a net loss on its war business. Neglecting to reveal the existence of

United's $28 million contingency fund, he stated that "the immediate requirement was an early delineation of an air power policy. Unless we expect to ride off in all directions at once, we need to know where we all are going."[14]

To help the nation find out, Wilson suggested a new version of the Morrow Board, which in the past had enabled America to lay the solid industrial base required for emergencies. But, just to keep the record straight, he informed the senators that according to the industry's new policy "the key to this cutback is a transition from a predominant air force to a predominant air commerce." To achieve Air Power for Peace, he concluded, the government must develop the air-transport infrastructure, foster technological change, and "train the youth of the country to understand the air as a vast new world for transportation and to fly the airplanes which use that world."[15]

After Wilson left the witness stand, his aviation colleagues echoed his plea for presidential commission.

In filtering through this testimony, Committee Chairman Senator James Murray of Montana apparently decided that they had presented a viable case. Soon afterward, he introduced a bill calling for a new presidential advisory commission along the lines of the Morrow Board.

Success was finally in Wilson's grasp when, despite his years of diligent work, the "U.S. aeronautical community split open five ways!" All hell broke loose because the Army and Navy, once again, were battling over the issue of air power. Just as in 1925, the Army Air Force wanted to eliminate the Navy Air Force. This in turn made it impossible for manufacturers to support one aviation policy, because they would risk losing their only serious market by taking sides. Moreover, the very air transport companies that Wilson was trying to assist were at one another's throats. At Pan American, Juan Trippe insisted on monopolizing foreign markets, while American, United, and Eastern Air Lines were urging the government to allow them to compete as soon as possible. The airlines did agree that implementation of Wilson's plans was bound to upset prospective legislative changes. The appointment of a national advisory committee meant losing control of Congress exactly when each side's sponsors were promoting its positions.

In Hartford, Eugene Wilson watched these battles with a deep sense of dismay. The president could hardly be expected to help him against the wishes of the airlines, when the military publicly fought about reorganization of its forces, and when America was still at war with Germany and Japan. Resigning himself to a long and conceivably futile fight, Wilson continued to accept engagements for himself and his speakers and put the finishing touches on his book *Air Power and Peace*, published in early 1945. Ironically, however, American pilots, employing weapons such as napalm, magnesium, and a bomb nicknamed "Fat Boy," would keep the destructive aspects of air power in the headlines.

With industry feuds stalling their public relations program, Wilson and Rentschler watched as aviation's future fell back into the hands of the military. As the nation moved into 1945, Army air force generals and Navy admirals were intent on shaping the industry's postwar posture in terms of peacetime armadas of close to twenty thousand planes. And what the military wanted had very little to do with the proposals so painstakingly developed by Eugene Wilson, Fred Rentschler, and the Aeronautical Chamber of Commerce.[16]

Air Power for War

As early as July of 1943 the Army Air Force, which considered itself the linchpin of America's postwar defense, settled on a minimum of 105 groups as a "reasonable estimate" of interim forces for its postwar posture. In November of 1944, When General George Marshall informed air-arm planners that no postwar budget could possible support that many planes, they reluctantly agreed to an "irreducible minimum" of 70 groups, an astronomical number for peacetime. As Army Air Force head of planning General Lawrence Kuter put it, "We must have another plan up our sleeve in the very probable event that the element of cost should become a principal consideration."[17]

Throughout 1945, continuous public attention enforced the air force's opinion of its own preeminence. On February 13, for example, the city of Dresden was attacked by 318 British and 311 American bombers; in one night, nearly three times the acreage destroyed in London during the entire war was devestated and anywhere from 50 to 150,000 killed. The next day pilots attacked Chemnitz "to finish off any of the refugees who may have escaped from Dresden."[18]

On March 9, it was Tokyo. According to General Curtis Le May, commander of the Twentieth Air Force, his pilots needed napalm because it "splattered farther" and magnesium because its hotter fires would "get things going where probably the napalm might not." The heat generated by explosions was so intense that liquid glass ran down Tokyo's streets and water in the canals reached the boiling point. Almost 100,000 people died. "We burned up nearly sixteen square miles of Tokyo," the general boasted in *Mission with Le May*. "There were more casualties than in any other military action in the history of the world."

"Congratulations," General Hap Arnold wired. "This mission shows your crews have the guts for anything."

Le May acknowledged that, yes, "it was a nice telegram, but I couldn't sit around preening myself on that. I wanted to get going just as fast as was humanly possible." And he did. By mid-June, 1945— two months before either atomic bomb was dropped— Le May and his men had crippled six of the most important cities in Japan. In Tokyo, 56.3 square miles were leveled; in Nagoya, 12.4; in Kobe, 8.8; in Osaka, 15.6; in Yokohama, 8.9; in Kawaskai, 3.6. All told, Le May's strategic bombing had left 105.6 square miles of Japan a charred abyss of death of desolation.[19]

To the Army Air Force, no more proof was needed that air power could vanquish any enemy, anytime, anywhere. As long as America rested its defense on strategic bombing, there was little to fear from any potential aggressor. When the horror of Hiroshima and Nagasaki was added to the toll at Dresden and Tokyo, it did seem that an independent air force would be the axis of America's national security. Nothing summarized the country's attitude more succinctly than a statement from the scientists who had created the atomic bomb called "Fat Boy": "Never has the offense become so entirely dominant. Never has there been a weapon whose first application will be almost certain not only to penetrate the defense, but also largely to demolish it. . ." It didn't matter that victory had little meaning if other nations could imitate General Le May's heated attack on Japan.

Although air power had won the war, Eugene Wilson and his colleagues nevertheless stubbornly retained their belief that they could win the peace— if, that is, the president and Congress helped the manufacturers broaden their base. As Wilson summed it up in an article in Aviation, "It must always be kept in mind that until the industry can develop a private market, the government is directly or indirectly its chief customer."[21]

The Terror Called Peace

Wilson knew what he was talking about. In 1937 and 1938, the last years before the war took hold, United did 58 percent of its business with Washington. From 1942 through 1945, the numbers skyrocketed to 86, 97, 99, and 97 percent. Like Siamese twins, the federal government and the United Aircraft Corporation were inextricably linked. Now, with peace a reality as of V.J. Day— Victory over Japan on August 14, 1945— neither offered a universally acceptable plan for separation.

On V.J. Day alone, the government had terminated over $750 million worth of United's contracts, whereupon Frederick Rentschler closed all United's factories for the remainder of the month. He only turned the machines back on in September— at "drastically reduced schedules"— when he learned what the government was willing to buy. Assured orders for 1946 totaled only $70 million. Although that was double 1938 sales, it still represented only one-seventh of the company's 1945 government business. United would have faced hard times were it not for the safety nets installed through the efforts of men such as Eugene Wilson and organizations such as the Aeronautical Chamber of Commerce.[22]

Despite Wilson's failure to establish his Pax Aeronautica as a national aviation policy, he did help create the financial cushions that eased the transition to peace. For example, United was left with nearly $54 million worth of "termination inventory," for which the government agreed to pay $52 million at once; meanwhile, a settlement was being negotiated on the remainder. And of the approximately $115 million worth of factories Washington had provided, the company intended to buy or lease facilities worth $65 million. Washington was willing to remove the other $50 million worth of factories at its own expense. As for taxes, United exercised the option that Wilson had demanded under the 1940 British contract (see Chapter 5). By electing to "terminate the amortization period with respect to emergency plant facilities owned by the Corporation," it wrote off an extra $8.5 million on its 1945 tax bill, entering 1946 without having paid for equipment that could be used profitably for many years into the future.

Out of the $36 million reserved for reconversion, United spent $732,001 and left the rest in the bank. As Rentschler told stockholders, "It was expected that the board of directors would give further consideration to the disposition to be made of this reserve during the current year. . ." Despite the government's funding of reconversion, it was best to wait another year before disposing of money Rentschler was never to label "war profits."[23]

For 1945, United earned a net profit of $12.8 million. Although that was the lowest rate of the war years, it capped a process that the New York brokerage house of White, Weld and Company called "unique in the financial history of this country." The aircraft manufacturing companies in general and United Aircraft in particular had effected extraordinary increases in working capital "with practically no increases in capital liabilities [such as bank borrowings] or sale of additional stock."

United possessed $12.9 million of working capital in 1940 and $112 million in 1945. Calculated on net worth, that came to $36.3 million and $118 million respectively. As Eugene Wilson described the company's financial position, "The net result of all this was that in spite of every effort we made to keep from being profiteers, the net increase in working capital in United Aircraft at the end of this whole operation was $93 million*— which in our view was unconscionable, but which was forced on us by the artificialities and the policies whose whole purpose was to convince the public that they were keeping those rascals in hand, and all they did was succeed in making rascals out of us against our better judgement."[24]

As in 1926 or 1941, of course, United could have returned the money instead of keeping it. But in his October 9, 1945, testimony before a special committee investigating the National Defense Program, Horace Horner explained that, if United was to keep producing the best equipment for America's air forces and world's airlines, its future research and development efforts would easily cost $40 to $50 million per year, a figure based on postwar sales "roughly three times our pre-war volume." Horner suggested that, unless the government gave United the money, "our only other alternative will be to drastically reduce our research and development program, which appears to be a shortsighted overall government policy just at

---

* Wilson was relying on memory when he made this remark in 1962. The actual working capital increase was $99 million.

this time." The reason it would be shortsighted, he continued, was that "unless appropriations were available to the armed services, they would be unable to support financially their forward developments even though they do feel they are necessary to our national defense.[25]

By waving the flag and hinting at an enemy in the bushes, Horner used a tactic common in defense hearings— senators found it hard to refuse when experts stated that a lack of funds led to a lack of defense. Yet, Horner was making a valid point about the nature of postwar aviation: even 10 percent of a company's total sales spent on research and development would be considered extraordinary today; had United followed such a course in 1946, spending $12 million— 10 percent of its anticipated sales of $120 million— it still would be at least $28 million short of its estimated research and developmend budget. Thus, Horner was correct in arguing that if government did not furnish the funds, no one would.

The real problem, of course, rested in the ongoing issue of subsidies. At a time when Washington and companies like United could have honestly discussed their mutual rights and obligations, they merely shadow-boxed around the crucial questions and entered the future without settling the issues that had divided them in the past. During the Delaney and Black hearings in 1934 (see Chapter 4), the government alternated between gladly providing public monies to United Aircraft and accusing United of profiteering and monopoly. Yet Washington openly fostered United's share of the early 1930's market and, at least in the Navy department, was well aware of the company's profits. With some justification, Rentschler felt he had been victimized in 1934, but now, in 1945, he still was not pressing the government for an explicit formulation of the terms of their relationship.

But research and development funds were only one aspect of Horner's request for government assistance. He also indicated that United Aircraft (and the entire aviation industry) "urgently required a definite and continuing production program for Army and Navy against which we can make our future plans." United needed "a satisfactory way by which we can acquire the facilities in which to produce that program." If Washington failed to help United pay for the government's war-built factories, they would not be used for postwar production.[26]

As for the $36 million set aside for reconversion and the $99 million increase in working capital, Rentschler tried to avoid spending it; and the government never forced him to do so. Instead of analyzing the long-range impact of heavily subsidizing research, Washington agreed to help carry the aircraft industry at a time when the increasing sophistication of weaponry guaranteed skyrocketing costs for research, development, and production. As a result, United tied its business future to the government more tightly than ever before and, in essence, became a peacetime ward of the state. That was never United's intention (remember the Pax Aeronautica) but, if the choice was to spend its own money or the government's, the company chose the latter, especially since neither the president, nor Congress, nor the general public precisely defined United's obligation. If the company produced an engine for the military and refined it for commercial markets, was that profiteering? Or, if it pushed new weapons to keep its factories in operation, did that constitute war-mongering or patriotism? And, by subsidizing United's factories, was the government obligated to keep them running even if America already owned sufficient weaponry?

In 1945, such questions were rarely asked and never answered.

1946: Losses Mean Profits

For United and the nation, 1946 was a year of transition: transforming the war economy became the universal order of business. The absence of a program such as the Pax Aeronautica led many aviation companies to diversify. Because government assistance alone could not adequately sustain the large manufacturers, Ryan Aeronautical attempted to make caskets from stainless steel; Grumman turned to dinghies; and Douglas lost money on its aluminum rowboat venture. Curtiss-Wright purchased Marquette Metal Products, a manufacturer of electric-razor parts, and a firm producing 16-mm film projectors. Glenn Martin concentrated on "Marvinol," a polyvinyl chloride coating for shower curtains and other domestic products, while Northrup acquired a motor-scooter operation. North American's "Dutch" Kindelberger combed the Sears Roebuck, Montgomery Ward, and Sweet's Building catalogues in search of products his company could make but "decided to stick exclusively to aircraft."[27]

At United, no one bothered to consult catalogues. Rentschler had always rejected diversification as a means of escaping Washington. His father's attempt years before to produce automobiles at the Rentschlers' Ohio machinery factory proved such a disaster that United's chairman was left with the unshakeable belief that new ventures "required a complete and ceaseless absorption." "Let's stick with our own things," he declared time after time. "We know them best, and we have only scratched the surface."[28]

Fred Rentschler was correct, both in forecasting aviation's future and in unearthing those areas in which United was likely to turn a profit. On jets, for example, he ultimately opted for boldness. With the huge 3,800 horsepower Wasp Major, developed to meet the military's needs, in Pratt & Whitney's stable, and a continuing market for piston engines a short-range certainty, Rentschler knew United could safely postpone production of a jet engine of its own. Because the government had previously restricted Pratt & Whitney's participation in jet research by withholding development funds, General Electric had had a large head start in America. The English, who intended to penetrate world markets as a technological leader, had abandoned work on piston-type engines in favor of jets; by 1948, they boasted, British jet planes would be crossing the Atlantic, rendering Pratt & Whitney engines obsolete.

Rentschler disagreed. Even if British claims were accurate, American and foreign airlines were forced to work off the considerable investment in piston engines such as the Wasp Major that they had ordered in 1945 and early 1946. During what Rentschler termed is "breathing spell," United could build an engine with slightly more thrust than existing power plants— or, alternately, much more. Instead of a straight jet, the company could develop a complicated high-compressor jet engine that would lower fuel consumption. Either choice presented difficulties, but opting for a bigger engine than any yet built involved using $15 million of its own funds and, particularly to the cautious Wilson, represented a huge gamble with no assurance of success. The competition, after all, was already years ahead in jet design and experience.

After a long and conflict-filled period of arguments with his colleagues, Rentschler decided to go for broke— build a jet engine as revolutionary as the Wasp was in 1925 or build nothing at all. United had the "time-honored right of eventual leadership," and

Fred Rentschler, unwilling to accept second place in the engine stakes, bet that Leonard Hobbs, United's engineering chief, would come through just as George Mead had done twenty-five years earlier. And, as always, Rentschler cut his risks by using other people's money whenever possible.[29] In explaining this jet course to United's stockholders, Rentschler stressed that much of the research and development work on the new jet engine would be conducted under development contracts with the United States government.

Late in 1946, when the Navy offered Pratt & Whitney the opportunity to produce the Rolls Royce Nene jet engine for a Grumman fighter plane, Rentschler readily accepted. It would be years before Hobb's engine was ready; in the meantime, Pratt & Whitney could gain valuable design and production experience from reworking the British Nene— and enhance its chances to leap-frog the competition.

United embarked on its jet experiments without the services of Eugene Wilson. Since his meeting with Navy Secretary Forrestal in the summer of 1943, United's vice chairman had spent most of his time promoting the Pax Aeronautica. Nevertheless, he took his nominal control of research so seriously that, when the jet decision went against him, he resigned. Although Wilson was still thoroughly committed to the concept of air power for peace, his chances of convincing the president and Congress to accept his air transport plan appeared dimmer than ever. Battles between the Army air force and Navy actually had increased in intensity, and the airlines, which never had reconciled their differences, were so optimistic about the prospects for passenger travel that they felt no urgent need for a policy emphasizing the transport of cargo. The sixteen major American airlines together operated about four hundred planes at the beginning of 1946, yet C.R. Smith, president of American Airlines, had told his fellow executives, in reference to his own company, "Anybody who can't see the day when we will fly a thousand planes damn well better get out right now."[30]

Despite *Fortune* magazine's accusation of "fatuous optimism," in 1946 all the air carriers signed contracts for over $380 million worth of passenger-carrying planes, engines and propellers— contracts that within a year would be called "Walkie-Talkies" because you can talk yourself into one but you can always walk out on it. For the aircraft manufacturers, however, that $380 million provided the "breathing spell" Rentschler had had in mind before jets took over— money that helped United achieve, in 1946, a feat that it was not to duplicate until 1968.

By the transition year of 1946, United Aircraft did a mere 60 percent of its business with the federal government. While Washington, slowly debating the future of the air force and the air industry, provided only stopgap funding, United took on all the airline business it could get. At year's end, the company had "sort of" lost money in 1946, but far less than it would have without the new commercial contracts. And the $36 million set aside for postwar reconversion remained almost intact— only 1.1 million was spent. With "reconversion and rearrangement substantially completed," Rentschler and Horner decided to rearrange the fund; $26.7 million was deposited in United's earned surplus account, and $7.5 million was placed in a "reserve for War and Transition Contingencies." Ever the clever businessman, Rentschler pocketed $26.7 million in wartime profits without anyone noticing yet left enough money to pay for expenses "which may yet result from the expanded level of operations and the complexities of the war and transition periods."

As for 1946 profits, Rentschler, quite legitimately, used the carryback provisions of the tax laws. On sales of $120 million, United had lost $4.5 million but was entitled to a government refund check for $10.5 million. That resulted in over $6 million in net profits. Rentschler promptly informed his stockholders that United "had emerged from the most critical period in our history" and declared a dividend of $1.79 per share of common stock. The loss-that-was-not-a-loss had been totally expected as a result of the rearrangement of the company's factories and the development of new products But, the annual report boasted, "Beginning in October and throughout the fourth quarter, in spite of our abnormal burdens, operations did turn the corner."

In 1947, on the other hand, United anticipated profits with no need to exercise carryback options. Some $285 million worth of orders were in hand, and the company was steadily pulling ahead of the competition. As Rentschler put it in *The 1946 Annual Report,* "United Aircraft is essentially an engineering operation. It has been in a definite position of leadership in its field to date, and no effort will be spared to fully maintain this position in the fast-moving period which lies ahead."[31]

Partners: United and the Air Force

Directly after the war ended, the soon-to-be-independent Army Air Force embarked upon an elaborate research and development program under the direction of General Curtis Le May. One of the first moves was a trip to Germany.

According to Le May, the Germans had built "a military machine the most impressive the world had ever seen." Hitler's mistake had been to halt research, which was far ahead of America's, after he had invaded Poland, France, and the Lowlands; otherwise, his scientist's weapons could have defeated the Allied armies. "The moment enemy resistance collapsed in Europe, we overran some of the research centers and started gathering up papers and files— and the scientists— and trying to get them back to the States," Le May wrote in his autobiography.

Despite the nation's reservations about admitting the Nazi scientists, except as prisoners of war, General Le May and his Army Air Force "rescued those able and intelligent Jerries from behind the barbed wire and got them going in our various military projects and fed them into American industry."[32] Although none of Le May's Nazi recruits were hired by United Aircraft, the general's quick thrust into Germany illustrates his conviction that singleminded pursuit of technological "progress" was required to win a modern war. Frederick Rentschler concurred. For twenty years he had preached that aviation equipment, unlike other products, did not wear out; manufacturers could not depend on replacement to sustain their businesses. Unlike the automobile industry, moreover, styling changes offered no hope of new orders. Thus, Rentschler continued to insist, better performance was the key to better business.

What was different in 1947— and of tremendous significance to United aircraft— was the attitude of the Army Air Force, Congress, the American people, and, possibly, the Russians. From the Marshall Plan to the containment of Communism, from concern about spies at home to support for the French in Indochina, the United States had declared the Cold War and supported the aspirations and recommendations of its military services— especially the Air Force.

Even before President Truman formally granted the Air Force its independence on July 26, 1947, Congress had sanctioned research on rockets, bombers, nuclear airplanes, and jet engines. The result for United was a substantial increase in Air Force orders.

Throughout World War II, Pratt & Whitney had been intimately linked with the Navy. Now, however, the Navy had strong reservations about jet engines at the very time the Air Force was determined to own the latest aeronautical equipment. The Navy supported United's jet research reluctantly and only partially; planes that flew with too much power and speed were unsuited for the small runways on carriers. Clearly, the Air Force was the business wave of the future.

United had no other customer able to keep its factories humming. As today, the airlines in 1947 were refusing to pick up options for more equipment. No matter how hard Eugene Wilson tried, it was increasingly apparent that no one wanted a Pax Aeronautica. Wilson had succeeded in convincing many military officers, executives, and congressmen to push for a new Morrow Board. Instead of long-range procurement policies based on commercial uses of the airplane, however, supporters of air power were more concerned with the status of aviation in the defense of America and the free world. Ironically, Wilson had gotten Congress and the president interested in aviation, yet the result of Wilson's efforts would be greater dependence than ever on the military customer United sought to escape.

Testifying on May 17, 1947, before a Senate committee eager to establish a National Air Policy Board, Horace Horner described United's problems. Exports totaled no more than 10 percent of postwar business, with no foreign orders whatsoever at the Vought division. On commercial orders United had fared better —its engines powered many of the new transports— but commercial production soon would end. "Our cutback in size will be tremendous," Horner stated, "and with that will necessarily go a tremendous reduction in the research and development which we now have underway."

"Does the situation look serious to you?" Senator Warren Magnuson asked.

"Terribly serious," Horner responded. "Not only for my company but for the industry and for our country. I want you to understand that we will take our chances under any program to survive as an individual company, but it is the industry as a whole that I am concerned about."[33]

Congress wanted action, and so did President Truman. On July

18, 1947, he established the President's Air Policy Commission, a new version of the Morrow Board charged with making "an objective inquiry into national aviation policies and problems" and "formulating an integrated aviation policy" to counter the danger that our national security may be jeopardized and our economic welfare diminished through a lowered aircraft production and a failure of the aircraft industry to keep abreast of modern methods. . ."

According to the interpretation reached by Truman's commission members, the president wanted both to "protect the Nation's security to the greatest extent practicable" and to "foster its economic and social interests."[34] The two goals were linked, but national security came first. In 1947, the needs of the air industry were clearly subservient to the needs of the Air Force and the Air Navy.

Rentschler's Advice

During a September luncheon with Thomas Finletter, chairman of the President's Air Policy Commission, Frederick Rentschler was asked to provide an analysis of the aviation industry's predicament based on his thirty years' experience in the field. Although Rentschler thought his statement, which was mailed to Finletter on September 25, 1947, seemed to be "too much of a personal narrative," he nevertheless felt "obligated to register certain strong convictions which are the outgrowth of an experience in aviation which I believe should qualify me to express my judgment. While I am approaching the end of my active business career, I am certain that these same objectives are burned deeply into our organization and my primary purpose is to point out certain hardly learned lessons which are fundamental and consistently true."[35]

Above all, Rentschler remained hopeful. "There was still time to do those things which will place our industry on a sound basis," he wrote. Though more complex, the industry's status in 1947 was "absolutely unchanged from what it was in 1920." Then, as now, financial support was essential for long-range stability, and only the federal government could offer it. The industry had floundered before the Morrow Board's five-year procurement programs permitted the research that made American equipment the best in the world.

Insisting that he was not bitter, Rentschler reminded the commission that, "through the twenties and thirties, men in my position as heads of aviation companies were literally looked upon as warmongers and munitions makers by a great number of intelligent people." In 1940, however, "overnight we were rather important."[36]

Unless the commission bettered the performance of the Morrow Board in 1925— the cost of research, development, and production, after all, had risen drastically— the industry would not produce the best possible equipment. And, it went without saying, "a second-best air force was just no good." The best air force, he continued, must be based on the oft-forgotten truism first learned in 1918: "The engine is the heart of the airplane." The European manufacturers now had a head start on the development of jet engines and would remain ahead, unless and until Washington furnished the most liberal support to private companies such as United Aircraft. While "certain research and exploration of a common nature could be done by the government," past experience indicated that only private enterprises successfully manufactured the engines and planes needed for the world's most powerful Air Force. Rentschler never addressed the issue of the success of British, French, and Russian nationalized aviation programs.

In a December 9 letter to Finletter, Rentschler made one last try at resurrecting Air Power For Peace. "Having available superior types of transports for an emergency had become a vital military requirement," he wrote. "There should be no reason whatever for considering this kind of assistance by government as coming within the scope of subsidy." Funding the development of air transport, in other words, indirectly aided the military. If it directly profited the manufacturers and the airlines, that was simply a by-product of any "generally sound" aviation policy.[37]

Whether Finletter ever gave Rentschler's suggestions serious consideration remains an open question. By January 1, 1948, the Air Policy Board had submitted to the president a report entitled *Survival in the Air Age* that displayed not a trace of Eugene Wilson's Air Power for Peace programs. The bellicose report, in fact, specified strategic bombing as the nation's best course. As Wilson recollected in *Kitty Hawk to Sputnik to Polaris.* "The only comfort to be taken from this effort lay in the fact that it did establish a military procurement program which not only assured the aircraft industry of survival, but induced a boom beside which the war production effort paled into relative insignificance."[38]

7

SAVED BY THE RUSSIANS

"In our opinion this Military Establishment must be
built around the air arm. Of course an adequate
Navy and Ground force must be maintained. But it
is the Air Force and naval aviation on which we must
rely. Our military security must be based on air power."

Survival in the Air Age,
President's Air Policy Commission

A National Aviation Policy

The advent of the atomic bomb presented military strategists with an insoluble dilemma: if each opponent in a war employed atomic-armed air power to devastate the other, both would be defeated. Victory was meaningless if the winner's cities resembled Dresden or Nagasaki.

One potential solution was to stop the enemy's planes and long-range rockets while destroying its battlefronts, but even the most fervent advocates of air power agreed that enough planes would get through to cause hideous damage.

Finally the strategists took a thoroughly original tack: use the military establishment not to win wars, but to avert them. Amass such an awesome arsenal that no sane enemy ever would attack, because his own country's devastation was a certainty. Of course, the enemy could be insane; or could miscalculate; or could decide that national honor required national suicide. No strategy ever guaranteed peace, but on January 1 and March 1, 1948, two separate groups— the President's Air Policy Commission and Congress's Aviation Policy Board— independently reached the same conclusion. The Air Force, powered by the products of the aviation industry, would provide the axis of America's future military policy. One flew the planes the other provided them and together they gave America the ability to survive in the Air Age.

The role of air power in World War II, after all, foretold what would occur in World War III. The next war would surely include what Congress described as a "sudden and indiscriminate attack on our cities, our factories, our transportation lines, our communications centers and water supply, and more important than all else, upon our lives."[1]

To protect America from the horrible effects of obliteration bombing with the atomic weapons enemies were right now developing, the best air defense was a mammoth air offense. This course offered some hope of stopping enemy planes; it assured a "crushing counter-offensive blow on the aggressor," and it also might avert the war no nation could win. "By serving notice that war with the United States would be a most unprofitable business, we may persuade the nations to work for peace instead of war,"[2] the Air Policy Commission's report read.

This aggressive stance, the cornerstone of popular American thinking, mocked Roosevelt's condemnation of United Aircraft's 1938 sales to Japan. In less than ten years, the odious had become commonplace. Granted, the United States never would attack first, but, if provoked, we too would bomb our opponent's cities and factories. Congress and the presidential commission, chaired by Thomas Finletter, rooted their recommendations in worst-case reasoning, and their pessimistic assumptions about enemy intentions made a vigorous and up-to-date air industry the key to national survival.

The president's commission envisioned an air defense created in two stages. Phase I, to be completed by January 1, 1953, would increase the size of the Air Force from its "hopelessly wanting" fifty-five groups to an absolute minimum of seventy groups (this was the same arbitrary figure devised by the Air Force in 1944, based on a 1943 War Department memo regarding a reasonable size for Interim Forces). Seventy groups meant an immediate increase of $350 million for 1948 Air Force procurement and $660 million for 1949. The purchasing program would be reviewed in 1950, but the long-term trend was to triple all Air Force appropriations, going from $2.8 billion in 1948 to approximately $8.1 billion in 1952.

Planning for Phase II depended on the nature of the assault a potential enemy such as Russia was likely to make. Although attacks could conceivably be localized, Finletter's presidential commission stressed that "we must assume, in making our plans, that if the enemy can do it, he will make a direct air assault on the United States mainland regardless of how or where the shooting first starts." Thus, Phase II specified an Air Force of even greater size and power than was created in Phase I.

In making their costly recommendations, both the presidential commission and Congress recognized that a "heavy strain" on the American economy was inevitable. *Fortune* magazine called the costs "staggering" and the program "the wildest blue yonder yet." But national security required the huge expenditures; the best hope for reducing expenses was to demand from the Joint Chiefs of Staff "the most rigorous efficiency in operations and in the consolidation of strategic functions."[3] To guard against abuses, it was essential to oversee the private companies slated to produce the weaponry. On this score, both panels echoed Fred Rentschler's oft-stated conviction: without question private industry would furnish the goods, and without government relief it wouldn't be able to.

The president's commission called attention to the optimistic predictions of 1945, which maintained that the supposedly growing demand for commercial and private planes would sustain the industry without a large injection of public funds. Unfortunately, the forecasters proved wrong. In 1948 and beyond, the president's Air Policy Commission responded, it was "certain that current commercial demands would not carry us through the present crisis. Whether we liked it or not, the health of the aircraft industry, for the next few years at least, was dependent largely upon financial support from Government in the form of orders for military aircraft."

Both aviation panels accepted the fact that Washington must shoulder the burden, and both stated openly that the government "had to create an atmosphere as conducive as possible to profitable operations in the aircraft manufacturing business." The requisite support involved five-year procurement plans to assure stability; "additional latitude" to procurement officers in negotiating contracts; federal encouragement of the "sale and use" of military aircraft by other nations and credit for those unable to pay at once; and, finally, keeping "a few marginal manufacturers in business who might be forced out if the normal laws of supply and demand were allowed to operate."[4]

The charter for what was later termed "the military-industrial complex" was not secretly formulated in a backroom by industrialists smoking Havana cigars. Like the Morrow Board in 1925, both the president's and congress's aviation panels indicated quite clearly and publicly the nature and extent of the federal support they anticipated giving to private manufacturers. But like the Morrow Board, both panels failed to confront a contradiction inherent in any capitalist society: Washington could not provide defense only to those who could afford it. Everyone got defended, and everyone paid the bill. Nothing had changed since 1925 except that, considering aviation's starring role in America's scenario for deterring the Communists, the price for ignoring this contradiction was far steeper in 1948.

Through the late twenties and thirties, the Air Force was an untested weapon that stood third in the funding line behind the Army and Navy during the worst economic crisis in American history. In Harry Truman's America, however, the Air Force reigned supreme. As Fred Rentschler reminded Finletter, after 1940 the nation needed United Aircraft. Instead of a depression dominated by New Dealers, Rentschler and his competitors faced boom times dominated by Cold Warriors. In 1938 United's total sales equalled $35 million; in 1947, the figure had increased sixfold to $207 million, 69 percent of it to the government. If the nation approved the aviation panels' request for still more, companies such as United would become wards of the state. From increased funding for research and development, to the lease of government machinery, to assistance with export orders to reduce domestic research and development costs, "Pentagon Capitalism" would be publicly endorsed.

All of this amounted to a *de facto* nationalization of the aviation industry. But rather than operating realistically from this premise, both Washington and the companies opted to continue what *Fortune* had called an "elaborate ritualistic dance."[5] Though it may have seemed the easier route, this eyes-closed pact between Washington and the manufacturers would guarantee the same kind of castigation for his successors that had driven Fred Rentschler into Florida exile after the Black, Delaney, and Nye hearings of 1934. For "Survival in the Air Age" spurred a headlong rush into a mammoth peacetime aviation buildup that ignored such questions as what constituted excess profit or what subsidy was too great a price to save the failing company. While neither party relished signing on to this agreement in 1948, neither has managed to extricate itself from it—nor, for that matter, to squarely confront the issues that continue to plague the aviation industry.

Vought Moves to Texas

With their highly publicized and well-received reports, the aviation panels had provided blueprints for defending America and nourishing the aircraft industry. National security was assured if the nation would foot the bill for Phase I of the Air Force's program, but it seemed as if the nation might not, at least not until no other choice remained. Congress intended to reduce federal expenditures by $5 billion in 1948. A fact we tend to forget today is that Harry Truman balanced most of his budgets and adamantly refused to spend more than he received in taxes. As long as the threat of war remained a threat, the military had to rest content with less than it wanted.

Appropriations, however, were reasonably generous, particularly if pre- and postwar budgets are compared. In 1938, $1 billion— 12 percent of total federal outlays— went for defense. In 1948, by contrast, the military received $11.7 billion, 36 percent of federal spending. In 1938, the Army's air arm and Navy purchased $69 million worth of new planes; in 1948 the Air Force was granted $550 million for new equipment, and the Navy, $338 million. For research and development, the air arm received about $18 million in 1938; in 1948 the figure was $312 million— 38 percent of all federal research and development funding. In a year when Congress was belt-tightening, in other words, the air services were given thirteen times more procurement money than in 1938. Nevertheless, they complained of deprivation.[6]

At the United Aircraft Corporation, Fred Rentschler and his colleagues had already decided to bet their business futures on the Air Force and Air Navy— in 1948, a hefty 81 percent of the company's sales were to the military services. A prime indication of the military-mindedness at United Aircraft and throughout the United States was Chance Vought's seventeen-hundred mile move from Stratford, Connecticut to Dallas, Texas. "Survival in the Air Age" had expressed the military's concern that the aviation industry's manufacturing capacity was largely concentrated in three locations: Los Angeles, Seattle, and Long Island/Connecticut. If the Russians attacked these inviting masses of closely packed plants, America— without the industrial resources required to mass production weaponry— might be forced to surrender at once.

The services wanted to disperse factories as widely as possible.

They began their campaign in Connecticut, where a major engine manufacturer (Pratt & Whitney), the world's largest producer of propellers (Hamilton-Standard), the best source for helicopters (Sikorsky), and a prominent producer of Navy fighter planes (Chance Vought) were located within forty miles of one another. As early as December of 1946, the Navy suggested that Vought move to a government-owned Dallas plant formerly occupied by North American Aviation.

Vought and United Aircraft had little choice in the matter. Not only was virtually all Vought's business with the Navy, but its current factory was somewhat antiquated, while the Dallas facility was as modern as federal funding could make it. The wide open spaces of Texas, moreover, permitted jet-sized airports some distance from residential areas.[7]

In the 1948 United Aircraft annual report, Fred Rentschler explained the financing behind Vought's $2.8 million move. The government had reduced United's taxes by $1.2 million; the other $1.6 million was deducted from the $7.5 million left in the World War II reconversion account! By tapping the World War II money set aside in 1940, Rentschler was preparing Vought for World War III. With the $5.9 million remaining in the account, he could pay the rest of Vought's migration bill. Because the entire sum was not required for the move, which was completed in 1949, leftover funds were devoted to what soon would become the largest privately owned jet laboratory in the world— the facility where Rentschler hoped to produce a jet engine as revolutionary and reliable as George Mead's Wasp.

If use of World War II reconversion funds to enter the jet age was not what the government had intended in permitting such reserve accounts, Rentschler's innovative action appears to have gone unnoticed. After spending $7.9 million of United's own money on the facility by the end of 1948, he merely changed the name of the reserve account in 1949 from "Reserve for Transformation to Post-War Conditions" to "Reserve for Development Facility Expenditures."[8]

The Andrew Wilgoos Turbine Laboratory was named after Pratt & Whitney's chief engineer, who had died on March 1, 1949, and who certainly deserved the recognition for his work on George Mead's Wasp in 1925. But Mead himself had died on January 20. Although United named its first entries into the jet field Turbo-

Wasps, the company did not otherwise honor the man who had designed the engine essential to its success simply because Rentschler never had forgiven Mead for resigning. He took his former partner's departure so personally that he thereafter ignored Mead's crucial role in the company's development.

The Pratt & Whitney Story, a company history celebrating Pratt & Whitney's twenty-fifth anniversary in August of 1950, consistently downplayed Mead's role. In one photograph, Wilgoos, Rentschler, Colonel Deeds, and Donald Brown are shown "studying design details on the original Wasp"; presumably Mead was occupied elsewhere.

Andrew Wilgoo's loyalty, in contrast, was rewarded amply, if posthumously. A full year before its completion, the new jet turbine laboratory named after him was used to test the engine— the J57— that once again would propel Pratt & Whitney to the forefront of its field.

In 1949, Pratt & Whitney, which contributed roughly 70 percent of United's total business, stood third place in engine sales behind General Electric and General Motors.[9] The company's market had been eroded during the war, but now bombers were strategic to America's military power, and a new Wasp could make all the difference. The J57— slated to deliver an unprecedented ten thousand pounds of thrust— promised to do just that. Although the original new engine was still undergoing tests as of July 1949, Leonard Hobbs, Pratt & Whitney's engineering chief, was confident that the company was developing "the new margin" in jet engine power.

While Rentschler awaited the production of the J-57, United's reliance on military business continued to increase; in 1949 and 1950, it did 87 percent of its work with the services. Pratt & Whitney sold Wasp Majors to the Air Force for its Boeing B50 bombers. Hamilton-Standard, which made propellers for every conceivable engine, was already concentrating on aircraft accessories in anticipation of the time when jets rendered propellers obsolete. The F-86D fighter produced by North American in 1950 employed a Hamilton-Standard air conditioning system. At Chance Vought, now solidly based in Texas, a new Cutlass fighter plane was in production by late 1949, and improved versions of the Corsair were on order for the Navy. Because of Vought, however, Pratt & Whitney lost some potential engine customers (Grumman and North American) reluctant to indirectly assist a competitor. Meanwhile,

Sikorsky's anticipated surge of postwar commercial helicopter business never materialized. And, to add to the company's woes, competitors at Bell, Vertol, (a Boeing subsidiary) and Heller were profiting from its experience to cut into its market. Although Sikorsky did sell its wares as far afield as South Africa and Argentina, it never fulfilled its promise.

The only other subsidiary was Joe Barr's export operation, which was formally reincorporated in Delaware in 1947. According to Barr, "Exports were a buffer between foreign customers and the manufacturers that would complicate any endeavors of foreign governments to tax our U.S. operations and also would prevent legal service on the American company in the event of suits for damages resulting from accidents."[10]

From his Brussels base, the well-traveled Barr went to Johannesburg to initiate sales to South African Airways and to Germany to provide the Air Force with engines for the Berlin Airlift in 1948. In the Belgian Congo, he helped Sabena install spray equipment on a Sikorsky S-51 to kill deadly malaria mosquitoes. Both Barr and Sikorsky took great pride in putting United's military equipment to peaceful use. Unfortunately, however, the military remained the company's best customer at home and abroad.

To simultaneously stimulate United's domestic and foreign sales, Barr devised "Joe Barr's Gold Party, known in all parts of the free world as the greatest thing since sliced bread and Alka Seltzer."

The annual tournament, initiated in Farmington, Connecticut in 1947, was scheduled to coincide with the June graduation and reunions at West Point. The first guests included the chief of the Air Force, two other generals, and two foreign attaches and their assistants, all of whom praised the experience upon their return to Washington. As an added attraction the following year, the company plane picked up Barr's guests in Washington on Monday morning and flew them back Tuesday evening. At later parties, potential clients who disliked golf were flown— by helicopter— to a trout pond fifty miles away. As Barr explained, because "we were actively selling helicopters, the party was an excellent vehicle to demonstrate its versatility."[11]

If Barr liked to golf and fish, he also like to sell. His high-profit export orders— about 10 percent of United's overall sales at the time— helped United through a period of slow growth in the military budget and, therefore, a slow increase in sales and profits.

United did slightly better than most airframe manufacturers, but profits on sales fell below the 6 percent average of all manufacturers and below the return on net worth of industries such as automobiles (15.7 percent), drugs (19.6 percent) or chemicals ($15.6 percent.)[12]

	1948	1949	1950
Sales	$208 million	$227 million	$269 million
Net Profit	$ 9.4 million	$ 10 million	$ 13 million
Profit as % of Sales	3.3%	2.7%	2.6%
Profit as % of Net Worth	8.1%	8.4%	10.4%
% of Business to Government	84%	86%	87%

As Fred Rentschler and Eugene Wilson always had feared, United's dependence on, and regulation by, the federal government often inhibited profits. At events such as Joe Barr's gold parties, United's men tried to influence policy but consistently got less than they wanted. By 1950, however, the corporation's commitment to the military was so overwhelming— nearly 90 percent of its business— that United Aircraft had no choice but to accept Truman's tight-fisted policies. Despite his commitment to air power, the president never initiated the spending spree desired by the Finletter and Congressional aviation panels until June of 1950.

Then, a politician famous for decisiveness made one of the most momentous decisions in recent American history by openly committing America to war in Korea and mandating such an increase in military spending that the Air Force finally received all the funds it demanded for survival in the air age. In 1950, the military budget was $13 billion; in 1951, $22 billion; in 1952, $44 billion. At a time when the inflation rate was 2 percent, America boosted its military spending by more than 300 percent in two years. Between 1951 and 1953 the Army's prime contract funds were cut by 50 percent, while the Air Force's were nearly doubled, from $8.9 billion in

1951 to $14.5 billion in 1953; Navy spending remained even. The boom was finally on.

By 1954, a delighted Fred Rentschler wrote that "despite the tensions that come and go with the cold war, the aircraft industry has found increasing stability, efficiency, and economy of operation under the relatively long-term blueprint of current defense requirements."[13]

The June Boom

On one level, Truman had already committed America to increased funding for air power months before the decision to police Korea. When he learned in August of 1949 that Russia had produced an atomic weapon, he consulted his advisors about moving ahead on the hydrogen bomb. Despite the unanimous negative response of the Atomic Energy Commission's General Advisory Committee, and despite Enrico Fermi's conviction that it was "wrong on fundamental ethical principles to initiate the development of such a weapon," the president expedited production of a weapon that theoretically would be delivered by Boeing bombers powered by Pratt & Whitney engines.[14]

Truman formally established the Federal Civil Defense Administration, a separate civil defense agency, under Frank Caldwell, a former governor of Florida, in December of 1950; previously, civil defense had been the province of the National Security Resources Board. A civil defense advertising poster of the period graphically illustrated both the government's mood and its commitment to air power. Boldly printed beneath the depiction of a gigantic steel fist speeding down from the sky to crush the unsuspecting citizens on the crowded streets of any American city was a simple warning- Enemy target number one: Civilians.

The president's ambitious military program was initially confronted with the same stumbling block that had hindered Roosevelt in 1940. The cautious aviation industry hesitated to act for fear of the overcapacity problems inevitably generated by wartime production. Because manufacturers insisted on assistance, Truman employed financial arrangements that his former Senate committee investigating the National Defense Program had recently termed "legal profiteering."[15]

Echoing Eugene Wilson's 1940 demands, the industry intended to write off all expenditures for machinery within five years. During the Korean emergency, the creation of capacity was stimulated by a device called the Certificate of Necessity. If a company could demonstrate that 75 percent of a new plant and its equipment would be devoted to military production, it was authorized to recover the total amount covered by its certificates by adding a 20 percent surcharge to the price of its products during each of the five years of the accelerated write-off. If a $10 million plant produced a thousand engines per year, in other words, the outlay was paid back through a two-thousand dollar surcharge on each engine for five years running.[16]

Military planners had immediately realized the advantages of such a scheme in 1940. No new or complex bureaucratic procedures were necessary; no special financing was involved; no factories would rest in the government's hands after the war. The certificates were simplicity itself, except that, as Air Force Planners maintained, they also were "an outright gift of a new plant." Thus, the idea was dismissed in 1940 but resurrected during World War II, and to such commercial advantage that the Senate committee investigating the national defense program stated that "many administrators of the Renegotiation Act think that the largest unjustifiable war profits were made as a result of the certificate of necessity program." Manufacturers emerged from the war with so many new, valuable, fully paid-for factories that the committee saw a need to "formulate a procedure under which war facilities could be financed by private capital to the greatest extent possible and at the same time unreasonable profits prevented."[17]

In theory, few Americans disagreed with the committee's desire to prevent excess profits but, during the Korean emergency, theory gave way to necessity. The nation needed weapons as soon as possible, and, as in 1940, the quickest method was to give manufacturers new plants. A supportive *Aviation Week* argued on June 25, 1951, that the certificates constituted neither a subsidy nor a gift; rather, they were "a tax incentive to take a risk which was beyond the normal." Even if the surcharge covered the entire cost of new facilities, after all, industry was guaranteed no orders in the postemergency period.[18]

Aviation manufacturers nevertheless decided to take the risk when plans were announced for government financing of over $3 billion worth of emergency expansion. United Aircraft not only returned to the Southington, Connecticut, facility built during World War II and the abandoned Vought factory in Stratford, but it agreed to new construction in East Hartford "involving 1.9 million square feet of floor space, including test buildings and other structures." Although this program would ultimately cost $40 million, stockholders were reassured that "certificates of necessity covering approximately 75 percent of the cost of these facilities had been obtained as provided for under the Internal Revenue Code."[19]

To fill the new and old factories with machinery, United also entered into other government-financed facilities contracts. Use of government equipment contradicted the corporate policy of owning all facilities required for normal operation but, in an emergency, "the corporation looked to the government to furnish any additional facilities required for its expanded production." United graciously deigned to accept "approximately $150 million" worth of public property. Moreover, given the government's "likely benefits" in the form of decreased engine costs, it negotiated a contract (No. A-1081) that stipulated "no cash payment would be required to cover the use of government-owned tools." In the national interest, United financed new factories with certificates of necessity and used public property to do the public's business. Once again, this private company made private profits from dramatic increases in public sales; from 1950 through 1952, its sales jumped by $388 million, with 85 percent of its business with the federal government.[20] Now, however, Fred Rentschler made the cover of *Time* magazine.

Suddenly United's chairman no longer was a profiteer. In its May 28, 1951 cover story, *Time* called him "Mr. Horsepower"— a man who had "probably done as much for U.S. aviation as anyone since the Wright Brothers." along with a sprinkling of personal tidbits— after 23 years Horace Horner still referred to him as Mr. Rentschler, for example, and top aides were informed of their raises by memo rather than in person— the article maintained that with his Wasp engine, Rentschler had transformed military and transport aviation; during World War II, moreover, his companies furnished "half the U.S. piston horsepower flown in the war." Thus, with the nation competing in "the global race to dominate the skies" America should heed Rentschler's warning that "The one thing that would destroy our country's leadership in the air would be for government to take a dominant part." Industry must be free "to do things in its own way," he insisted. As long as Washington continued to give the industry free rein, the United States would remain ahead of the Russians— and ahead of the world."[21]

America had Fred Rentschler's word. And the respect *Time* accorded that word points to a supreme irony in Rentschler's (and United Aircraft's) relationship with the federal government. In 1934, when United was far less dependent on Washington, Rentschler was labeled a profiteer, war-monger and merchant of death. In 1951, when the government clearly dominated the company's affairs on everything from sales to profits to facilities, Rentschler became a national hero on the order of the Wright brothers.

Fred Rentschler received the public's esteem for taking more from Washington; and United Aircraft received a high ranking on *Fortune's* list of the largest industrial corportions in the United States. By the early fifties hot and cold war had transformed United Aircraft into the forty-first largest industrial corporation in America.[22]

	1951	1952	1953
Sales	$417 million	$668 million	$817 million
Net Profit	$14.2 million	$17.8 million	$21.2 million
% Profit Sales	3.3%	2.7%	2.6%
% Profit Net Worth	10.73%	12.51%	13.9%
% Sales U.S. Government	84%	86%	87%

Using 1950 as a benchmark, United's sales had climbed 300 percent in three years. In 1953, defense expenditures were nearly double those of all other federal agencies combined; double those of all state and local governments; and the near equal in terms of public employment of all federal, state, and local governments combined. The military purchased 73 percent of the more than fifteen thousand planes manufactured in 1953, and paid $7 billion for 90 percent of the monetary value of the year's domestic airframe, engine, and propeller production.[23]

For United Aircraft, the rapid increase in sales and profits led to "comparatively good years," yet nothing like the figures for 1939 or 1940. Washington's underwriting of 75 percent of the company's expansion did contribute to a return on net worth that compared favorably with that of any established industry in America, but in the early fifties many of the airframe manufacturers such as Boeing and Northrop consistently achieved more than 35 percent profit on net worth— double United's return— in part, by extensive use of government-owned plants and equipment. Fred Rentschler was adamant about checking Washington's power over his company; from his experiences at Wright in 1924, he had learned the dangers of letting others shape his business destiny.[24] However, his insistence on maintaining complete ownership reduced United's profits considerably during the Korean years, especially compared with other segments of the aviation industry.

Despite Rentschler's attempt to keep Washington at bay, United's payroll had nearly tripled since 1949; of the sixty thousand-odd employees, 87 percent were paid from federal revenues. Rentschler might have worried if the new president of the United States— *the* general of the U.S. Army— threatened the current supremacy of the air power and instead based national security in a massive army, thereby leaving United with the dreaded problem of overcapacity. But Eisenhower did nothing of the sort.

In fact, in the early days of his administration in 1953, Ike honored three civilians who had helped the Air Force "fulfill its role as this nation's first line of defense." Along with Frederick Rentschler, the new Air Force secretary, Harold E. Talbott, praised Donald Douglas and Dutch Kindelberger, president of North American Aviation, for performing such a vital role in aviation's history that they deserved to be considered master builders of industry. "A man's contributions in life depended on his viewpoint and his idealism," said the secretary— the man who, with his father, had helped Colonel Deeds establish the Dayton-Wright Airplane Company and the Wilber Wright Airfield and who, in 1955, was "accused of shady dealings with firms holding Air Force contracts and resigned under a cloud."

"Three stonemasons were asked what they were doing," Talbott continued. "The first replied, 'earning my wages.' The second replied, 'cutting stone.' And the third one replied, 'building a cathedral.' Each of the three men— Don Douglas, Dutch Kindelberger, and Fred Rentschler— has built a cathedral."[25]

The B-52, The J-57, and Massive Retaliation

President Eisenhower inherited a budget that worried him. As he explained in this memoirs, *Mandate for Change,* he agreed that "security based upon heavy armaments was a way of life that had been forced upon us. "But by devoting 68 percent of the budget to defense in 1954, the nation risked its long-term future. If the commercial side of the economy deteriorated, military security would be paid for with economic weakness. Perhaps the Russians would never have to fight; they could simply watch Americans spend themselves into oblivion.

Ike, who was much smarter than history remembers, immediately tried to fashion a budget reflecting that "national security could never be measured in terms of military strength alone." The "new look" in national security that he devised reallocated resources among the armed services by placing an even "greater emphasis than formerly on the deterrent and destructive power of improved nuclear weapons, better means of delivery, and effective air-defense units." The former Army general favored the Air Force because it provided the least expensive military posture and because he saw no way to employ large numbers of ground forces effectively. During the first few months of a nuclear war, he argued, it would be both impossible and insane to deploy a huge army; the awesome power of nuclear weapons turned concentrations of soldiers, like sitting ducks, into a passive target.

The president did admit a need for "reserves of sufficient strength to meet a brush-fire war in one— or at most, two— localities," but a widespread outbreak of fighting equalled a general war, "which was a different problem entirely." In that case, his "intention was firm: to launch the Strategic Air Command immediately upon trustworthy evidence of a general attack against the West." He intended to deter the Russians as inexpensively as possible by threatening to blow them off the face of the earth if they initiated a general war.

Despite the criticism of his massive retaliation strategy, Ike's policies were never as ridiculous as opponents argued in the face of the question that plagued every postwar president: How do you fight a war that nobody can win? Because he accepted annihilation as a definite possibility for America, he concentrated on air power to deter the Russians without ruining the economy. His critics wanted to build up the Air Force and, at the same time, spend money on tactical nuclear weapons and maintain ground forces ready to fight brush fires before they ignited general conflagrations. Instead, the president attempted to stimulate the commercial side of the economy at the same time that he institutionalized enormous expenditures for the aviation segment of the defense economy. During his two administrations, the Army or Navy never awarded more prime contracts than the Air Force. Toward the end of the decade, in 1958 through 1960, the Air Force consistently gave companies such as United Aircraft almost twice the business of either the Army or Navy.[26]

Unintentionally, Eisenhower helped create the military-industrial complex. United Aircraft's sales grew significantly, both because of the president's strategy and because it had a splendid product to sell. Unlike Curtiss-Wright, United had moved into the jet age with by far the best jet engine on the military or commercial markets. The J-57 produced ten thousand pounds of thrust, far more than any of its competitors. Just like George Mead's Wasp, moreover, the power plant produced by Leonard Hobbs and his colleagues proved to be exceedingly reliable. And, as a bonus, it was exceptionally fuel-efficient. In comparison to its jet-engine predecessors, the J-57 offered unusual economy in a period when costs were a serious consideration.

Flown on a Boeing B-50 as early as March of 1951, the engine underwent a series of rigorous tests on April 15, 1952. Boeing's giant bomber, the B52, took off from Seattle powered by no less than eight prototype J-57s. When the engine legitimately earned high marks on every phase of the flight program, United had a winner. On December 17, 1953— the fiftieth anniversary of powered flight— President Eisenhower presented the aviation industry's Collier Trophy for the greatest achievement in American aviation in 1953 to Leonard Hobbs, the first person in twenty-one years to be honored for the development of an aviation engine.[27]

After the J-57 went into production in 1953, orders accumulated so rapidly that United doubled its annual output of jet engines between 1953 and 1956, from 1,557 to 2,905 (the total also includes other jet engines, such as the T-34 and J-48, all of which went to the military). Pratt & Whitney now stood far ahead of its competition. From a 21 percent share of the military market in 1950 and 20 percent in 1953, the company jumped to 54 percent in 1957. General Motors' share had slipped to 9 percent and General Electric's to a nominal 3 percent.[28]

Because the J-57 was essential to the Strategic Air Command— the linchpin of Eisenhower's massive-retaliation strategy— and because Pratt & Whitney was contributing 70 percent of United Aircraft's business, Fred Rentschler's corporation was more dependent than ever on Washington.

	1954	1955	1956
Sales	$654 million	$697 million	$952 million
Net Profits	$ 26 million	$ 31 million	$ 37 million
% Profit Sales	4%	4.5%	4%
% Profit Net Worth	17.4%	18.7%	17%
% to U.S. Government	88%	89%	86%

This familiar pattern repeated itself at each of Pratt & Whitney's sister subsidiaries. Hamilton-Standard was compensating for the decline in propeller sales, which constituted 70 percent of its 1955 business, by producing a variety of equipment for military planes: air conditioning systems, refrigeration units, jet-engine starters, fuel controls and pumps. When the company received a small contract for work on the Army's Nike program, missiles were included on its product roster.

At Sikorsky's new Stratford plant, which opened in 1955, business was "satisfactory," never spectacular, because of stiff competition at home and low returns on its mostly military orders. Fortunately helicopters were increasingly being used for mail and passenger service, so there was some hope of reducing Washington's influence.[29]

At United Aircraft Exports, Joe Barr was busier than ever exploiting the growing market for engines, propellers, and especially military and commercial helicopters created by Europe's gradual recovery from the war. Following in Tom Hamilton's footsteps, Barr did business with high-ranking ex-nazis.

In search of a local company with which to cooperate in filling German helicopter orders, United settled on Weserflug of Bremen, a subsidiary of the great Krupp complex. Alfred Krupp, now out of prison, did not participate in the lengthy negotiations. Once an agreement had been reached, however, Barr and the visiting Bill Gwinn, Pratt & Whitney's managing director, visited Krupp at his Essen castle, where they toured the grounds and enjoyed their lunch— and where Gwinn suffered a memory lapse that might have destroyed the deal. "With the very best intentions," he said to Krupp, "I hope you'll come over to Hartford and let us reciprocate your hospitality."

According to Barr, who nearly fell off his chair, Gwinn apparently "didn't know that another part of Krupp's penance was to be forbidden entry into the United States, and this was a mighty sore subject to him." But Krupp reacted gracefully, and United purchased 43 percent of Weserflug, thereby giving Krupp an American connection and the legitimate claim that he was making weapons in the free world. Barr also signed helicopter licensing agreements with Westland Aircraft in Great Britain, Société Nationale in France, and Mitsubishi Heavy Industries, Reorganized, Limited, of Japan.[30]

Back in the United States an awkward situation had developed between two of United's most valuable subsidiaries. As airplanes became more complicated and jets replaced conventional power plants, air-frame and engine manufacturers required precise knowledge of one another's designs. Buyers of Pratt & Whitney's engines were suspicious that their airframe engineering secrets were being passed on to Chance Vought to give that United subsidiary an edge in the fighter-plane market. As United's president, Horace Horner, explained, these suspicions of industrial espionage "were brought forcibly to our attention when our very good customer, North American, in a certain competition, happened to have a variable-incidence wing, and so did Vought, and when Vought won it, North American just wouldn't believe that the information on the variable wing hadn't leaked via Pratt & Whitney to Vought."[31]

Because Pratt & Whitney's importance to United's balance

sheets outweighed Vought's, Rentschler and Horner reluctantly decided to sever a bond that had lasted almost twenty-five years. In a July 1, 1954 stock exchange, over $17 million was added to United's accounts for its holdings in Chance Vought Aircraft.

With the Vought connection broken, United focused more than ever on the manufacture of aviation engines. In 1956, to maintain Pratt & Whitney's lead on the competition, the company established a new research facility on a seven-thousand-acre plot in a wildlife preserve located seventeen miles from West Palm Beach, Florida. The site was chosen because "in this remote area accoustical requirements in test facilities would be at a minimum." The military approved the idea that "secret turbine projects" would be conducted in a remote, easily policed area where potential espionage would be minimal.

United paid for the Florida facility with its own funds, using certificates of necessity to write off the project long before it had to be rebuilt. As far as the government was concerned, peace in Korea had not ended the national emergency. Whether it was Florida purchases, Sikorsky's new plant, or additions at Hamilton-Standard, United's stockholders almost always found the same statement toward the end of every annual report during the late fifties: "Substantially all addition to fixed assets during this emergency period have been covered by Certificates of Necessity as provided for under the Internal Revenue Code. The portion (as high as 75 percent) of that cost covered by such certificates is being amortized on the books and for tax purposes over a five-year period."[32]

As much as ever, United was insuring itself against overcapacity with the financial safety nets erected by the federal government. From 1950 through 1956, an average of 87 percent of the company's business was with Washington. The only hint of change occurred in the last major transaction Frederick Rentschler ever made. A few months before his death in April of 1956, Rentschler personally committed United Aircraft to the sale of engines for Boeing's and Douglas's commercial jet transports.

The airlines had embarked on a jet-buying spree that promised light at the end of the government tunnel. So what if commercial customers provided none of the government's guarantees? So what if signing a contract with Pan American meant fulfilling its terms or, as with Sikorsky's clipper ships in the thirties, delivering to Juan Trippe every minute feature his specifications called for? Fred

Rentschler had seen a "hole in the market,"[33] and he jumped in without the safety nets to which he and United long had been accustomed.

Flying the Skies with the J-57

A February, 1956 *Fortune* article entitled "The Airlines' Flight from Reality" accused the carriers of an "equipment-buying binge that was phenomenal even in the burgeoning post-war economy." As of December 31, 1955, they had ordered seventy-five jets at $5 to $6 million each; 170 turboprops; and 222 piston-engine planes. Including ground installations and other requisite equipment, the industry expected to spend a "literally staggering" $2.5 billion.

Fortune advised the airlines to look at Ford, which, despite five years of explosive growth, never spent more than 5 percent of its annual sales for expansion, modernization, and replacement. Ford kept expenditures down to $200 million per year, whereas the airlines had committed themselves to $500 million per year through 1960— 31 percent of their current gross revenues. Like planes in the twenties, *Fortune* warned, airlines could soon be dropping from the business sky.[34]

Some airline executives agreed. As C.E. Woolman, then president of Delta Airlines, complained, "We are buying airplanes that haven't been fully designed, with millions of dollars we don't have, and we are going to operate them off airports that are too small, in an air-traffic control system that is too slow, and we must fill them with more passengers then we have ever carried before."[35]

It was a time for caution, yet the airlines joined the buying boom one after the other. When Fred Rentschler followed suit by agreeing to jet-power the industry's overexpansion he tied his company to a commercial market that, as *Fortune* had suggested, was every bit as unstable as a military market turned on and off by presidents, Congress, and war.

United would emerge unscathed only if the J-57 and its offshoots proved to be as good as George Mead's Wasp.

Boeing had a prototype jet liner ready for testing in July of 1954. Using fifteen million dollars of its own funds, Boeing had built a thoroughly new plane that promised great improvements in air travel. To protect itself against loss, the company planned to build any planes ordered by the airlines in facilities leased from the federal government. Boeing's president, William Allen, was a shrewd operator. While the jet liner was still under construction, he urged Washington to fund a jet tanker to refuel jet bombers in mid-air; that way, tankers and commercial jets could be built with the same tools used on the Air Force's planes.

In June of 1954, when Air Force Secretary Harold Talbott announced a design competition for a new jet tanker, it seemed that Allen would receive half of what he desired. By August, Boeing had a firm order for twenty-nine of the new planes, with the likelihood of at least another eighty-one to come from the Air Force. By March of 1955, the order had increased to four hundred.[36]

Allen's next obstacle was Juan Trippe, who had shown by far the most interest in Boeing's jet liner, but was masterfully manipulating, in turn, Boeing, Douglas, Pratt & Whitney, and Rolls Royce. Through insinuation and pressure, Trippe had each manufacturer design a plane to his specifications, then complained that neither the Boeing prototype nor Douglas's entry was a truly transatlantic jet. If the competitors wanted Pan American's business, Trippe suggested they they build a plane around an engine even more powerful than Pratt & Whitney's J-57; despite its ten thousand pounds of thrust, it lacked the strength necessary to carry hundreds of people over thousands of miles at nonstop jet speeds. Over the industry grapevine, he had learned that Pratt & Whitney, under an Air Force research-and-developmet contract, was building a successor that promised double the thrust of the J-57. Although this J-75 engine still required years more development Trippe insisted that, if Boeing and Douglas designed a plane around it, he would provide the orders needed for a production go-ahead.

Boeing and Douglas hesitated at fulfilling such seemingly absurb requests. For Boeing, it would involve millions of dollars in development and design costs on its prototype. Douglas, which had no prototype in early 1955, was also reluctant to combine an untested engine with an untested plane. Besides, all parties were aware that the Air Force still considered the J-75 secret. Trippe's assurance that he could obtain a release contributed yet another uncertainty.

While the airframe manufacturers pondered, Juan Trippe devised a scheme that was to leave them little choice but compliance. Pan Am's president traveled to Hartford, where he wanted to order approximately 120 J-75's for use on his transatlantic jets. Trippe knew that Rentschler knew that such planes did not exist, yet he asked Pratt & Whitney to expedite production.[37]

Rentschler knew his man. He had purchased fifty thousand shares of Pan Am stock in 1929 and had sat on the Pan Am board for several years; United, moreover, had been burned by Trippe on each of Sikorsky's clipper ships. Although he mistrusted Trippe, Rentschler found it difficult to resist a commercial order. If Trippe bought the J-75, other orders surely would follow, and United Aircraft might become the world's leading manufacturer of commercial as well as military aviation engines.

Rentschler, exercising characteristic caution, nevertheless refused Trippe. He was reluctant to leave United liable for specification failures on an engine still in the testing stage, even though the J-75 was based on the successful design pioneered in the J-57, and although Air Force development contracts were allowing United to learn at the government's expense. The already proven J-57 was in production and ready to go, Rentschler reasoned. If Trippe wanted those, fine; if not, he would have to add 120 nonexistent engines to his nonexistent planes.

Trippe thereupon went to England, but with no real intention of purchasing Rolls Royce engines. Rather, he was relying on the airline grapevine to pass the word that Pan American "was no longer considering Pratt & Whitney engines at all because the J-57 was too small and the J-75 not available."[38]

Trippe's tactic succeeded. After they had absorbed this information, Rentschler and Gwinn and Horner and Hobbs reevaluated their previous conclusions. The J-75, after all, was "only a bigger version" of the J-57. Inspired by a vision of the first American commercial jets flying with engines provided by Pratt & Whitney, a company whose longtime trademark was the American bald eagle, United's engineers surely would finish the remaining work in record time.

The next time Trippe and Rentschler met— at the Cloud Club atop New York City's Chrysler building— they agreed to a deal whereby Pratt & Whitney was guaranteed $1 million for each J-75 produced. But the deadline, the summer of 1959, alarmed Pratt & Whitney's technical staff. If the engine failed to meet Trippe's specifications in what amounted to record time, they protested,

Pratt & Whitney still would have to make good on the contract no matter what the further costs. In that event, the $40 million expected for the initial order might be offset by the untold costs to bring the engine up to standards— in the end generating a possible loss that might undermine the entire United Aircraft Corporation.

Rentschler, however, was insistent. Besides the government, only the airlines provided a market for United's products, and only Juan Trippe had the courage— some said recklessness— to forge ahead where others feared to fly. By cooperating with Trippe, United would earn a significant head start on all commercial business, domestic as well as foreign. By refusing, United would remain crippled by its reliance on the government.

Now that Trippe had the upper hand, he proceeded to manipulate the air-frame manufacturers according to his own accurate assessment of their business situations. Once one company accepted his terms, the others risked losing one of the only two markets for their products unless they followed. After Boeing refused him once again, Trippe went to Douglas and threatened to order his planes abroad. Douglas promptly agreed to build Trippe's plane, and Trippe agreed to buy 24 DC-8's— as long as the deal was kept secret temporarily.

The secrecy was essential because Trippe intended to coerce Boeing, too, into building his plane. When Trippe agreed to buy twenty-one of the smaller Boeing prototypes powered by J-57's, Boeing assumed Trippe had caved in. Bill Allen was unaware that Trippe had signed both plane contracts on the same day.

Allen, who learned of the Douglas contract from the newspapers, suddenly was lodged between a rock and a hard place— his 707 seemed obsolete even before leaving the factory. Not only would Douglas obtain most of the business sure to be generated by Trippe's order, but Boeing could lose a fortune because Trippe's twenty-one-plane order was contingent on Boeing selling the additional twenty-nine planes needed to break even on its huge development and production costs. If Boeing failed to enlarge its planes to accommodate the J-75, it could look forward to nothing but losses.

Bill Allen bit the bullet and called Juan Trippe to announce that Boeing would build six of the smaller 707's with all possible speed to guarantee Pan Am's lead in jets. After that, however, Boeing would deliver the balance of Trippe's order with its soon-to-be-enlarged planes, with Pratt & Whitney's soon-to-be-delivered J-75's.

Juan Trippe got his engines, his planes, and had the first commercial jets in the air; and when American, Eastern, TransWorld, and United Airlines all followed Pan Am's example, United received an extraordinary number of commercial orders. Pratt & Whitney was contracted to supply 90 percent of the jet transports that Douglas and Boeing planned to build, thereby virtually eliminating the competition. Pratt & Whitney's subsequent ability to produce the J-75's on schedule and without major problems led to its fifteen-year reign as the undisputed king of the enginemaking industry. Although it would be 1959 before the airline orders showed up on United's balance sheets, Rentschler's gamble provided the perfect finale for a fascinating career.

After Rentschler's death in April of 1956, his successors were willing and able to sustain the principles their chairman had ingrained so deeply into the United Aircraft Corporation. The new chairman, Horace Horner, boasted of having witnessed the first production ever shipped from Pratt & Whitney's tool-company headquarters in 1926. Along with an obvious love for the company, he possessed the business savvy one would expect in Fred Rentschler's hand-picked heir. William Gwinn, United's new president, had joined the company as an "air-struck kid" in 1927. His aviation education at Pratt & Whitney had included time spent as a go-fer, a salesman, an assembly man and, since 1943, the managing director of engine operations. Gwinn displayed his status as a member of United's home-grown management team with this assessment of the company's future: "Our business is aviation. What we supply is the power. If they ever decide to fly 'em with rubber bands, we'll make the rubber bands. But we stay in aviation."[39]

And why not? The commercial sales engineered by Rentschler would decrease United's dependence on Washington. In the meantime, government business— 87 percent of the 1957 total— was so good that the company finally entered the billion-dollar club; on sales on $1.2 billion, United earned $51.3 million. The annual report bragged that 1957's operations had "reached their highest level." The corporation stood prominent among engine-makers, and its new leaders were prepared for any and all challenges, even a project Secretary of Defense Charles E. Wilson publicly called a "shitepoke."[40]

The Nuclear Airplane

The development of the nuclear airplane was indirectly related to the jet tankers Boeing used to help underwrite production of its 707's. The tankers assisted Strategic Air Command pilots in remaining in the air by providing in-flight refueling. But the Air Force wanted to go one step farther with a self-fueling bomber that stayed airborne as long as pilots stayed awake. SAC commanders eagerly proceeded with this project, for which they coined the acronym CAMAL: continuously airborne missile-launching and low-level penetrating weapon system. According to Major-General Donald Keirn, director of the CAMAL project, a nuclear-powered bomber could stay in the air for a week or more. Such bombers, fully armed and prepared for instant retaliatory action, could cruise anywhere in the world, immune to surprise attack or sabotage. Even if the United States went up in a mushroom cloud, this fail-safe weapon system would immediately destroy the Soviet Union.[41]

The prospect was so appealing to Strategic Air Command officials that they (and the Atomic Energy Commission, Congress, and the president) ignored a host of obstacles. No matter how efficient an engine Pratt & Whitney created, for example, pilots would inevitably be exposed to heavy doses of radiation— one study estimated a minimum of 20 REMs per year (REM, which stands for Radiation Equivalent Man, measures amounts of radiation received). Because this exceeded the occupational dose considered permissible for industry, project personnel formulated two potential solutions: a pill to immunize the crew against radiation damage or, more likely, crews composed of senior volunteers who had already produced children and thus would be willing to risk sterilization.

And despite "current operational plans which called for the nuclear aircraft to be flown under carefully controlled flight conditions," the possibility of crashes also concerned project officers. For the pilots, they devised "escape capsules which would protect them from wind blast and provide a habitable environment during descent and rescue operation." No escape capsules would be provided for the public, but if the SAC "painted the aircraft distinctively," it would be easy to find; thereupon, "the firefighting, rescue and clean-up job probably would be done with remote-controlled, shielded vehicles." As yet, no such emergency devices existed, but engineers were working on it.

Continuously airborne, senior pilots were sure to experience "physical and psychological problems." To ease their burden, "the nuclear aircraft cabin would be considerably more luxurious than normal large aircraft crew compartments," and "designers planned to pipe in music."[42] There was no hurry to choose the program, however, because the engine for the CAMAL bombers was too heavy. And when the "shielding required to protect the crew and equipment against radiation" was added, the nuclear airplane did seem to be the "shitepoke" described by Defense Secretary Wilson. Even if it finally flew, it would be far too slow to offer SAC the performance characteristics essential to any bomber's success.

Headquarters for the CAMAL program was Pratt & Whitney's CANEL HOT Laboratory— Connecticut Aircraft Nuclear Engine Laboratory— in the Middletown facility that had cost the federal government $30 million to build. There, Pratt & Whitney's staff analyzed nuclear fuels and their containers; studied the physical, chemical, and metallurgical effects produced through the transfer of reactor heat; and studied the damaging effects of "intense nuclear radiation" on structural metals and other material likely to be used in a nuclear power plant.

The work demanded "good housekeeping" along with careful technical planning. When radioactive materials entered the lab, "the sealed shipping cask was lowered into the cell by an overhead crane through a removable concrete roof block and opened by a remotely controlled crane inside the cell after the roof block had been replaced." As an alternative, workers sometimes used what Pratt & Whitney called the "hot pass" technique; workers dressed in protective clothing and wearing a mask that resembled a dog's muzzle used mirrors to locate the experimental capsule within the sealed cask. Once they located their radioactive mark, one man lifted the capsule from the cask with a "grasping tool"; a second man then "seized it with a pair of tongs" and swiftly shoved the capsule into an experimental cell. As one engineer explained, "The hooker in a hot laboratory operation is that we are never able to touch the material with our hands. It is frustrating, but in spite of all you may read, it is not dangerous."[43]

The research also was not particularly productive. Through 1958, the nuclear aircraft program had cost Washington over $681 million. B.A. Schmickrath, manager of the Pratt & Whitney project, estimated that despite progress on the advanced reactor research and development work, it would take another three to four years before CAMAL officials could "probably discuss the flight program." Nevertheless, Schmickrath assured the Joint Committee on Atomic Energy that "a vigorous engineering program would permit the establishment of a feasible power-plant design suitable for militarily useful nuclear flight."

Although Pratt & Whitney received government funding for its CAMAL laboratory through 1960, the attitude of the Eisenhower administration toward the nuclear aircraft program in particular, and military research and development in general, had changed significantly. By 1959, Ike harbored serious doubts about CAMAL's work; no materials were yet available with which to fabricate a useful reactor unit, and the potential hazards of a nuclear plane crash remained as ominous as ever. Under intense pressure from congress— and especially from Melvin Price, chair of the Research and Development Subcommittee of the Joint Committee on Atomic Energy— the president agreed to fund the development work at the minimal rate of $140 million per year, just enough to bequeath the nuclear "shitepoke" to the next administration.[44]

Ike had more important problems to deal with. Russia's launching of Sputnik in late 1957 had embarrassed American scientists at the same time that it demonstrated sufficient technical competence to conceivably threaten national security. If the Russians could create and deploy missiles first, they also could destroy America and lose only a few million people to the inevitable retaliatory bombs.

As early as 1955 Val Patterson, the nation's Civil Defense director, had suggested that the government install along all major highways "miles of concrete pipe, either four feet in diameter or more as our funds would provide, and cover that pipe with three feet of dirt." Ideally, Americans would crawl into the pipe in search of protection both from fallout and from intercontinental ballistic missiles. Now that Sputnik was encircling the globe, Patterson's idea seemed less farfetched. America's race to catch up with Russia added a totally new element to Ike's plans— and to those of United Aircraft.[45]

To achieve at least parity with the Russians, the president added nearly $2 billion to the budget for missile development and production in 1959. But Eisenhower was as reluctant as ever to weaken the economy in order to arm the nation. Between 1958 and 1960, the defense budget had remained even, and defense as a percentage of the total budget had actually declined from 62 to 60 percent. To keep expenditures in line he reevaluated programs such as the nuclear airplane, reduced appropriations wherever possible, and cut back research and development funding for private industry. As United Aircraft informed its stockholders in 1960, "Because of limited funds, the military services in the past few years have given financial support only to those development projects which are of most critical importance to them in the light of funds available."[46]

The consequences of Eisenhower's restraint were painful to United. Bombers, one of the company's mainstays, had receded into the background in importance. If missiles could reach their destination in thirty minues or less, why build expensive bombers that would get to Russia long after it had been obliterated? The president however, also refused to underwrite the research necessary for United to exploit missile production and the potential market in outer space.

If United intended to proceed, there was no choice but to spend a great deal of its own money and accept the reduced earnings that implied. If the company failed to make the leap into space it could be left behind on earth, building a few jet engines while its competitors were manufacturing rocket engines. Even the commercial coup achieved with the J-57 could never compensate for erosion in the annual nearly one billion dollars of government business.

Along with America, United Aircraft entered the missile age. Horace Horner reluctantly financed the takeoff by spending over $100 million on research, buying Norden Industries, and creating the first new subsidiary in twenty-five years— The United Technology Corporation.

The Sikorsky factory as it looked in the late thirties. The operation would soon turn into Vought-Sikorsky. *The Hartford Courant*

Eugene Wilson (second from right, back row) huddling with heads of other aviation companies. The picture was taken in early 1944, shortly before Wilson began to barnstorm for his Pax Aeronautica. Donald Douglas is not in the picture but J.H. Kindelberger, head of North American Aviation, is at the far left of the bottom row. *United Press International*

Frederick Rentschler, then chairman, and Horace Horner, then president of United. The picture was taken about 1951. *The Hartford Courant*

Joe Barr, head of United's export operation, receiving an award after thirty years of service to the company. In the background is William Gwinn, then chairman of the company. *The Hartford Courant*

Arthur Smith, then president, and William Gwinn, then chairman of the United Aircraft Corporation. *The Hartford Courant*

Building a jet engine at Pratt & Whitney Aircraft. *The Hartford Courant*

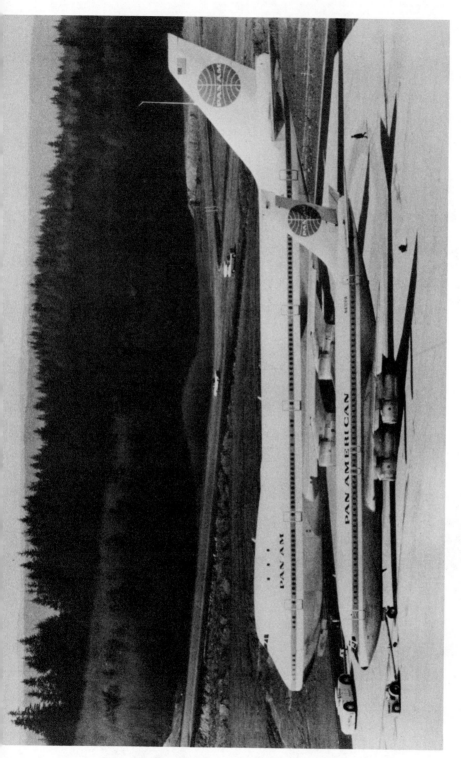

A Boeing 707 beside a Boeing 747. United's job after 1965 was to jet power a plane that was literally the biggest and heaviest ship in the sky. *Pan American World Airways Photo*

The King Kong and Frankenstein cartoons were done by Tim Atseff of the *Syracuse Herald Journal* when United tried to buy the Carrier Corporation. Mr. Atseff says the original King Kong cartoon was purchased by Harry Gray, apparently to hang in his Hartford Office. *Courtesy of Tim Atseff*

Harry Gray presiding over the 1982 annual meeting of United's stockholders. *The Hartford Courant*

Edward L. Hennessey, Jr., chairman of Allied, announced that Allied is the new parent company of Bendix Corp. in 1982. *United Press International*

Alexander Haig served as United Technologies president during 1980. Because of a serious illness, however, Mr. Haig's impact on the corporation's high policy was understandably diminished. *The Hartford Courant*

Cartoon done by Tim Atseff when United tried to get its share of the Bendix Corporation. Notice General Haig in the right foreground. *Courtesy of Tim Atseff*

8

McNAMARA AND MISTAKES

"Military sales constituted, as usual, most of Pratt
and Whitney's 1961 product sales."

Annual Report, 1961

"A substantial loss was recorded for 1971. . . This loss
reflects the decision made at the year end to provide
in 1971 for estimated after-sales costs and other
obligations related to the JT9D (the 747's) engine."

Annual Report, 1971

A New Ballgame

To keep up with military demands for improved armaments (and to keep their factories in operation), the executives at United Aircraft were obliged to keep up with everchanging technology. It was a simple facts of defense life: if you ignored the latest developments, you faded into aviation obscurity like the once-prominent Curtiss-Wright Company.

United's Horner and Gwinn took the competitive ideology fostered by Frederick Rentschler quite seriously. Despite the tight money policies of the Eisenhower Administration, they were determined to acquire technological capabilities conspicuously absent at the world's premier aircraft company.

One significant gap was in the rapidly developing and increasingly important field of avionics: the electronic equipment used in aircraft for weapons delivery, navigation, detection, communications, and other functions. To enhance its business prospects, United acquired the assets of the Norden-Ketay Corporation on July 1, 1958, in exchange for 64,934 newly issued shares of United's common stock at $57 each. The purchase price of this immediate entry into avionics was $3.7 million.

Carl C. Norden was a bombardment pioneer. Until 1941, formal bombardier training was nonexistent and so too the technology necessary for precise positioning of bomber pilots' deadly cargo. One reason Winston Churchill authorized terror bombing in 1942 was that a study of the British air arm's effectiveness revealed that, in June and July of 1941, only one third of the pilots had come within five miles of their targets. Norden changed all that by creating the instruments that permitted pilots "to put a bomb in a pickle barrel from 20,000 feet." His "football," so called because the actual bomb sight was roughly cylindrical in shape, helped win World War II. It gave bombers more precision, and it gave Norden a great deal of business; by war's end, some twenty-five thousand bomb sights had been produced at a cost of ten-thousand dollars each.

The Connecticut-based company soon was manufacturing radar, decoding equipment, airborne television, computers and, by 1958, missiles. Norden supplied components for the Atlas, Polaris, Nike, Redstone, Jupiter, and Snark missile systems. Although it never made much money— on 1957 sales of $27.2 million, Norden actually lost $5 million— it did have a toehold in a market that aviation analysts deemed essential to future defense procurements, and that United deemed essential to its future. Theoretically, Pratt & Whitney could provide the engines for tomorrow's planes, Hamilton-Standard the air conditioning, and Norden the avionics. At the very least, United had purchased a great deal of experience for what then seemed to be a relatively small paper investment.[1]

The opposite situation prevailed at United's new Missiles and Space Systems division, which was established in the East Hartford headquarters on July 1, 1958. With no inexpensive means of buying into this market, the company was forced to hire well-paid scientists and provide the facilities for them to work in. "Study contracts in general were not profitable," Horner conceded, but at least, if the scientists covered United's costs with research awards, they would help with cash flow until— with luck— their research translated into production contracts for space and missile vehicles.

Because missiles were apparently the key to eventual profits, Horner also authorized the creation, in the fall of 1958, of what soon became the United Technology Corporation. Headed by Lieutenant General Donald Putt, formerly Air Force Deputy Chief of Staff for Development, the first UTC was originally based near California's Stanford University, an area occupied by defense-minded researchers. United simply helped itself to the local talent, paying a team of "outstanding scientists" to initiate a solid-propellent research program. When Putt soon afterward requested the spacious facilities necessary to test and produce rockets providing 60,000 or even 100,000 pounds of thrust, United purchased over three thousand acres near San Jose and added a twenty-nine-acre tract near Sunnyvale for offices and laboratories.

Until the new United Technology subsidiary obtained government funding for its missile development activities, it would continue to drain United Aircraft's treasury. Over $17 million was soon sent to California for research and all the while Horner pleaded for patience from stockholders.

Horace Horner readily agreed that United Aircraft's huge research tabs ($11 million in 1958, $28 million in 1959) were a big gamble, but he pointed to 1959's sales figures: down nearly 10 percent, management had correctly forecast that military orders would decline unless United moved into areas where the government promised to spend large amounts for research and missile vehicle procurement. For the next few years net profits might continue to drop —United eventually netted $42 million in 1958, $28 million in 1959— and so too the company's return on net worth. When it fell below 10 percent for 1959 with another $40 million in corporate funds for research to come out of 1960's earnings, United's stockholders were braced for some very lean years.[2]

Not all of United Aircraft's expenditures were coming from the company treasury during this period. Because Pratt & Whitney's Florida research facility was used for development of the government's Centaur rocket program, Washington had paid $43 million in 1959. Overall, the company still did $845 million worth of government business— 78 percent of its total. There was a $1 billion backlog, and substantial new orders were under negotiation. Eisenhower never cut off government funding entirely; he merely demanded that United spend its own money to pave the way for entry into government programs that promised the lowest returns in its history.

As it moved into the sixties, United tripled the size of its professional— and highly paid— technical staff in order to provide the increasingly sophisticated development work required for procurement contracts with shorter production runs than ever before. In the past, development money was recouped when profits increased at the back end of the learning curve. Now, however, fewer procurement contracts were signed, and those that were did not stipulate the large orders essential for large profits.

United was burdened with high research costs and low profits at the very time that President Eisenhower called attention to the dangerous influence of the military-industrial complex. While critics complained about United's high profit years after the boom times, Americans failed to anticipate the predictable consequences of their insistence on scientific breakthroughs. It was as if a company were instructed to produce revolutionary products immediately, then criticized for technological errors.

United Aircraft was committed to aviation and willing to satisfy its customers' demands for the most sophisticated equipment possible. The problem for Horace Horner and his colleagues was the breakneck pace of change and Washington's new rules. "The government was depending more and more on rapid application of technical innovation and less and less on mass procurement," Erle Martin (United's vice president for research and development) told unhappy stockholders. To make matters worse, instead of permitting manufacturers to add development costs to the price of a product, "the government had drastically restricted overhead allowances through which such costs might be recovered."[3]

The result was that companies now competed on the basis of research and development projects rather than of "finished hardware." The administration was perpetrating a gigantic contradiction: because of its heated demands for technical progress, its desire to eliminate unfair profits, and the high cost of prototypes, Washington had made paper proposals the key to procurement at the same time that it insisted on weapons that stretched the state of the art. Such policies and priorities promised trouble for United Aircraft, its competitors, and the nation. Technical progress involved mistakes; new planes could not be produced by snapping one's fingers and saying "presto." As with United's Centaur rocket program, the product might explode— not because of anyone's incompetence, but merely as part of the learning process.[4]

The price tag on progress often soared when paper proposals were translated into reality, especially since contractors competing for business were pressed to promise far more than they could deliver: recall Eugene Wilson's "promising contest" in 1937 on the Vought plane that became the Japanese Zero. Although Wilson exaggerated the plane's potential, at least he offered a working prototype developed at United's expense. Because the government did not at once resolve the contradictions between paper proposals and the inordinately complex machinery they were supposed to become, the same problems face us today: inevitable cost overruns, ongoing disputes over the funding of research, conflicts of interest, and "excess" profits. As in 1948, Washington once again sidestepped crucial issues and made policy on an *ad hoc* basis.

Eisenhower's second administration had seen the continuation of bad business for United Aircraft. On 1960 sales of $988 million, net return was $13.8 million— 1.5 percent net profit as a percentage of sales and a disappointing 4.8 percent as a percentage of net worth. Although Horace Horner conceded that "net income for 1960 was the lowest for the past ten years," he reminded stockholders that earnings had absorbed another $39 million for development costs (on a new jet engine, missiles, and space work) with no "contractual or other customer support." United already had booked $50 million for development work in 1961 and $60 million for 1962; stockholders should expect "no lessening of these amounts for a few years." Unless the new president suddenly reinstated the policies of the Korean emergency, United Aircraft was in for a stretch of hard times.[5]

The Bow-Tie Bastards

John F. Kennedy entered office commited to a new defense posture radically different from Eisenhower's. For years, critics had argued that Ike's massive retaliation strategy had one great flaw: prepared to fight only nuclear wars, America either threatened catastrophe when trouble occurred— or backed down. There was no middle ground, no provision for tactical nuclear war or, equally important, for the small guerrilla conflicts that were cheaper to mount and, supposedly, easier to stop.

In contrast, Kennedy insisted on national security planning on three levels: for all-out nuclear war, tactical nuclear war, and conventional conflicts of every sort. Ideally, the nation would employ the lowest level of deterrence and, if successful, never have recourse to the alternatives. Along with his three-pronged defense strategy, the new president was firmly committed to technological progress. Because the "balance of terror" was everchanging, the best way to best the Russians was to remain far ahead.[6]

Robert McNamara, Kennedy's secretary of defense, was as committed to change at the Pentagon as he was to the new strategy. Because the military failed to understand business in general and

skills such as systems analysis in particular, McNamara was determined to streamline their procurement methods. To get a more
efficient bang for the buck and save millions of taxpayer dollars, he
would institute a method he called "commonality"— a policy of
making one weapon's design serve the needs of two services.

McNamara chose the TFX, or Tactical Fighter Experimental,
program to implement his budget-cutting joint-procurement program. The TFX was a fighter plane that functioned like a bomber,
thereby exemplifying Kennedy's desire for alternatives to full-scale
nuclear war. Originally designed to engage in air-to-air battles, the
TFX had been modified by the Air Force to make "nuclear interdic-
tion," or air-to-ground missions, its primary goal. Flexible enough to
use small air fields, theoretically it would take off from a three-
thousand-foot unpaved runway, fly for long distances at fuel-
efficient high altitudes, and then, if the order came, "make a 400-mile
supersonic dash under defensive radar screens to deliver nuclear
bombs."

Like the Air Force, the Navy had been considering its future
tactical needs. But instead of a fighter turned bomber, the Navy
envisioned the Missileer, a fleet air defense plane that could
"loiter" at high altitudes on a perimeter 150 or more miles from the
fleet. If it sighted an enemy aircraft threatening the fleet, the
Navy's plane would unleash its air-to-air missiles. Pratt & Whitney's
new turbofan engine, the TF 30, had won the Navy's Missileer
competition in 1960. But because Eisenhower had refused to commit
his successor to a major new weapons system, the Kennedy administration would have to approve any engine contract.[7]

The two ongoing Navy and Air Force projects offered
McNamara the opportunity to apply his commonality goal by purchasing two planes for the price of one. On February 14, 1961, after
less than a month on the job, he issued a formal directive to his staff
to study the development of two versions of one fighter aircraft.
Although both the Army and Navy would be forced to compromise,
McNamara assumed that small sacrifices in performance were easily
outweighed by large savings in public funds. Each service would
still obtain a sound plane, but one version would cost about $1
billion less than two.

Not surprisingly, the military protested McNamara's TFX
decision, arguing that performance, not cost, was the most crucial
element in weapons procurement. McNamara and his Whiz Kids,

whom soldiers called the "bow-tie bastards," displayed their ignorance in attempting to couple the incompatible. To spot the enemy at distances of up to 150 miles, for example, the Navy needed a five-foot diameter nose in the plane to accomodate long-range radar antennae. The Air Force, in contrast, required a needle-nosed plane in order to achieve 400-mile distances at supersonic speeds. And to withstand the intense pressures of terrain-hugging flight at extraordinary speeds, the Air Force's plane had to weigh more than eighty-five thousand pounds, whereas the Navy stipulated a compact aircraft thirty thousand pounds lighter.

The military accused McNamara of wanting the impossible, and manufacturers agreed. "The art of aircraft building used to be defined as the art of building things that almost don't work," said one of the contestants in 1961. "The designing of a multipurpose aircraft is so difficult as to be impossible." Nevertheless, there were no withdrawls from the competition. After all, the Air Force planned to buy 1,473 planes, the Navy another 231— the TFX was the procurement buy of the decade. McNamara held the purse strings; the military either complied with his orders or gave none to manufacturers.

The manufacturers, in turn, found it impossible to resist the lure of such a long production run at a time when orders were scarce. To Pratt & Whitney, over three thousand engines meant $1 billion of assured business. United Aircraft could not possibly dismiss that kind of money, particularly since the competition offered only a design proposal. General Electric's power plant looked fine on paper, but Pratt & Whitney's could be assembled and tested. Thirty million dollars of Navy development money and substantial sums from United had given Pratt & Whitney a head start.

For the promising contest that followed, Pratt & Whitney linked up with General Dynamics, a manufacturer of planes, and Grumman. Politically, this triad had every base covered; General Dynamics worked with the Air Force, Grumman worked with the Navy, and Pratt & Whitney supplied engines to both services. Together, they had a chance of producing a plane with the commonality McNamara demanded.

Boeing, the primary competitor, was using the theoretically more powerful General Electric engine and striving for quality rather than commonality, giving each service what it actually needed. "Boeing was ready to gamble that the old way, pleasing the services, was still the best way, and that a bi-service TFX would ultimately be recognized as impractical," noted Richard Smith in *Fortune* magazine.[8]

Boeing was wrong. Despite the unanimous recommendation of Boeing's design by the Source Selection Board on January 19, 1962, the Air Force insisted on using the Pratt & Whitney engine because it would take too long to translate General Electric's paper proposal into reality. While Boeing redesigned its planes around the TF-30, the Navy, which felt it would be shortchanged by Boeing, obtained approval of a second competition, this one between Boeing and General Dynamics-Grumman. Pratt & Whitney, of course, won no matter who lost— the TF-30 was everyone's power plant.

Through three additional competitions Boeing remained the unanimous choice because its plane offered the best performance. But price, not performance, had always been McNamara's priority. On the Boeing planes, roughly 60 percent of the parts were interchangeable; on the General Dynamics Grumman entries, the figure exceeded 80 percent. That, not politics, was what prompted the secretary of defense to reverse the Selection Board's decision. On November 24, 1962, the Defense Department awarded the TFX contract to General Dynamics, Grumman, and Pratt & Whitney.

Although the triad had won the competition, they were soon to rue the day they became involved with Robert McNamara and the "bow-tie bastards." Previous governments had eliminated the aviation industry's noncompetitive practices and reduced its profits. On the TFX project, McNamara moved beyond economic issues to pursue unprecedented control of private corporate affairs. In the name of free enterprise, he forced companies to assume more responsiblity than ever before for the results of their work. Ironically, on a project that the manufacturers never wanted (and that the military privately agreed could not be accomplished), the secretary made them play by rules that were among the strictest in Defense Department history. With the TFX, the secretary of defense actually attempted to resolve some of the issues that had been neglected by the Morrow Board in 1925 and again by the Finletter Commission in 1947.

To cover their possibly infinite liability for potential errors, for example, the manufacturers struggled to negotiate the best contracts possible. Robert McNamara, who refused to provide them with the government safety nets they requested, instead insisted on the principle of accountability. Although Washington did agree to pay for retrofit items— "It was reasoned at the time the contract was let that no contractor could sustain the cost of that"—the secretary included an unusual provision in General Dynamics' TFX contract: a cost of deficiency clause. If General Dynamics or one of its subcontractors made a mistake, the company paid at least part of the cost. If you bought in, in other words, you might also have to pay your own way out.[9]

Unlike General Dynamics and its subcontractors, Pratt & Whitney was not worried about a cost of deficiency clase —its separate Navy contract for engines at $273,000 each contained no such provision. Somehow, McNamara had only focused on the airframe manufacturers; that left Pratt & Whitney free to use its Navy contacts to write a traditional contract. Pratt & Whitney bought into far fewer risks than its competitors but, since all parties to the TFX's anticipated failure, Pratt & Whitney could have a hard time turning a profit on the decade's largest production order —especially if Secretary McNamara ever turned his attention to the engine manufacturers.[10]

More Trouble, A Little Sunshine

As usual, United Aircraft was wearing a uniform. The company's participation in four separate design competitions over two years exemplified its desire for more military business to compensate for unprofitable government-sponsored research-and-development work. United did 72 percent of its business with Washington in 1960, 77 percent in 1961, 80 percent in 1962, and 79 percent in 1963. But despite increased military sales, it was manufacturing fewer weapons than ever before.

United was quickly becoming a federal research agency. From 1961 to 1963, the government supplied nearly $768 million for a wide array of research and development projects, including nuclear reactor work for the Atomic Energy Commission, the creation of a forty-three-foot tall four-segment rocket booster for the Air Force, and the development of fuel-cell power plants for NASA's lunar excursion module. Although such research contributed 28 percent of United's 1963 sales, it not only was unprofitable, but it was supplemented by large infusions of company money— almost $100 million in the same three years. The government provided 7½ dollars for every one of United's, but net income nevertheless was suffering. As Horner repeated to his stockholders yet again in 1962, "The substantial corporation-financed development costs were being provided directly from earnings in an effort to bring along new products both in United Aircraft's traditional areas of activity and in the growing sphere of space and rocketry."[11]

In 1961, United's profits plunged to another new low, five times less than in 1957. On *Fortune's* list of the five hundred largest industrial corporations, United ranked 25th in the number of employees and 39th in sales. The company scored high in every area but profit, where it took 380th position in terms of profit as a percentage of invested capital and almost fell off the board with 441st place for profit as a percentage of sales.

	1961	1962	1963
Sales	$1.1 million	$1.2 million	$1.3 million
Net Income	$10 million	$18 million	$21 million
% of Profit to Sales	.9%	1.6%	1.7%
% of Profit to Net Worth	3.5%	6.2%	7.2%
% of Sales to Government Research and Development	13%	23%	28%

"The importance of commercial sales to United Aircraft cannot be stressed too strongly," Horner maintained, but airline orders had been disappointing: from 171 Pratt & Whitney-powered planes in 1955 to a mere 55 in 1962. Pratt & Whitney did supply engines for 90 percent of Boeing and Douglas airlines, but the carriers as a group went into the red for the first time since 1947. Until the airlines managed to solve their own problems, Horner would continue to stress their importance as he continued to see their contribution to United's total sales decline.[12]

To Horace Horner, the supersonic transport was an apt symbol of the airlines' (and America's) flight from reality. Because France and England were at work on the Concorde, the United States felt obliged to produce an SST of its own— and, as usual, "in one grand leap." Horner, who predicted the same major problems that characterized the TFX project, announced that "We do take gambles, but we don't want to have the dice loaded." Assuming the supersonic transport actually could be built, United might have to spend $100 million of its own money. Although Horner was quite correct in insisting that such a staggering investment never could be recouped, he gave in to the Federal Aviation Authority's pressure to participate. As of 1963, its preliminary work on the SST had already cost United $3 million. Unless the government agreed to underwrite the project completely, Horner could only hope that Pratt & Whitney would lose a competition allegedly vital to the nation's prestige. In his opinion, United's path to profits lay with the Boeing 727, a technically sensible plane with a potentially huge commercial market.[13]

Boeing conceived of the 727 in 1958, when an industry survey indicated the need for a medium-range jetliner capable of carrying approximately 150 passengers at speeds up to six hundred miles per hour. Because airlines did their best business on traffic between cities, not between continents, any manufacturer able to increase operating efficiency significantly was sure to sell at least five hundred planes on the world market, especially now that the public was demanding jets whether or not the airlines could afford them.

For a power plant, Boeing naturally turned to Pratt & Whitney, the undisputed leader in the aviation engine field, which thereupon funded development of another remarkable engine, the JT8D, at its own expense. By November of 1963, the 727, powered almost exclusively by Pratt & Whitney, embarked on a seventy-six-thousand-mile world advertising tour covering forty-four cities in twenty-six nations. The new plane met with such widespread approval— backed up by firm orders— that even its designer, Jack Steiner of Boeing, remarked in surprise, "It appears that we've got a lot more airplane than we bargained for."[14]

The 727 provided United with hopes of once again reducing its reliance on military business, and at a particularly opportune time America suddenly seemed to be at war in a place called Vietnam, and for United Aircraft war inevitably brought increased dependence on Washington.

Brushfire Wars

As a result of John Kennedy's three-pronged military strategy, nuclear stockpiles were increased from 28 ICBM's to 1,054 by November of 1967 (the Russians had 250 ICBM's in place in 1966). The Air Force, moreover, was fortified with a dozen new wings, and the TFX was under development. The president intended to avoid large-scale conflicts through the use of the Army, which potentially could extinguish brush fires before they became major conflagrations.

Kennedy had been strongly influenced by *The Uncertain Trumpet*, published in 1960 by former Army Chief of Staff Maxwell Taylor. Critical of Eisenhower's massive retaliation strategy and disturbed that the Air Force was overshadowing his relatively unemployed service, Taylor suggested the subsitition of "flexible response." The nation must recognize that "the active elements of our military strategy" were the Army forces that could contain Communism without precipitating total world destruction. Using rifles and tanks, cluster bombs and napalm, helicopters and transport planes, the Army (backed up by the Navy and Air Force) "could provide the flexible sword for parry, riposte, and attack." The president found *The Uncertain Trumpet* so convincing that he made General Taylor his military advisor. The general provided the ideas, while companies such as United Aircraft produced the new weaponry essential to success in small wars.[15]

Vietnam— and the larger emphasis on guerrilla war— was giving Sikorsky aviation a chance for solid profits. The company's S-58 helicopter, designed originally as a Navy search vehicle, was popular among the Marines in Vietnam in 1962. With the addition of the armor plate needed for combat assignments and the emergency flotation gear for amphibious operations, the Navy's Sea Bat became the Marine Corps's Sea Horse almost overnight. Unfortunately, the S-58 was the only one of Sikorsky's helicopters that interested the services. Since 1951, its competitors had won all major military competitions, leaving Sikorsky to pick up the procurement crumbs. Although the company never caught up with Bell or Vertol, a Boeing subsidiary, it finally won a military competition in 1962 when its Sea Stallion (CH-53A) was selected by the Marine Corps as a heavy assault transport. The Marines would probably buy at least one hundred Stallions at approximately $1 million each.

Sikorsky hoped for a real business resurgence if only it could find a customer for its recently unveiled Sky Crane, which was developed for roughly $10 million of United Aircraft's money. It was necessary to sell perhaps sixty of the unique vehicles just to break even, but by 1961 Sikorsky had managed to unload only three, with two of those going to the West German government (United's 1958 purchase of the Krupp subsidiary Weserflug provided the contacts required for "emergency" sales). The new military strategy, however, generated Army interest in a helicopter able to carry light armored vehicles, or combat troops, or a complete field surgery unit. The Army bought six Cranes in 1963 and, if they proved as valuable as Sikorsky boasted, they might help the company recoup its heavy investment.

Sikorsky's final victory came courtesy of the Air Force, which ordered a search-and-destroy vehicle in 1962. The "Jolly Green Giant," complete with rear loading ramp and General Electric's six-barraled minigun, would be delivered by 1965, and more were likely to come if the Vietnam fighting heated up. As company officials proudly announced in 1964, "For the second successive year, Sikorsky Aircraft produced helicopters for all the nation's military services and the Coast Guard."[16]

But Sikorsky never contributed more than 10 or 12 percent of United's overall business. The really good news was that Pratt & Whitney, accounting for roughly 75 percent of sales, was about to start work on a huge plane for the small brush-fire wars of the future.

According to Robert McNamara, the Johnson Administration was seeking a means to contain disturbances "conceivably at widely separated points in the world." The options were "to maintain very large conventional forces stationed around the globe near all potential trouble spots," or, preferably, to "maintain a smaller central reserve of highly ready forces, supported by the means to move them promptly wherever they might be needed." Clearly, a fleet of gigantic planes able to transport thousands of troops and their equipment anywhere in the world within forty-eight hours would provide the most flexible military response possible. Thus, in 1964 McNamara asked the aviation industry to submit proposals for by far the largest aircraft in history.

Called by its boosters "the biggest, cheapest lift ever," the C5-A would weigh twice as much as the eight-jet B-52, then the heaviest production plane in existence. Its incredibly powerful engines would deliver forty thousand pounds of thrust. Its "cavernous fuselage" would hold a thousand passengers or fourteen supersonic jets; it had the space and gear with which to release "at least thirty jeeps in a single pass over a drop zone."

Like so many weapons of the time, the C5-A was a military dream on the verge of easy realization. Advocates pointed out that "apart from the engines, the C5-A would be a state-of-the-art design embodying no new technological principles. . . ." It would be a cinch to build, except that boosters forgot Fred Rentschler's sound advice: "The power plant was the heart of the airplane." Even if the rest of the C5-A could actually be built with ease, what use was a plane without an engine? With the C5-A, manufacturers were entering a new realm of power plant technology. They had to watch their guarantees because the largest airplane in history could also be the biggest gamble the aviation industry had ever taken.[17]

Pratt & Whitney's only competitor for the C5-A engine contract was General Electric, still attempting to enter the large-jet market. Both companies were obliged to follow the military's Request for Proposals document, a massive volume containing 1,287 pages of specifications. The document soon proved so confusing that the manufacturers bombarded the Systems Program Office with 1,783 questions. The response was 1,600 pages of clarifications and revisions— including 294 specific changes in requirements. The paper race was on.

While they awaited a decision on the C5-A winner, United's executives reported some very good news. Commercial business for 1964 had reached an all-time high: airlines had accounted for 29 percent of sales, and more commercial orders could be forthcoming. Even the loss of the lucrative C5-A couldn't shake a company that, at long last, had two baskets in which to put its many engine eggs.[18]

Good and Bad News

In 1964, air passenger miles had increased 17 percent, air freight by 20 percent. Planes such as Boeing's 727 permitted airlines to transport more passengers for less money than ever before. The carriers suddenly were so properous that TWA, for one, paid its first cash dividend in thirty drought-striken years. For United, the airline boom brought a 100 percent increase in Pratt & Whitney powered jetliners. New plane contracts climbed from 111 in 1963 to 227 in 1964. To exploit increased air traffic and boost commercial sales still further, Horace Horner resurrected ideas originated by Eugene Wilson in 1944 and stressed the advantages of air freight in expensive ads in national and international publications. In 1964, the airlines' share of freight tonnage remained less than 1 percent of the world's yearly volume, and Horner meant to do all he could to increase the airlines' —and United Aircraft's— freight business.

Reporting the "gratifying" airline news to stockholders, Horner still had to balance it with a moderate-to-heavy dose of poor government statistics. By 1964, United's investment in space and missiles had produced $184 million worth of billings, but mostly, as on the TFX, for research and development; 30 percent of sales had come from government research and development contracts. Although the research and development work had provided the best return yet, it nevertheless was responsible for a sharp dent in an otherwise encouraging bottom line. On sales of $1.3 billion, net profit was $29 million— almost 5 percent profit on sales and, much more important, over 9 percent on net worth.

As Horner had promised for so long, United finally seemed to be turning a corner.[19]

Major Mistakes

The TFX had serious problems— lots of them— and it was clear that the unrealistic twenty-five-month production deadline would not be met. The Navy plane, now called the F-111B, had put on so much weight —fully sixteen thousand pounds— that Grumman engineers put the Navy ship on a strict diet. But, when even CWIP —the Colossal Weight Improvement Program— failed to peel off the pounds that were essential to the (also overweight) Air Force plane, Grumman appealed to Pratt & Whitney for a more powerful engine to attain the speeds originally specified.

While Pratt & Whitney agreed to try, they had their own problems with the original TF-30 engine. When the contractors signed on, they agreed to put the first plane in the air within twenty-five months. Under any circumstances that was much too fast. But, when the F-111's weight problems were added to demands for an instant engine, the result was a power plant that looked good on paper yet awful in flight.

When the TF-30 was tested, the engine refused to work properly. While one writer jokingly called the stall sound it made an "almighty hiccup" what it meant to Pratt & Whitney was an expensive power plant that literally stopped in flight. At once Air Force officials pointed out (to *Aviation Week* in March of 1965) that the TF-30 "was the most complicated engine ever mated to an airplane." Soldiers tried to shift the blame onto the inevitable complications associated with technical progress, but by 1965 many Senators no longer wanted to hear about the performance heights the F-111 would soon scale. The issue was an engine that worked— Now! What did the contractors plan to do to fix the F-111?

Pratt & Whitney engineers set to work on the P-3, a second version of the TF-30 designed to provide extra power at the same time it solved the "erratic engine behavior" that continued to appear at various phases of the "flight envelope." A team of General Dynamics engineers proceeded with a new series of air inlet ducts to reduce stalls by improving air flow. These alterations had little impact on the F-111's weight problem. By April of 1965 it was apparent that the new engine lacked the thrust needed to adequately power any version of the TFX; Pratt & Whitney was obliged to develop a third engine. Senator John McClellan, along others, was "scathingly critical" of the refusal of the Secretary of Defense and General Dynamics to halt F-111 production and "get the aircraft right."[20]

Expenses were accumulating as fast as the plane's weight. Two engines slated to cost half a million dollars now cost one million,— and still were not sufficiently powerful. When Congress responded by cutting back the program, Pratt & Whitney's profits were dissolving even before the engine hit the production line. Although the company was protected from liability by the Navy contract, it had anticipated hefty profits on at least two thousand engines. Now, in mid-1965, that number was out of the question, and Pratt & Whitney's best people were engaged in solving stall problems. Aggravating the situation was the determination of Congress— and Robert McNamara— to keep a very close eye on the progres of the F-111.

Because of a plane it never wanted, Pratt & Whitney was experiencing almost unprecedented government scrutiny. Yet, smack in the middle of one engine controversy, Horace Horner signed on for another.

This time the buyer was Juan Trippe, president of Pan American Airlines, who made Robert McNamara seem like a gentle lamb. Trippe was a fox. And Pratt & Whitney was his willing prey.

The C5-A Equals the Boeing 747

The C5-A design proposals soon turned into a paper mountain. Because the Air Force demanded forty copies of each submission, a transport plane was required to deliver Douglas's sixty thousand pages in 625 volumes. Each competitor sent its own jet to Air Force headquarters in Washington with its own version of a C5-A encyclopedia.

After hundreds of thousands of hours spent poring over the 35 tons of paper, the Air Force based its decision on political considerations.

Boeing, which enjoyed a huge backlog of business, would survive easily without the C5-A contract; Lockheed might not. (A technical dispute with Air Force officals left Douglas a distant third.) So, mainly to keep Lockhead in business, and thus help maintain the industrial base needed in the event of war, Washington awarded the order to Lockheed on September 30, 1965.[21]

Pratt & Whitney had already learned that General Electric's engine, which appeared more advanced and much more fuel efficient than its own, had won the C5-A power plant competition. Boeing and Pratt & Whitney were left with detailed designs for a huge military transport plane that, just possibly, could be transformed into a commercial jet liner.

Boeing immediately established a "preliminary design group," which soon submitted three possibilities. After a whirlwind tour of all the airlines, Boeing's Joe Sutter explained that the company selected the design "closest to the largest concept we had in our studies. . . a plane that would weigh 700,000 pounds or more, capable of carrying double the payload of existing airline-type aircraft then in use."[22]

This jumbo jetliner, by far the biggest in aviation history, would require the most powerful engine in aviation history. And that could be the JT-9D, a new commercial version of Pratt & Whitney's military power plant. Like Boeing with its airframe, Pratt & Whitney had done so much preliminary work for the C5-A contract that it was only logical to proceed with development. The only thing missing was a customer.

To no one's surprise, Juan Trippe expressed instant interest in the "next step" in commercial aviation. But instead of approaching the losers, Trippe went to the winners. He called Lockheed's Courtland Gross the day the Air Force announced its C5-A decision to request a commercial version for Pan American.

Gross refused; building the military plane provided business enough. When Douglas insisted on stretching the DC-8 rather than developing a new plane, Trippe was obliged to turn to Boeing. Boeing accepted the order and then, just like Trippe, approached a C5-A winner. But General Electric was uninterested in contributing the engine for Boeing's plane. Occupied with its own military work, General Electric wanted the Air Force to pay for the inevitable errors during development. Boeing refused Rolls Royce's intriguing design proposal because of doubts about the British firm's abilities to deliver, then belatedly chose its long-time partner, Pratt & Whitney Aircraft.

During a series of three-way conferences in late 1965, representatives of Boeing, Pan American, and Pratt & Whitney designed and redesigned, negotiated and renegotiated a plane that Lawrence Kuter, a Pan Am vice president and former Air Force general, called "The Great Gamble." Like the C5-A, he maintained, the jumbo jet was possible only if manufacturers "pushed the state of the art in several respects as to air frame, the aircraft engine, and to some extent airline salesmanship, management and ground handling equipment and techniques."[23]

A fascinating question is why supposedly rational executives willingly, even eagerly, made such a long-shot bet. The F-111 fiasco was unfolding before their eyes. At United Aircraft, they were especially aware of the risks of moving too fast, yet plunged right into development of the 747— and without the government safety nets that General Electric had wisely obtained.

One reason the participants gambled is that they supposedly had no choice. Passenger travel still was growing at a rapid rate— a Pan Am study predicted a 200 percent increase by 1980— and airways were dangerously congested. A plane that could cruise at higher altitudes would fly over the traffic jams while carrying more passengers for less money than previously possible. The 747 promised Pan Am increased profits and promised the Boeing-Pratt & Whitney team control of the commercial airplane market.

Despite the jumbo jet's business appeal, it nevertheless involved two steps in one and the concomitant risks. Boeing was obliged to construct a mammoth new factory, connect it to the main Seattle facilities with a new rail spur, and provide special locomotives able to climb the steep hill with its heavy load of parts. Prudent men might have pulled the emergency cord then and there. But the chief executives of the three companies concerned, all in their sixties and facing retirement, made their bold bids for very different reasons.

For Juan Trippe, the 747 would cap a long career filled with firsts. He was willing to finance Pan Am to the maximum and give Boeing a huge down payment plus crippling installment fees in order to be first with the world's biggest jet; besides, he expected to employ his considerable negotiating skills to transfer as much risk as possible to Boeing.

Boeing and United Aircraft ignored the risks, arguing that the 747 was simply an improved C5-A. They already had done their homework; now they merely would finish what they'd started. If they refused to build the plane, moreover, Trippe would look elsewhere; to retain their commercial lead, the premier plane makers must build the latest premier plane. Perhaps most important, the 747 provided the means to reduce United's twenty-year reliance on Washington.

Thus, Pan Am agreed to buy twenty-five of the new planes— at the then-staggering price of $550 million— if Boeing offered some special guarantees. Because in the past airframe manufacturers had tried to pass the buck by blaming poor performance on the enginemaker, Trippe demanded one contract only— with Boeing. Boeing was free to sign separate contracts with any company it pleased, "but the final combined power plant and airframe performance would be Boeing's sole responsibility.[24]

Boeing reluctantly assumed full responsibility for the 747 but, as in a game of hot potato. Boeing's Bill Allen in turn demanded solid legal assurances from United's Horace Horner. Because engines would be the most likely culprit if trouble arose, Pratt & Whitney must guarantee the required thrust to jet-propel whatever

Boeing produced, no matter its weight, and make the largest engine in history virtually smokeless and extremely quiet to boot.

Horner's decision to fill this giant order would plague United Aircraft for the next six years. With military planes, customers rewrote their contracts when technical problems made it impossible to meet the original terms. Hormer may have assumed that his old friend Bill Allen would do the same. But neither Bill Allen nor Juan Trippe wore a uniform, and United was low man on the 747 totem pole. Because of his own contract with Pan Am, Allen had no options; if it came to a choice between Boeing's survival and United's, he would choose Boeing's every time. As Eugene Wilson had warned thirty years earlier, "Pan American with respect to the manufacturing part of the industry was a predatory object."[25]

In a letter of intent signed on December 22, 1965, Boeing agreed to present Pan American with a plane able to lift 350 to 400 passengers to 35,000 feet and carry them 5,100 miles at close to supersonic speeds. In December, Boeing's prototype weighed 550,000 pounds at takeoff. By the turn of the new year, it had gained 100,000 pounds. In the contract finalized on April 13, 1966, Boeing specified a plane weighing roughly 655,000 pounds. Whether or not it would ever be scaled down, Pratt & Whitney was obliged to power it.

As Horace Horner informed stockholders, United had acted "to protect its competitive lead in providing power plants for the next generation of long-range, large-capacity jet transports." Despite an initial investment of $21 million for engine development in 1966, there was no cause for concern. United was so confident of success that it had purchased a new factory in which to produce the JT-9D1— the Middletown plant formerly used for development of the nuclear airplane.[26]

"Should Cost" Accounting

While United was making its largest commercial gamble ever, government orders still provided nearly two thirds of its overall sales— 66 percent of its 1965 business and 64 percent in 1966. The Vietnam war brought Sikorsky more than $209 million of business in fiscal 1966. The majority, $169 million, resulted from Marine Corps orders for Sea Stallions; the Army bought $39 million worth of helicopters. As long as the war continued to escalate, Sikorsky was assured of substantial business.

Norden accumulated only $15.6 million in prime military contracts in 1966, but the smallest United subsidiary finally broke into the big leagues in 1966 as a subcontractor to North American Aviation's Autonetics division, which had agreed to furnish the most advanced avionics system possible— the Mark II— for the F-111D. Norden's job was to fabricate "the heads-up vertical display and the integrated cockput display."

North American, in turn, was a subcontractor to General Dynamics, the company that held the government contract. According to Secretary of Defense McNamara's requirements, very much like Juan Trippe's on the 747, General Dynamics must supervise the work of its subcontractors or ultimately pay the bills.

On the Mark II system, all parties involved "grossly underestimated" the technical challenge presented by such an extraordinarily complex navigation and bombing system. Testifying before the House Committee on Appropriations in May of 1969, Major General T.S. Jeffrey, Jr., said that North American and Norden, along with the Air Force, failed to appreciate "the magnitude of the job involved in developing and building this system,"[27] In his opinion, because of the artifically low bids engendered by fierce competition in the aerospace industry, a system that was slated to cost $132 million had jumped within a matter of months to an estimated price of $357 million. As with the F-111 planes, higher costs meant fewer purchases than originally planned. The order for 761 Mark II systems had been reduced to 210 by early 1967.

At this point, the Air Force specified a ceiling of $245 million; North American and Norden pleaded for a minimum of $357 million and tried desperately to convince the Air Force to accept full financial responsibility for the Mark II system. If the government refused to rewrite the contract, Norden's losses could easily outweigh any profits it had ever contributed to the United Aircraft Corporation.

United's biggest moneymaker was in trouble, too. As costs on the F-111 engines continued to climb, Navy employee Gordon Rule was authorized to conduct a "should cost" audit of Pratt & Whitney's manufacturing practices. Robert McNamara, annoyed that Pratt & Whitney's engines stalled in flight, was enraged when their price was nearly tripled, from $273,000 to more than $700,000 each. The secretary thereupon sanctioned a virtually unprecedented "interference" in Pratt & Whitney's everyday operations. If Rule found inefficiency, McNamara intended to rewrite Pratt & Whitney's contracts himself— with costs going down rather than up.

Rule's study, completed in mid-1967, indicated that the TF-30's cost 50 percent more than they should because Pratt & Whitney used its labor and machinery in a sloppy manner; lacked an efficient purchasing system; and was thoroughly inept at deciding whether or not to buy parts. Navy officials unilaterally reduced Pratt & Whitney's total contract by $180 million and demanded a $20 million price adjustment on engines already delivered.[28]

Although Pratt & Whitney officials did their best to dispute Rule's damaging analysis, their primary problem remained a less-than-powerful engine on a severely overweight plane; the Navy now was demanding a third and fourth version of the first Pratt & Whitney engine. Grumman, meanwhile, proposed scrapping the F-111B and instead developing a reliable fixed-wing fighter, tentatively called the VFX-2.

Criticized from every conceivable angle for the company's work on the TFX program, United's executives were required to submit to more abuse at mandatory biweekly Defense Department sessions called "Project Icarus." McNamara had initiated the meetings in August of 1966; throughout 1967, he urged executives from the participating manufacturers to repair the F-111 immediately. Congress, too, was applying increasing pressure. As Navy Secretary Paul Nitze remarked at a June 24 meeting, "The program could be in deep trouble if significant slippages should occur."[29]

Senator McClellan, Chair of a Subcommittee on Investigations and an outspoken opponent of McNamara's policies, could use congressional testimony as a basis for his accusations that the defense secretary intended to approve F-111 production "without any sound basis for believing the airplane would be suitable for service;" and McClellan was absolutely correct, especially on the Navy plane. Unless the manufacturers somehow managed to meet performance specifications, they had better renounce the dream of profits at the tail end of the learning curve— or Congress might cut off the F-111's funding.[30]

Despite further attempts to salvage an impossible program, United Aircraft no longer was devoting its full attention to the F-111. The 747 had caught the F-111's disease. Not only was the plane still substantially overweight, but Pratt & Whitney was fully liable for its shortcomings. Lacking a government contract as cover, Pratt & Whitney was as exposed as the Navy's fleet in search of TFX protection.

Trippe Turns the Screw

On June 9, 1967, Boeing informed Pan American that the 747 would be thirteen thousand pounds heavier than expected. Juan Trippe saw red. That much extra weight meant fifty-eight fewer passengers on each of twenty-five daily international flights. Boeing's error would cost the carrier 1,450 potential passengers— a revenue loss of half a million dollars for every day the 747's were in operation.

According to General Kuter, "Pan Am's letter in response to the June 9 declaration contained a clear and cold-eyed reminder that the full responsibility of meeting all agreed contract terms was the direct obligation of the Boeing Company." Trippe maintained that Boeing "became pregnant" with the 747 and therefore was obliged to make amends for its mistake; if the manufacturers refused, he threatened to withhold his next installment payment. Boeing would get the $12 million when Juan Trippe got satisfaction.

Now Bill Allen saw red. His options were limited. Delaying delivery was out of the question; to satisfy Trippe, the estimated cost to Boeing alone would total $400 million. The idea of planes built around Pratt & Whitney's first engine was rejected because the JT-9D could not propel even a thirteen-thousand-pound lighter version of the still very overweight 747. And, unlike the government, Juan Trippe clearly would not accept delivery of a plane that did not at least come close to meeting the specifications of his contract.[31]

A beleagured Boeing finally passed the buck to Pratt & Whitney. As Pan Am's General Kuter remarked after many meetings with the Seattle manufacturer, "All of Boeing's courses of action were based upon the provision of more power; none were premised on any major reductions in weight."[32] Boeing was satisfied that it had done its part satisfactorily— now Pratt & Whitney had no choice but to do the same. If the enginemaker was unable to power the 747's with its JT-9Dl's, let it use a second version. Whatever happened, Pratt & Whitney had the ball.

The company had alloted $21 million for engine development in 1966, $59 million in 1967, $58 million in 1968, $52 million in 1969, and $37 million in 1970. Besides $87 million of Navy development money, Pratt & Whitney stood to spend $227 million of its own funds because of Juan Trippe's demands. In mid-1967, Boeing threatened to cancel the entire 747 program, a course that also would have cancelled Pratt & Whitney's chance to recover its already substantial investment. Because it was under the gun whether it stopped or continued, Pratt & Whitney arranged with Boeing and Pan American to develop at its own expense a series of ever-more-powerful engines. Although they too might fail to power the overweight 747, they constituted the company's only hope.[33]

Long before Horner paid the costs incurred by Pratt & Whitney's failures with the Boeing 747, he was obligated to inform stockholders of unexpected charges that had arisen in connection with Douglas's DC-10's.

To compete with Boeing, Douglas had decided in 1967 to build its own jumbo jet. The DC-10, a wide-bodied three-engine passenger/cargo transport, was very different from the 747; one of its engines, for example, sat atop the tailfin, and all of its engines were manufactured by General Electric. "To take a necessary and vital position in the important and highly competitive trijet field," United Aircraft agreed to power the DC-10's purchased by Northwest Airlines, which used only Pratt & Whitney engines and would buy the planes only under that condition. Douglas had no objection— if United would "assume costs associated with the incorporation of the engine in the DC-10 of up to $100 million."

Horner's acceptance of Douglas's terms cost United $47 million in 1968. Pratt & Whitney had real problems getting its engines into Douglas's odd design with the result being pure loss because present estimates indicated that the $47 million "would not be recovered through sales of engines within a time period we can reasonably project."[34] General Electric controlled most of the DC-10 business, after all, and Northwest's loyalty could not compensate for such a staggering initial loss.

After the $47 million writeoff on the DC-10 and the $59 million for development costs on the 747, Horner admitted to stockholders a $35 million loss on Norden's Mark II avionics system: "Unfortunately, the system design, in order to meet objectives, had been more costly to develop and produce than originally contemplated,"[35] The government had followed through on its initial refusal to provide significant financial assistance, so Norden was left with the bill. All told, United subtracted $140 million worth of mistakes from its 1968 earnings. But an even more incredible figure appeared on the company's bottom line: despite so many simultaneous fiascos, United had earned a net profit of $61 million on sales of $2.4 billion. That was only 2.5 as a percentage of sales, but a surprising 12 percent as a percentage of net worth.

The profits that offset the red ink came from the huge commercial market for two superb Pratt & Whitney engines. The JT3D powered the majority of Boeing's 707's and Douglas's DC-8's; the JT8D powered most of Boeing's 727's and 737's and Douglas's DC-9's. Over a period of three years, 1965 to 1967, the world's airlines ordered no less than 1,847 jet transports with Pratt & Whitney engines. Far more important than volume, however, was that many of these engine orders fell at the back end of the learning curve. By 1968, having manufactured over four thousand of each power plant, Pratt & Whitney had its production process down pat.

Pratt & Whitney accounted for 75 percent of United's overall sales, $1.8 billion, in 1968. Hamilton-Standard contributed $216 million; Sikorsky, $264 million; and Norden plus the United Technology Center— whose promise never materialized— about $216 million. A generous net profit of 8 percent (based on past returns) on this $600 million of non-Pratt & Whitney business would result in a total of $48 million, enough to write off the Douglas loss against. The other losses plus the profits had to come from Pratt & Whitney Aircraft.

Of the $1.8 billion in engine sales, roughly $760 million came from military prime contracts. Calculating the same generous profit of 8 percent, the earnings total was $60.8 million, leaving $31 million to compensate for losses and development costs. Thus, to reach $61 million in profit, Pratt & Whitney must have earned over $92 million net profit on over $1 billion of commercial engine work— only 9 percent. These conservative estimates suggest how United Aircraft managed to make money in the otherwise disastrous year of 1968.

Adding just the $82 million in losses, United's 1968 profits would have been $143 million. But instead of glorying in a fantastic last year, the retiring Horace Horner handed over the reins to William Gwinn and new President Arthur Smith on October 1, 1968, at a time when the company could anticipate only more loss.[36]

Old Faces and New Problems

In 1969, United's old hands found themselves trapped in a hopeless situation. To attain the thrust demanded by Boeing and Pan American, Pratt & Whitney's engineers were forced to run the JT-9D's at higher temperatures, thus burning extra fuel. The only way to restore efficiency was to push the already overworked engines that much harder. Ultimately the engines "ovalized"— they became so hot that they changed shape while powering the 747, thereby losing thrust and, once again, burning more fuel than the contract specified.

Pratt & Whitney had to pay up. The charges against earnings for 1969 repairs came to $21 million, linked to another $52 million for development, linked to unforeseeable costs ahead. At the very time that United was succeeding in its eternal struggle to escape the government, the price of commercial work was threatening ruin. As soon as one 747 problem was solved, another appeared. After public relations people had created the necessary fanfare, the first 747 flight, on January 19, 1970, was grounded temporarily due to "hot start" problems with Pratt & Whitney's engines. The repaired Pan Am plane arrived three hours late in London; the demonstration trip to Frankfurt, Rome, Paris, and Lisbon was cancelled; and an empty 747 finally flew back to New York for further repairs to the too-hot-to-handle power plants.

Although that first plane's problem was quickly solved, even the world's best engineers could do nothing rapidly or inexpensively about the 747's terrible daily service record. Pratt & Whitney's solution to the ovalization phenomenon came slowly. Planes frequently were taken out of service while highly paid personnel installed the equipment that kept the engines flying at the specified speeds— and in only one shape.

Even worse, the JT-9D proved far less durable than Pratt & Whitney had promised. Because pilots ran the power plants at higher-than-normal temperatures to obtain the required thrust, parts wore out more quickly, and entire engines were replaced with "alarming frequency." What's more, Pan Am was complaining about reduced fuel efficiency. Boeing decided to offer its new 747's with a choice of engines; competition from general Electric and Rolls Royce would increase while Pratt & Whitney's commercial reputation continued to decline with every new 747 breakdown.

United Aircraft shouldered the blame for three companies' problems and paid for the solutions. The profits United would have made without Juan Trippe's jumbo jet or Robert McNamara's C5-A were eliminated. The corporation wrote off a loss of $46 million against the 747 in 1970. And, finally closing the books on Pan American's and Boeing's claims, United wrote off $137 million in 1971.[37]

	1969	1970	1971
Sales	$ 2.4 billion	$ 2.4 billion	$ 2 billion
Net Profit	$52.2 million	$45.5 million	$44 *million loss*
Profit as % of Sales	2.2%	1.9%	(2.2% loss)
Profit as % Net Worth	9.5%	8.1%	————
747 Losses	$21 million	$46 million	$137 million
747 Development	$52 million	$37 million	————

The cumulative effect of these losses was thoroughly demoralizing. United actually did only 48 percent of its business with Washington in 1971. In what should have been a year for celebration, however, United Aircraft recorded its first loss in thirty-seven years— all because of the commercial sales it had craved for so long. Instead of offering financial assistance, the government reduced military sales significantly as the Vietnam war wound down. The biggest drop in military prime contract awards, almost $500 million across four fiscal years, affected Pratt & Whitney, but the outlook for each of United's money making subsidiaries was either flat or dropping.[38]

	1968 (millions)	1969 (millions)	1970 (millions)	1971 (millions)
Pratt & Whitney	$891	$471	$541	$401
Norton	12	12*	13	9
Sikorsky Aviation	234	290	129	111
UTC (Sunnyvale)	47	39	44	15
Florida Research Facility (West Palm)	54	109	108	124
Hamilton Standard	55	47	32	27
Total (in millions)	$1,293	$968	$867	$687

*In 1969 Norden had to accept an additional $23.4 million loss on the Mark II avionics system. Total losses came to $58.4 million.

Nothing was going well in aviation, United's only area of expertise. As they moved into the new decade, the corporation's board of directors began a serious reevaluation of United's past performance and future prospects. With William Gwinn scheduled to retire in 1972 and Arthur Smith a few years later, perhaps it was time to question the corporate policies instilled by Frederick Rentschler and maintained by his hand-picked successors.

If United could learn from its long string of failures, the seventies might offer some hope of resurrecting what many observers considered a dying corporation. Perhaps Juan Trippe had actually done United Aircraft a favor.

The TFX and The 747

While United was reassessing its position, Congress was doing the same. Projects such as the TFX had proved so disastrous that even an industry periodical such as *Aviation Week* in a 1970 editorial advised the government to institute regulations: "A major lesson of the TFX case was that the Congress must not hesitate, in the exercise of its oversight function, to examine major procurement procedures, decisions and programs... The Congress must be ever watchful, because there could be recurrences of the serious and damaging mismanagement that attended the TFX program from its inception, as reflected in the subcommittee hearings. . ."

Aviation Week blamed the TFX fiasco on the former secretary of defense and wanted Congress to prevent direct involvement by future secretaries in technical decisions; if Robert McNamara had not overruled his generals, the TFX might have flown to everyone's satisfaction.[39]

Although many congressmen agreed with *Aviation Week*, Congress decided to exercise its "oversight function" in a more dramatic manner, a manner that threatened to fundamentally alter government procurement practices.

Specifically, the TFX project had demonstrated the inherent contradiction between the use of paper proposals and the incessant demand for technical innovation. For the seventies, Congress intended to institute "fly-before-you-buy" procurement procedures, whereby the military would develop new planes when they were needed and government would pay reasonable research and development expenses. The TFX was proof that a plane should never be put into production before it functioned exactly as its manufacturer promised.

The "fly-before-you-buy" philosophy would be accompanied by a new outlook on contractor liability. Although McNamara had inserted a "correction-of-deficiencies" clause in the TFX contract, it had been enforced only on Norden's Mark II system. In the seventies, COD clauses would become standard. If contractors wanted to buy into future military work, let the buyer beware.

If Congress had learned a lesson during the sixties, so had the manufacturers: to produce any new airframe or engine required an enormous expenditure of company funds. A mistake as big as United's on the 747 could lead a manufacturer to the verge of collapse. But with only two serious markets for their goods— the military and the airlines— the aviation companies had no alternative to taking frightening risks. As Frederick Rentschler had insisted for so long, the only way to sell new equipment was to advance the state of the art. A company either bet on progress, went out of business, or tried to cover its bets through diversification.

United Aircraft's board of directors anxiously debated the few available options. The seventies had to be different, because no sane businessperson was willing to face another decade of poor profits, poor performance, and poor prospects. The time for change was now— or, perhaps, never.

9

WHAT'S IN A NAME?
THE UNITED
TECHNOLOGIES CORPORATION

"So far, technology is the common denominator of
just about all the things we do —or plan to do."

Roy Ash, President,
Litton Industries, *Fortune,* 1966

"High technology is the common denominator
of all we do."

Harry Gray,
Chairman, President, and Chief Executive Officer,
United Technologies Corporation, 1982

Corporate crises, whether real or imagined, generally prompt even the most confident board of directors to reevaluate the company's direction. In 1971, United Aircraft registered losses for the first time since 1934, when the red ink had been someone else's fault: Franklin Roosevelt and his cronies, out to get Fred Rentschler, had dismantled the company subidiary by subsidiary. But now, with no American president to blame for its miserable performance, United accepted sole responsibility for overall losses of $250 million on the 747 engine alone.[1]

After forty-five years devoted exclusively to aviation, United's board determined to break with the past— and the principles of Fred Rentschler. Abandoning its policy of drawing top brass from the company well, United turned to executive recruiters for candidates for its presidency; and, ignoring its previous opposition to diversification, it thereupon hired Harry Gray, the number three man at the most controversial conglomerate in American business— Litton Industries, which produced everything from frozen foods to office furniture to dental equipment.

Though old-timers were puzzled by the selection of a man whose corporate experience reflected none of Rentschler's priorities, United's board offered a convincing explanation. The company's poor showing on capital investment since 1958, compounded by huge losses from Norden on the F-111 and from Pratt & Whitney on the 747 threatened catastrophe. If United's only specialty was unprofitable, why not try the one course —diversification— consistently rejected by Rentschler, Horner, and Gwinn? With Chairman Gwinn and President Smith soon to retire, 1971 seemed a promising time to rejuvenate an old company for the new decade.

Harry Gray, meanwhile, wanted the job. With Litton since 1954, Gray had used his public relations and financial talents to successfully climb the corporate ladder right up to the number three spot. But Litton's president and its chairman, Roy Ash and Charles Thornton, had no intention of retiring. If Gray, a man sky-high on ambition, meant to run his own show, it would have to be somewhere else. As he told *Fortune* magazine, "I took the job for one reason, a career opportunity."[2]

Indeed, he accepted United's offer in September of 1971 without signing a contract and with no guarantee he would become chief executive officer. Gray took this risk, a significant one for a fifty-one-year-old man, because he relished the challenge and because he intended to get quick results. "Results," he believed, "cause you to be valued."

Gray had achieved results based on his intelligence, attention to detail, and a capacity for work that was extreme even by American standards. According to Litton employees, after Gray almost lost both legs in a motorcycle accident, he set up shop in his hospital room. Dismissing the danger of permanent damage, he not only walked, "he carried on as if he had never left the job. Nothing got in his way."[3]

The same held true at the United, where he soon created an atmosphere of unprecedented informality. Whereas Rentschler's boardroom was regarded as a shrine where one worshipped the corporate gods, Gray —who to one and all was Harry— talked eye-to-eye rather than pontificating from on high.

At the same time he was revolutionizing the atmosphere at United, then ranked by *Fortune* as the nation's thirty-sixth largest industrial corporation. Gray spent his first year evaluating the company's strengths and weaknesses. Visiting his employees' turf, he actually listened to their complaints about company policy or about United's long bumpy ride on the federal and commercial aviation express.

Through 1972 Gray digested divergent opinions but relied for counsel primarily on Edward Hennessy. Like Gray, Hennessy was a man on the move. Formerly employed by Textron, ITT, Colgate-Palmolive, and Heublein, Hennessy joined United in 1972 as senior vice president of finance and administration. By February of 1973, Gray and Hennessy had established their philosophical blueprint for United's thrust into the seventies.[4]

The major order of business was reducing United's reliance on the federal government and on aviation. At a time when a new engine still represented a bet-your-company proposition, another 747 fiasco could result in bankruptcy. Although Gray intended to vigorously pursue military and commercial aerospace business, he also sought to minimize risks by investing in other areas. After analyzing attractive targets for diversification, Gray and Hennessy settled on four compatible industries— transportation-automotive; communications; electronics; and energy and environmental equipment— whose common denominator was high technology. "The most important part of any merger is the ability of the two managements to get along and to do something constructive together," Gray noted. "There are those possibilities that we might provide them something, but I think it is more important to understand their business."[5]

Once the decision was made to acquire high-technology companies, other aspects of United's merger philosophy fell neatly into place. On the issue of size, no maximum annual sales figure would bar a firm from consideration, but $100 million became the buying floor. Gray also sought mature management, international sales prospects, and the potential synergistic benefits of joining forces with another high-tech outfit. But besides size and compatible management, the only other essential criterion was profitability. Any prospect for acquisition had to make money.[6]

The search for appropriate candidates fell to Hennessy. As he and his staff accumulated data on companies, they assigned each a code number "in order to prepare a secret environment so that only a very limited number of people would be knowledgable about what was being done."[7] Expecting to assume the aggressor role, United determined that such "industrial intrigue" was necessary to prevent speculators— of whom there were plenty awaiting just such an opportunity— from buying stock in the target company and driving up United's purchase price. Moreover, with advance warning a candidate that cherished its independence might find time to apply "shark repellent," as NAT did in 1930 by altering its bylaws to frustrate Rentschler's takeover aims. If the firm slated for acquisition lacked "shark repellent," it could always seek a "white knight," a friendly second bidder who would up the ante or, even worse, snatch the company away from United.

Anything could happen, but Harry Gray's primary goal was to win, even in the face of determined and free-spending opposition. As Gray put it, "We have a policy where we would like to join with people who want to join us, but it is not a written policy."[8] Gray's intention, like Rentschler's before him, was to reduce United's dependence on Washington; and, like Rentschler, Gray put his interpretation of stockholders' interests before those of reluctant managements or the apprehensions of a community fearing absentee ownership.

It would be nice, in other words, if merger candidates embraced United's offers. If they refused, it would just take longer for the merger to occur, and it would also cost more money. Sweeteners were integral to any strategy designed to reduce a target company's resistance; the initial offer for stock would be raised, funds might be guaranteed for capital investment, or any number of bonuses could materialize. Once a determined bidder increased its floor offer and the target company's resistance alerted other interested investors, additional bidders might enter the fray and eventually eliminate the alleged advantages of buying an established concern rather than starting up a new one. With seventies stock prices down, the net value of a company's assets plus its potential profits usually amounted to far more than the cost of its outstanding shares. And if a bidder negotiated a good deal, the acquisition would become even more of a bargain.[9]

But this argument made sense only as long as the bidding stayed within the bounds of reason. With a determined opponent and one or two white knights in the picture, an aggressor could ultimately spend more than the target company was worth. Whereupon, the pressure would be on the acquisition to quickly produce a revolutionary product and recoup the new parent company's investment. Otherwise, the primary profits would go to temporary stockholders who bought as word of the proposed merger spread and sold as soon as they profited sufficiently from other people's bidding wars.

Mergers, in brief, were hazardous. The end sought— profitable diversification— could easily be sabotaged by the means used. Although Gray recognized that he might have to overpay for companies with solid but not spectacular prospects, his decision to diversify was irrevocable.

Speaking at a meeting of securities analysts, in New York in February of 1973, Gray made his merger philosophy public. As a result, while Hennessy continued to compile his list of merger prospects, brokers in search of commissions also sought out attractive candidates. Harry Gray intended to transform Fred Rentschler's company into a conglomerate in the Litton mold— if he could avoid serious financial problems with Pratt & Whitney's troublesome new engine, the F-100.

The F-100's Second Test

The new Pratt & Whitney power plant looked like a disaster in the making. The F-100 stalled, exploded and disintegrated in the wind tunnel during crucial tests on March 14, 1973; as the Air Force noted in its official report, "the engine damage was extensive and occurred with sufficient force to cause some damage to the test chamber."[10]

Harry Gray had inherited another bet-your-company engine. Yet again Pratt & Whitney had power-plant problems rooted in the "design deficiencies" that had plagued the F-100 from the outset. If Gray was to even have the chance to implement his merger plans, he had to finesse an engine whose potential for loss was every bit as great as that which powered Boeing's 747.

The F-100 was a joint Air Force–Navy program. The Air Force needed an especially powerful engine for its F-15 fighter interceptor fighter bomber, whereas the Navy sought an updated power plant for its F-14B long-range interceptor. Unlike the F-111 project, combined procurement for the F-100 made so much sense that the military willingly awarded initial development contracts to both Pratt & Whitney and General Electric in August of 1968. This "fly-before-you-buy" program, in contrast to earlier and less rational procurement policies, stipulated that each contractor provide a joint selection board with a demonstrator engine. After actual testing of the prototypes, the company whose engine triumphed would obtain the military's business.[11]

Pratt & Whitney won the competition and, in April of 1970, received a contract— the military engine plum of the 1970s and early

1980s— to formally develop the power plant crucial to its long-range success. The decline in military prime contracts begun in 1969 had not reversed itself. In fiscal 1970, United's subsidiary did over $540 million worth of military business, but that was $350 million less than in 1968; without the enormous F-15 commitment (the Air Force intended to build 1388 planes), Pratt & Whitney would remain in trouble.[12]

To develop the F-100, Pratt & Whitney initially received a $275 million research-and-development contract. When, among other problems, the initial compressor design was found to be deficient, that budget was increased by $122 million in 1971, with the Air Force and Navy each contributing $55 million and the remainder coming from Pratt & Whitney's profits.[13] But escalating development costs were common on new engines and, in any case, the military considered itself financially protected because of ironclad guarantees built into its contract. According to the "correction of deficiency" clause, Pratt & Whitney was obligated to correct problems "by virtue of design, workmanship or material."[14]

Despite the company's strenuous efforts to improve the engine, serious deficiencies remained. In February of 1973, an engine with a second compressor design failed the Air Force's 150-hour qualification test. In March, on another test try, an F-100 blew up on the test stand. Pratt & Whitney was grounded because under the fly-before-you-buy regulations, the Pentagon could award no production contract until the F-100 had successfully completed its mandated tests.

The Air Force, however, was reluctant to further delay a program that was already significantly behind schedule. And Pratt & Whitney, if it failed to proceed with production, might retard Harry Gray's merger plans. To provide a universally satisfactory solution, the Air Force followed the example set by Admiral Billy Moffett in the twenties: it authorized a new test. To ensure that the F-100 passed, it lowered the performance specifications by approximately 25%, reducing the required speed from Mach 2.3 to Mach 2.2.[15]

When General Benjamin Bellis, head of the F-15 program, and General Otto Glasser, Deputy Chief of Staff for Research and Development, appeared before the House's Armed Services Committee, they attempted to minimize the significance of the test changes. Nevertheless, it become clear that once Bellis had accepted the lowered performance as satisfaction of Pratt & Whitney's requirements, the government had no choice but to give Pratt & Whitney the go-ahead.

In defending the general's actions, Secretary of the Air Force Robert Seamans reluctantly acknowledged that Bellis had dug a hole for the Air Force and the government. He rejected the suggestion that the contract be renegotiated: "As Pratt & Whitney was well above target, we could anticipate a new target price which would probably match the ceiling of the current contract. That would mean a considerable cost increase."[16] Seamans reassured Congress that the correction-of-deficiencies clause still applied to any problems uncovered in the modified 150-hour endurance test and, therefore, still protected Washington's interests.

Despite Seamans's assurances, some committee members remained unconvinced. General Bellis had admitted that his test changes exposed the government to a "minimum risk program"; in for $93.6 million, Washington might well be risking much, much more. "I think that is what is disturbing," said Congressman Les Aspin of Wisconsin. "It. . . has happened before, when somebody makes a judgement that the risks are minimal and goes ahead with the production before we have it all worked out, and we have gotten into trouble. So that is why we have fly-before-you-buy. And that is why it is so disturbing to see that fly-before-you-buy is being breeched in this case."[17]

General Glasser, while agreeing in theory with the gist of fly-before-you-buy, argued that the government's risk was minimal. Indeed, he informed Congress that "I have been in the development business as long as anybody around, and I wish to goodness that the problems that I have had in the past on other programs had been as trivial as this one is technically."[18]

In any event, Congress had no option but to fund the program. Pratt & Whitney was temporarily out of the woods with an engine crucial to its financial well-being and to Harry Gray's long-term plans.

Another Engine, Another Problem

With the F-100 program underway. United's prospects were looking up when the comptroller general suggested that Pratt & Whitney, with the Navy's approval, had improperly used $87 million of government research funds to develop the JT-9 engine. The money had been obtained through the insufficiently publicized Independent Research and Development Program, which pertained to work "initiated by a contractor without any direct government involvement." No prospective purchase was anticipated, only the contention that the independent research would eventually benefit the military.[19]

Although contractors theoretically were obliged to demonstrate the application of their research to the government's needs, Admiral Hyman Rickover testified that Independent Research and Development proposals generally underwent no more than a "window dressing review." Defense Department officials, he maintained at a 1982 hearing before the House's Committee on Appropriations, "readily acceded to almost any contractor claim of relationship to the military."[20] In Pratt & Whitney's case, the comptroller general contended that, because funding for an engine designed for commercial use had not been carefully reviewed, the military received nothing for its $87 million. Pratt & Whitney, therefore, should return to the public treasury the money improperly authorized by the Navy.

Harry Gray refused. In a letter to the General Accounting Office dated July 13, 1973, he insisted that the government sponsored research and development "which was not covered by a contract, grant or other arrangement." In other words, United did have contracts to sell engines to Boeing, but no contract to develop the engine it planned to sell. "Under our commercial contracts for the sale of the JT9D engines," Gray continued, "our customers did not sponsor the development of the engine." The Independent Research and Development money merely helped United develop the finished product for which it did have contracts.[21]

The comptroller did not appreciate Gray's technically accurate reading of the regulations. Citing the intent of the law, he repeated that the use of public funds for commercial development was specifically forbidden; Gray's argument that the Boeing contracts excluded development meant that the public should pay for preparation of the engine but relinquish any share in the eventual profits.

The comptroller had a valid point; then again, so did Harry Gray, whose interpretation ultimately won the day. Gray did not return the $87 million; United was not forced to write off yet more losses on an already disastrous engine; and the public never was informed of this heavily funded program that consistently nourished private companies like United Aircraft.

Chairman, President, Chief Executive Officer

In United Aircraft Corporation's 1972 annual report, a photograph of Harry Gray, president and chief executive officer, appeared beside that of Chairman Arthur Smith; William Gwinn, the former chairman, had retired that year. By 1973, both Smith and his image had disappeared. A smiling Harry Gray, depicted next to a huge globe and a copy of "Who's Who," informed stockholders that, after thirty-eight years of distinguished service, Mr. Smith had retired but would remain on the company's board. To fill the vacant post, "The directors assigned me the additional duties of chairman effective January 1, 1974."[22]

A month after assuming his new responsibilities, Gray took advantage of his total control to exchange preferred stock for his first acquisition: Essex Industries. Essex made wire, which it sold to the telephone, automobile, appliance, and electrical industries. It produced no weapons and did little business with Washington, but in 1973 it earned a $40-million net profit on sales of $845 million. As Gray noted, Essex "provided additional momentum to United's drive to extend its market interests to a growing breadth of industrial and non-governmental opportunities."[23]

With Essex on board, Gray turned to the commercial aviation sector in hopes of generating sales equivalent ot the Air Force's order for 799 F-15s. To that end, he established the Delaware-based United Aircraft Credit Corp., a subsidiary designed to extend credit to less-than creditworthy customers. If Gray failed to subsidize the shaky airlines, after all, Pratt & Whitney would ultimately share their troubles. Lending money seemed preferable to closing factories and laying off the workforce.

Military sales were idling at United's other subsidiaries. Sikorsky, Norden, and Hamilton-Standard together averaged approximately $200 million annually in 1972 through 1974 in military prime contract awards,[24] but Gray hoped to boost sales further through aggressive marketing efforts. Sikorsky, for example, could enter military helicopter competitions worth billions of dollars to the winner. Gray pushed Sikorsky's staff to produce equipment superior to that offered by Boeing, Bell and Hughes.

At the end of 1974, Gray reported a net income of $105 million on sales of $3.3 billion, which amounted to 3 percent on sales and 12 percent on net worth.[25] "United," he boasted in the annual report, "had achieved the best operating results in its history." The increase in sales did come from the acquisition of Essex and a huge increase in Pratt & Whitney's military prime contract awards ($828 million in fiscal 1974 compared with $374 million in fiscal 1973[26]), but it was a fact that Harry Gray was responsible for increasing military sales while simultaneously reducing United's overall dependence on Washington through purchases like Essex.

To emphasize changes made and changes planned, Gray requested that stockholders approve a new corporate name; the "aircraft" label masked "the corporation's widening world of industrial and commercial horizons." The name "United Technologies," on the contrary, had everything. The word "United" formed "an identifying bridge with the achievement of the past," whereas "technologies" underlines the subsidiaries' one common demoninator. To emphasize the corporation's commitment to airplane engines and magnet wire, helicopters and space, Gray even displayed a new logo: "a graphic disc symbolizing the broadening technological interests in the corporation."[27]

The name change was approved in April of 1975. By May 1, the United Technologies Corporation was a reality, and by August 1, Harry Gray had made tentative plans to pursue a billion-dollar addition to its technological base. But this time the target fought rather than merged.

Otis vs. United

In July of 1975, Felix Rohatyn of the investment banking firm of Lazard Freres and Company called Edward Hennessy to suggest that the Otis Elevator Co., was vulnerable to a takeover. Hennessy informed Harry Gray, who, on the basis of a reading of Otis's annual report and a few questions about Otis's products, gave Hennessy the okay to pursue the merger.

That was it— nothing more occurred until early September.

The absence of any detailed studies surprised the Otis lawyer who later questioned Gray about the origins of his merger offer.

Mr. Axinn asked, "Did he show you any documents or studies, memos or anything like that?" Mr. Gray replied, "No. He at one time showed me an annual report, and I don't recall if it was that time or not, whether it was the annual report that has the photographs of very tall buildings on the front."

Axinn then asked if Gray had had "any reaction to the concept of studying Otis." "A favorable one," Gray answered. "It was a name that I had heard a lot about, a respected company. I have always had reasonably favorable recollections of using the service. I have never been stuck in an Otis elevator, for example. I just had a generally positive feeling." "Didn't you see any advantages whatsoever in discussing the combination so far as Otis was concerned?" Axinn inquired. "We didn't see any advantages,"[28] Gray replied. The only goal was to help United, and to that end Gray and Hennessy helicoptered to New York on September 8 for breakfast with Felix Rohatyn. En route, Gray studied documents provided by Hennessy, including another copy of Otis's annual report and, as Gray put it, "an array of figures setting forth a combination of common shares and cash in order to preserve a tax-free transaction."

At that point, United intended to offer a "40/30/30 package plan": it would buy 40 percent of Otis's common stock for cash, exchange 30 percent of its own common stock for Otis common stock, and issue convertible preferred stock for the remaining 30 percent of Otis. According to Gray's sworn deposition in later litigation, "the thesis was to find a package that would be attractive to all shareholders alike. We do not have a universality of interest among shareholders. Some people want cash dividends, some people want appreciation; it depends what they want."[29]

Of particular import was the selling price offered to those shareholders interested in a quick cash dividend. Neither Otis's management nor its shareholders were likely to accept United's bid unless it was substantially higher than the existing market price of Otis's stock, which was then selling for $29 per share. Hennessey's research indicated that Otis's projected earnings were, in Gray's words, "kind of clouded." Substantial losses were possible in nonelevator operations, and share price had been declining since the late sixties. Therefore, Gray concluded, "considering the earnings, the book value, the public statements about the prospects for the future, $37 a share seemed like a good price."[30]

Because Rohatyn argued that Otis would demand a price greater than its book value, Gray approved a $39 figure to give the investment banker some bargaining leverage. Rohatyn's next step was to arrange a meeting for the United officers with Ralph A. Weller, chairman and chief executive officer of the New York-based Otis Elevator Co. When Rohatyn had first informed Weller of United's possible bid earlier that summer, Weller displayed no interest in merger negotiations, claiming that the market price of Otis was too depressed. But, he added, Otis would talk to anyone who understood that a price of $45 to $50 per share would be necessary to appease Otis's stockholders.[31]

Whether or not Rohatyn had quoted different prices to each party, by the time Gray, Hennessy, Weller, and Rohatyn met for their September 11 luncheon, the "floor price" had jumped from a maximum of $37 to a minimum of $42 per share. Throughout the three-hour meal, Weller steadfastly maintained his distance. After receiving Grays's assurance that "United was not interested in going forward in the negotiations without the warm good wishes of Otis's management,"[32] Weller promised to contact Gray after the next meeting of Otis's board of directors on September 24.

In that meeting, Otis's management concluded that "no substantial advantage could accrue to Otis through merger negotiations with United." The board instructed Weller to inform United that, until such time as Otis solved its internal problems, they would pass on further discussions.

When Weller called Gray the next day, however, instead of announcing the board's decision, he asked about a rumor coming out of Otis's New York office that United intended to make a cash tender offer for Otis's shares.

Gray denied that accusation but asked Weller about a rumor he had heard: that a foreign company wanted to buy Otis.

Weller, in turn, assured Gray that this was not so. Even if it were true, moreover, the board had moved to reject any merger bid at this time. Gray expressed his disappointment but reiterated that United "had no action underway for a cash tender, and if we ever change our mind and ever do anything differently, I will call you and let you know."[33]

Eight days later, on October 2, Weller learned from Felix

Rohatyn that United had, in fact, changed its mind. Alarmed by persisting rumors of another company's interest in Otis, Gray had decided to create an obstacle by buying as much as 20 percent of Otis's stock in the open market. Though this move wouldn't eliminate other parties, it would certainly make them think twice before entering the competition for Otis Elevator Co.

While Weller resisted the idea of Gray owning any substantial block of Otis stock, he did feel more secure after reading the message from United in the October 13 issue of Barron's: "On the margin: Rumor of the week: United Technologies plans to acquire Otis Elevator. Answer of the week: It's news to us. United Technologies."

This Barron's item was among the United statements that Judge Pierce was to call "not only misleading but false" during subsequent hearings in federal district court. Hennessy argued that, when the Barron's reporter called, he had told the truth about United's having no merger plans. But, as the Judge believed Hennessy was well aware, Hennessy's disclaimer would not appear until the next issue of the periodical, which meant that readers would be told United had no designs on Otis at the very time United was slated to bid for at least 20 percent of Otis's stock. As the judge interpreted United's action, the company feared that, if Otis's stockholders knew a merger bid was in the offing, they might hold back their stock in anticipation of the tax-free advantages of a simple stock swap. With no knowledge of the potential merger, on the other hand, many stockholders were apt to do exactly what Harry Gray wanted: sell their stock at once, enticed by the $13 premium United was offering.[34]

On the same day he was being reassured by the Barron's piece, Weller received a summons from Felix Rohatyn to meet him and Gray. Weller, who had no intention of refueling any fires, refused. Later that afternoon, after a more insistent call from Rohatyn, he relented.

When the men met at Weller's apartment, Gray announced that he had called a special meeting of United's board the following morning. Though he had not yet determined the specifics of his offer, he definitely expected to make a bid for some percentage of the Otis stock. He was only telling Weller because he considered it polite.

Weller responded equally politely but, despite the threat of a public bid, he offered no help to Gray. If he was going to lose control of his own company, he meant to go down fighting.

The following morning, United's directors were informed for the first time of Gray's new acquisition plan. The board had little time to closely consider the material placed before them; indeed, Hennessy had prepared only a "rough draft" of the proposed offer for their consideration. When later asked in hearings about the amount of discussion that had taken place among the board members, Gray responded, "not much."[35]

Although Gray had only decided "what price to recommend to the board while shaving before the board meeting," he easily obtained the directors' approval to purchase up to 4.5 million shares of Otis, at $42 a share, as long as stockholders turned in at least 2.5 million shares —over 30 percent of Otis's total.[36]

When United made its offer public on October 15, shareholders learned the share price. Paragraph 12 of the offering statement said that "United had not formulated any plan or proposal to merge the company with United."

Weller, who never believed this statement, asked stockholders not to tender their shares; whereupon Otis decided to sue for an injunction against United's offer based on Gray's allegedly false statements about his intentions.

Meanwhile, on October 17, Gray made what he termed a "sales pitch" to Weller and the Otis board of directors, describing what United could do for Otis in terms of research and development. More specifically, he promised that a merger could give Otis a technological edge over Westinghouse, its primary competitor. Though his speech failed to impress the Otis board, it did assist the Otis lawyers in their suit against United. If Gray's statement was true and United Technologies indeed could help Otis, Westinghouse might be eliminated from the market. The merger would be denied, they hoped, because of too much "synergy" between Otis and United.

When Gray was questioned about such synergy, he admitted that he'd mentioned technical assistance in his sales pitch but denied saying anything that hinted of monopoly. On the contrary, when asked to tell the court how United's technology would be of advantage to Otis, Gray said, "We have no specific knowledge that it would be. We have done some conjecturing that it might be. . .but we do not know that we can do it better or. . . more cost-effectively."[37]

On the issue of false and misleading statements as a basis for denying the merger, the judge sided with Otis. Based on his opinion that Gray and Hennessy had withheld vital information from Otis's stockholders and that "Only an entirely new offering statement could cure the problem presented here," Judge Pierce issued an injunction against United on October 29.[38]

Gray quickly did as he was asked. In its new proposal, United offered to buy any and all Otis shares; instead of the $37 previously considered a maximum reasonable bid, moreover, he boosted the offer to $44 for each share of Otis common stock.

After a last-ditch effort to locate a white knight armed with sufficient cash, Ralph Weller and his board accepted the inevitable: the takeover of Otis by United Technologies. Ralph Weller became Harry Gray's employee, and United happily added $1.2 billion to United's sales figures. At this point, Gray had created a company with potential sales of over $5 bilion and decreased the government's share of United's business to 33 percent. While he was negotiating the Otis sale, Pratt & Whitney had arranged to rewrite its F-100 contracts in a manner that assured a substantial (yet risk-free) growth in government business.

Harry Gray was a man who had his cake and would be able to eat it too. His new acquisitions supposedly protected him from one customer he simultaneously rejected and embraced: the United States government.

Capping United's Corporate Liability

By mid-1975, the F-100 was once again in trouble. Although the revised performance test had permitted Pratt & Whitney to enter production in 1973, the engine continued to present so many problems that the Navy finally withdrew from the joint procurement program. On the assumption that compromise was preferable to paying for a power plant whose costs increased while its deficiencies remained, the Navy instead settled for an available but less powerful Pratt & Whitney engine.

In 1974, the cost of an F-100 had nearly doubled, soaring from

$1.4 million to $2 million each. Even more upsetting was its performance. As *Aviation Week* reported on May 12, 1975, "the engine was still having compression stall problems" and actually required an in-flight shutdown; in fact, the military had assigned a team of thirty Air Force and NASA experts to locate the source of the difficulties. Clearly, the F-100 program was proving to be anything but the "minimum risk" predicted by General Bellis when he altered the qualification tests.[39]

Not surprisingly, Pratt & Whitney officials were growing anxious about the guarantees they'd given the Air Force when they opted to proceed with a program that ultimately meant the manufacture of one thousand engines. The Air Force estimated that, for the first seventy-two engines built as a result of the test change, Pratt & Whitney would spend $7 million of its own funds to fulfill the terms of the comprehensive correction-of-deficiencies contract that made it responsible for any design, material, or workmanship problems. For a company that had only recently spent a quarter billion dollars to repair the 747's engines, the F-100's troubles once again threatened disaster. If the government, like Juan Trippe, demanded fulfillment of contractual obligations, United might have to follow Harry Gray's words: "Once we have signed a contract with the government to make certain products for them, we have got to complete that contract. If it was a bad contract, that is too bad. You have got to complete it."[40]

Unless, that is, you can convince the government to erase the clauses that promise loss to the manfacturer. In mid-1975, Pratt & Whitney filed suit against the government to recover $37.6 million spent on producing the F-100's. And, as long as the company and the military were discussing the F-100, Pratt & Whitney once again brought up the guarantees mentioned in the initial contract. Now that the military had decided to ignore the performance problems and buy even more engines, it was high time to link settlement of Pratt & Whitney's cost clauses to the new order— and to the old correction-of-deficiencies clauses.

Colonel R. Steere, Deputy for Propulsion, Aeronautical Systems Division, told Congress that "there were repeated negotiations during several years over the prospect of relieving Pratt & Whitney" of the correction-of-deficiencies clause. So, because "the contractor was obviously concerned that we might, in fact, present a risk that was just totally unacceptable," colonel Steere testified that the Air Force had placed "a cap on Pratt & Whitney's liability." On September 18, 1975, while Harry Gray was occupied with the purchase of Otis to minimize his risks on defense business, the government was helping United Technologies by changing the F-100 correction-of-deficiencies clause to a supply warranty.[41]

"The only thing we relinquished at that point in time was a claim for deficiency of design," Colonel Steere told Congress. Which, of course, was exactly what Pratt & Whitney wanted. According to the revised contract, Pratt & Whitney paid for engine changes up to $20 million; above that the government stepped in where a businessman like Juan Trippe had been too cost-conscious to tread.

In justifying his decision to eliminate the design guarantee just as the F-100 was enduring compressor stall problems, Colonel Steere faced some tough questions. "How many flying hours did the Air Force have on this engine at the time the warranty was cancelled or an agreement made with the company?" asked Committee on Armed Services member Senator J. James Exon of Nebraska.

Colonel Steere guessed that "we were back in the 100,000, 125,000 flight-hour range at that time." But when the senator insisted on a precise figure for the record, the actual number of hours flown totaled only 14,754. Though that was about eight times less that the colonel recollected, it was nearly seventy times less than Robert Carlson, Pratt & Whitney's president, estimated was necessary to make a military gas turbine engine reliable. According to Carlson, "wisdom far more experienced than mine" indicated a military engine needed "about one million hours" of flight before it could be judged dependable.[42]

Yet, after fewer than fifteen thousand F-100 flight hours, the military relinquished its design guarantee and immediately entered into a component-improved program that eventually committed the government to over $500 million on F-100 improvements through 1982. Thanks to pliable procurement officers, Pratt & Whitney had been able to make a bet despite the high risks involved and, once it was apparent they'd drawn a losing hand, transfer the cards and the risks to the government. Had the company used its monies to repair the engine, a company-funded component-improvement program might have wiped out all of United Technology's net profits— $353 million— for 1976 and 1977. It was infinitely preferable to publicly laud the free enterprise system while making double profits on the F-100: on both the manufacture of the engines and on the cost-plus fixed-fee component-improvement program. With Juan Trippe, who meant business, United had been forced to slug it out line by contract line. With the federal government, United merely used erasers.

By eliminating "bet-your-company" risks, Washington gave Harry Gray a clean slate plus the assurance of substantially increased defense busineess only weeks before the new United Technologies Corporation achieved synergy through the purchase of Otis Elevator Co. As Harry Gray told stockholders in the 1975 annual report, "Your corporation is making highly satisfactory progress and we are pleased to report its results in this first annual report bearing the new corporate name. In the troubled economic climate of 1975, which brought setbacks for some companies, United moved strongly ahead."[43]

Old and New Business

Because of Securities and Exchange Commission regulations, Harry Gray began the new year by issuing a report on an old practice: United Technologies had made nearly $2 million worth of questionable payments to foreign sales representatives or to representatives of foreign governments or foreign corporations. In pursuit of orders, United had "induced" people to buy its products, but had restricted such activities to nonindustrialized areas of the world where "commissions" were a regrettable but understandable fact of underdeveloped business life.[44]

Soon afterward, he issued a detailed policy statement accompanied by procedures designed to implement and enforce his ban on bribes. Although Gray meant what he said, the bribery problem reappeared in the even more damaging form of "co-production agreements," which were not confined to back rooms or dimly lit alleys. NATO nations openly demanded a slice of the production pie, and sometimes went a step farther— they refused to buy your products unless you also bought theirs.

Licensing other countries or companies to produce its products was no novelty to United—consider Germany and BMW in 1934 or Japan and Mitsu in 1940. And "offset agreements" dated back to Tom Hamilton's acceptance of Persian rugs instead of money for Pratt & Whitney power plants. But as the oil crisis illustrates, what changed in the seventies was the international business balance. Along with the less developed nations, formerly weak industrialized countries suddenly had unprecedented control over their own— and United Technologies'— future. To sell their wares to the NATO nations, United and its competitors were obliged to accept terms that would have been unthinkable for Fred Rentschler or even Horace Horner. NATO nations refused to buy F-16's, for example, unless they manufactured 40 percent of the dollar value of the 348 airplanes specified. When Belgium held out for a sweeter deal, the federal government assisted the aviation industry by agreeing to buy $30 million worth of machine guns from the Belgian company Fabrique Nationale.[45]

Despite its mammoth size, United could not avoid making production payments to these foreign companies to obtain the orders necessary to keep its factories in profitable operation. Ironically, the company's technologically sophisticated products severely limited its markets; any terrorist could buy a machine gun, but only industrialized nations or oil-rich sheiks had the wherewithal to purchase planes costing, in the aggregate, hundreds of millions of dollars.

In addition, United's competitors— General Electric, Rolls Royce, the French Societe Nationale (SNECMA) d'Etude et de Construction de Moteurs d'Aviation— offered engines just as advanced as its own. Fred Rentschler had cornered the market in his time because the Wasp and J-57 were the best of a small lot. In 1976, though the number of manufacturers was still modest, no one engine eclipsed the others; thus competition was based on factors such as financing, or buying Belgian, or keeping the military-industrial base of nations besides America in good working order.

Two months after he'd made public United's bribery problems, Gray's new Otis subsidiary admitted its own "questionable payments" of $5 to $6 million in 1971 through 1975.[46] Again, Gray acted to eliminate bribery and again he found himself facing a far-reaching situation that, in being corrected, threatened another United subsidiary's long-term profitability. Otis did roughly 50 percent of its business abroad, in places where cities were expanding rather than deteriorating as they were in many parts of the United States. A major reason the company resorted to bribery was the industrial competition in world markets. In Switzerland, Schindler built fine elevators; in Germany, Siemans did the same; and in Brazil, where a local company built an elevator factory, Otis followed suit. Although Otis lost money in Brazil, relinquishing a larger share of the market to locals might mean losing out in those countries where the company's products would most likely find advancing rather than declining markets.[47]

For Otis, like Pratt & Whitney, was caught in the changing balance of world power, competing at home and abroad on increasingly difficult terms. As a result, United Technologies showed a steady but hardly spectacular growth in sales and profits during the first half of the 1970s. Subtracting the $2 billion contributed by Essex and Otis from United's 1976 sales left $3.1 billion. Harry Gray had inherited a $2 billion corporation in 1971, and a substantial part of the increase at the old company came from the F-100 order. In 1973, Pratt & Whitney held $354 million worth of military prime contracts; in fiscal 1976, the figure was $897 million ($713 million of that from the Air Force), which amounted to an increase of $543 million. Sikorsky and Hamilton-Standard's military prime contracts remained steady, while the losses at the Florida research facility were roughly balanced by gains at Norden and at United Technologies' Sunnyvale, California, operation. As for space activities, United's share of NASA funding actually had dropped from $39.6 million in fiscal 1974 to $17.4 million in fiscal 1976. Although United intended to increase its share of NASA contracts, as in other areas, it had to compete with capable peers for a space budget that remained roughly the same from 1970 through 1976.[48]

To Harry Gray, who titled the 1976 annual report "Five Years of Achievement," United "had evolved from an aerospace company into a high-technology designer, manufacturer and management organization holding a leading position in the power (Pratt & Whitney), industrial (Essex, Otis) and systems (Sikorsky, Norden, Hamilton-Standard) areas." United strengths— its technological expertise and the ability to advance, apply, and manage it successfully— had allowed the corporation to prosper. In the years ahead, Gray predicted, stockholders would see more growth in United's share of the defense budget, more growth in the industrial sector and, most important, more growth through acquisition.

Harry Gray aimed for $10 billion in sales by 1985, the year in which he was scheduled to retire. Considering the sluggish performance of the companies he already owned, his only means of achieving his goal was to purchase other large companies, including, it seemed, the one that built the nuclear reactor for a plant at a then-obscure site called Three Mile Island.

Babcock-Wilcox

Babcock-Wilcox was a large industrial company that concentrated on coal-fired boilers and nuclear steam systems for electric utilities. To cut dependence on oil in general and OPEC in particular, coal and nuclear power promised the best long-range solution. Three years into the oil crisis, Babcock-Wilcox made a product everyone wanted; 1976 sales totaled $1.7 billion.

After an intensive study of Babcock-Wilcox as a merger prospect, Harry Gray used a back-door approach in late February, 1977. When Babcock-Wilcox agreed to discuss research and development concepts with United, Gray had his foot in the door. He talked acquisition "in the hope that a friendly merger could and would be affected."[49]

Like Ralph Weller at Otis, Babcock-Wilcox's management considered Gray's proposal, decided they shared none of his enthusiasm for a merger, and told Harry Gray he was an unwelcome suitor.

As usual, Gray refused to take no for an answer. Once again he reversed his policy that "we would like to join with people who want to join us,"[50] gave Babcock-Wilcox a copy of his tender offer before it became public and, when Babcock-Wilcox's bosses again refused, he publicly announced an offer, on March 29, 1977, to buy all Babcock-Wilcox's outstanding stock at $42 share— a 20 percent premium on the previous day's closing market price.[51]

Gray had intended to entice stockholders into a quick sale for a hefty profit. But, before stockholders could react, Babcock-Wilcox sued United Technologies in Ohio's federal district court. Although the suit ostensibly addressed antitrust issues, it also gave Babcock-Wilcox's management time to seek a white knight. In the meantime, a federal injunction kept Harry Gray at bay.

After nearly five months, the court found no merit in Babcock-Wilcox's suit. The merger, it ruled, offered no threat of horizontal or vertical monopoly nor of eliminating potential entrants into the energy field. United was free to bid on Babcock-Wilcox if it still wanted this very reluctant partner.

It did. But so did Charles Graves of J. Ray McDermott & Co., a New Orleans-based company that enjoyed huge profits in its offshore oil-drilling operations. While the court case dragged on, Graves had purchased roughly 10 percent of Babcock-Wilcox stock on the open market, thereby raising the stakes so much that, when Gray reentered the bidding, he found himself offering $58.50 per share— nearly double the market price in March and $8 per share more than even optimistic analysts considered a fair price.[52] But Gray wanted the company so desperately that, in the auction-room atmosphere of this hotly contested takeover, he went higher still, to nearly $60 per share. When Graves countered with a bid of $65, even Harry Gray had had enough. "When the bidding got to $62.50, it was time to get off the bus," he told Business Week. "The ride wasn't worth that much."[53]

In analyzing his setback, Gray claimed he never bid more than the company's actual or potential value based on a detailed analysis of Babcock-Wilcox's strength and potential. A stock analyst, moreover, had convinced him that President Carter's ambitious plans for coal promised a boon for companies like Babcock-Wilcox. Taking Gray at his word, an observer must question the quality of the advice he received. Carter's energy bill never materialized, and when Babcock-Wilcox's reactor at Three Mile Island produced a near meltdown, the firm sustained losses that, added to the incredible costs of the stock, made Gray's defeat United Technologies' victory. Harry Gray's own summary of the Babcock-Wilcox episode is particularly apt: "Sometimes you have to be born lucky. I'd rather be lucky than smart."[54]

Luck, however, has been known to run out. Gray's eagerness to expand through acquisition made him the prisoner of a process he could never completely control. At one price a company could look attractive, but once the bidding began, matters could quickly get out of hand. According to *Fortune* magazine, "The contest for Babcock-Wilcox generated $6.3 million for the investment bankers." And Felix Rohatyn, Gray's representative on the Otis deal, noted that acquisitions "are a very seductive business. The fee you get when a deal closes compared with the minimum processing fee when it doesn't is so enormous. The incentives to do a deal are much too great. There is a dangerous push, conscious or un-conscious, to get the thing to go."[55]

More Military Business

Unable to acquire more companies in 1977, Harry Gray had to rest content with substantial growth on the weapons front. At Pratt & Whitney the F-100 program was in high gear: Military prime contracts for fiscal 1978 grew by over $610 million. The enormous increase in Air Force orders alone accounted for United's increase in 1978 sales. But, if the Air Force helped Pratt & Whitney, the Navy and especially the Army gave unprecedented business to Sikorsky Aviation.

Despite its sterling reputation, Sikorsky averaged only $123 million per year in prime military contracts from 1970 to 1975; in 1976 the company manufactured only 19 production aircraft. Considering the dismal military and commercial prospects, "it became questionable how long Sikorsky could stay in that mode,"[56] said Robert Daniell, the company's president.

To avoid disaster, Sikorsky was counting on its new helicopter. Developed with United's and the government's funds, the S-70 incorporated advanced "fly-by-wire" technology and extensive fiberglass construction. It looked like a winner, and it flew like one when Sikorsky beat Bell and Hughes for two of the most lucrative helicopter contracts in United States history.[57]

Like its helicopters, Sikorsky's sales went soaring straight up. For the Navy's LAMPS (Light Amphibious Multi-Purpose System) program, the company was commissioned to build two hundred helicopters at an estimated $3.7 million each, over $700 million worth of assured Navy business. And for the Army's UTTAS (Utility Tactical Transport Aircraft System) program, Sikorsky was scheduled to produce over one thousand helicopters at $4.8 million each. This meant almost $5 billion worth of business; in fiscal 1978, the booming sales at Sikorsky were brightening United's overall picture. Between fiscal year 1976 and 1978, the company increased its military prime contracts by almost 400 percent, from $110.5 million to $389.9 million.[58]

Despite these huge increases, military sales continued to decline as a percentage of United's sales because, even after so many rejections, Harry Gray was still intent on diversification. In July of 1978 he succeeded in buying Ambac (American Bosch Magneto Corp.), a manufacturer of diesel fuel injection systems as well as medical, scientific, and environmental equipment. Ambac, which was founded in 1906, made $16 million in net profit based on sales of $225 million. Gray won this prize by paying $220 million, $92 million above the "underlying net assets" of the company. While awaiting a bonanza to redeem his faith in Ambac along with his stockholders' money, he used his financial training to good advantage. The $92 million was written off as "goodwill" to be paid over twenty-five years. Stockholders were to be satisfied with the knowledge that his costly goodwill was part of their equity in United Technologies— Gray had decided to include Ambac's extra cost in the corporation's net worth.[59]

Gray's brand of accounting wizardry led Abraham Briloff, the City University of New York's Emanuel Saxe Distinguished Professor of Accountancy, to a harsh conclusion: the figures seemed "absurd on their face." Briloff, who was unable to "warrant the booking of an enormous $92 million blob of goodwill," was especially distressed by the prolonged writeoff period. United had used a ten-year span to write off $3 million of goodwill in the Otis merger. Now, without fanfare, Gray prolonged the Ambac amortization by 60 percent.[60] Gray had seized the opportunity to make United's short-term outlook far better than it actually was or, more accurately, better than if Ambac's goodwill had been written off before the twenty-first century.

In response to critics like Briloff, Gray denied he was "playing with accounting mirrors." The cost of goodwill was fair, given Ambac's sales, for their investment, stockholders received dividends plus an increase in United's equity.[61] Had United devoted the purchase price of Ambac to a new company, "We'd have spent a lot more than that on an after-tax basis to get it." (Then again, a new company making a new product might yield a far greater return than Ambac's projected 9 to 15 percent. The real question was how to warrant the $92 million, given Ambac's relatively low yield.)

Considering that the equity increase came from the goodwill, Gray's justifications failed to convince Briloff. Nevertheless, Gray expected to repeat his Ambac strategy with other purchases— even one as large as the Carrier Corp.

Once again employing what Wall Street analysts term the

"bear hug" approach, Harry Gray pursued yet another company that had no intention of joining United Technologies. Carrier, which had been based in Syracuse, New York, since 1937, was a hometown outfit with impressive balance sheets; on 1978 sales of $2.1 billion, it netted $95 million from its air conditioning and heating equipment operations. In 1972, Carrier had concluded its own first acquisition (Inmont, a manufacturer of inks and automotive paints), and neither Melvin Holm, Carrier's chairman, nor the people of Syracuse were inclined to witness years of their work pass into the hands of an absentee owner, especially one with a reputation as a "takeover artist."[62]

Undaunted by the heated opposition he immediately encountered, Gray purchased Carrier stock on the open market for $28 per share (a 40 percent premium on the then market price) and, by late 1978, held 47 percent of its common stock. That would have clinched the deal, except that United once again was called before the federal district court.

This time the allegation was the antitrust violations a Carrier-United merger was sure to occasion. Desperate to escape Gray's clutches, Carrier suggested "that it would receive significant competitive advantages if it were able to offer its heating and air conditioning equipment in a package deal with an Otis Elevator and Hamilton-Standard management system."

Although this might seem a reasonable supposition, United produced evidence that easily convinced the New York court that no packaging advantage was to be gained from the merger. As the judge noted, "GE and Garnett Airesearch were engaged in the manufacturing of both jet engines and air conditioners. The availability of jet engine technology had not catapulted these two companies into the forefront of the air conditioning business."[63]

Carrier's request for an injunction was denied because "the injury which Carrier might suffer if a preliminary injunction was denied was remote and speculative in nature. On the other hand, the injury which United and Carrier shareholders would suffer if a preliminary injunction were granted was real and immediate."[64]

Investors had a perfect right to profit from Harry Gray's tender offer and, like good capitalists, United's and Carrier's shareholders made the most of their golden opportunity. Trading stimulated stock prices and Harry Gray's purchase price for a company that came, by United's own admission, with no significant synergy benefits. Gray paid over a billion dollars, $263 million more than the value of Carrier's underlying net assets. Reviewing Carrier's three-year earnings average, Abraham Briloff saw enough money to pay the dividends required by the preferred stock (United had paid part of the sales price with $540 million of preferred stock). However, he found "nothing (probably less than nothing) left over to pay for the interest cost (actual or imputed) incurred on the $459 million paid to acquire the 49 percent bought for cash."[65]

If Briloff had a point, Gray and his accountants ignored it. They wrote off the $263 million over twenty-five years, once again adding the extra cost of the merger to the equity of United's shareholders. In under a year Gray had increased the value of his corporation with $355 million of goodwill.

Briloff asked, "How much water can a balance sheet hold before it sinks?" Harry Gray responded by buying yet another very expensive company.

Gray's new target was Mostek, a manufacturer of RAMS— random access memory semiconductors — founded and, in 1979, still operated by L.J. Sevin. Although Mostek had had its ups and downs, (losing over $1 million in 1975, its long range prospects look-ed promising in 1979. The company had earned over $9 million in 1978, and with semiconductors so vital to future technology, Mostek looked like a company worth buying if Gray could get it at a reasonable price.)[66] Sevin had spurned Gray when he first came courting in 1978 and, a year later, still wanted to remain indepen-dent. His problem was William Ylvisaker of Gould Incorporated, who had purchased 20 percent of Mostek's stock and meant to get the rest. Enter Harry Gray in the unfamiliar role of white knight. Within a matter of weeks Sevin relinquished his independence for a very sweet deal. As Juan Trippe did with planes. Sevin watched his suitors accelerate the price of his stock and then, when one dropped out of running, tried to extract additional concessions from the "winner."

For stock selling at $24 per share, Gould had opened with a bid of $42. Gray countered with $50. Sevin asked for more; Gray offered $55 and Gould came back in at $61. When Gray responded with $62, Gould dropped out and Sevin assented to the merger, especially after Gray agreed to put up $200 million for Mostek's expansion.

This was Gray's most audacious purchase of all. Not counting the extra $200 million, Gray paid $234 million more than the value of Mostek's underlying net assets. On United's books, the balance sheets showed (on a *pro forma* basis) Mostek losing $19 million in 1978 and $11 million in 1979.[67]

As with Babcock-Wilcox, Gray had entangled himself in a bidding war. To justify its inflated price, Mostek needed to contribute large profits as soon as possible. Otherwise, how could United's shareholders receive a fair return on their investment with twenty-five-year financing? Accountant Abraham Briloff's answer was "no way" —he found it "literally impossible to see even a glimmer of Mostek's presumptive earnings bonanza." United and its auditors were "playing with Silly Putty" rather than dollars, which they demonstrated once again by adding the extra $234 million that Mostek cost to stockholders' equity in United Technologies.

By the end of 1979, the acquisitions of Ambac, Carrier, and Mostek had cost United over $530 million in goodwill. From 7.5 percent of common stockholder's equity in 1978, the goodwill figure had jumped to 32 percent of equity of 1979.[68] That was a lot of water under the balance sheet, especially for a company about to drown in Mostek's red ink.

Japan's Chip Victory

Nobody saw them coming. Like his colleagues in the semiconductor industry, Mostek's Sevin never expected the Japanese to compete so aggressively and effectively. "They won the memory market," he admitted. "It was the thing we were all dreading. Here it had happened. Bang."[69]

Japanese semiconductor producers had appropriated a substantial share of the billion-dollar word market for 16K RAM's— a market America assumed it had locked in— by copying Mostek's 16K design, improving it, and selling it at a price far below American manufacturing costs.[70]

Aware that chip users preferred to assure a dependable supply through close relationships with manufacturers, the Japanese reasoned that once they'd attracted customers, they'd keep them. They were right. And the effect on companies like Mostek was devastating. Mostek's manufacturing costs were $1.40 for a chip that retailed at $5. When Japan started cutting prices, Mostek found itself selling 16K RAM's for anywhere from eighty cents to one dollar each. Although unit volume was up, at those prices Mostek was awash in a sea of red ink— one analyst placed United's 1981 losses from Mostek at $100 million.[71]

In the 1981 United Technologies annual report, Harry Gray blamed "overcapacity and the intense price erosion in the semiconductor industry." As of February 1, 1982, "the expected improvement in the semiconductor marketplace had not yet occurred, and the timing and rate of recovery was uncertain."[72]

Gray knew what he was talking about. His luck had run out, and he and Mostek (and United's shareholders) were in a battle that might require government intervention to bail out the semiconductor industry. Although American and Japanese chips were competitive in quality and price by August of 1982, analysts assumed that the Japanese were keeping a low profile, deliberately and temporarily, in fear of import restrictions. Once their fears subsided or they chose to compete despite the consequences, their American competitors might be selling chips below cost once again. Even more ominous for all was the prospect that huge American firms such as IBM and Western Electric, that made chips for internal use, would enter the semiconductor marketplace.

As of this writing, the situation remains too volatile to risk predictions of a final outcome. The only certainties are the huge and continuing losses at Mostek; according to United's third-quarter 1982 report, "Our Mostek subsidiary had made significant progress in reducing costs and developing new products, but Mostek continued to operate at a loss."[73]

Harry Gray had problems that extended beyond Mostek. Hard times in the automobile industry adversely affected Essex and Carrier. And in aviation, United Technologies faced its most serious challenge of all: A European consortium called Airbus Industries threatened to significantly reduce Pratt & Whitney's share of the commercial jet engine business.

Airbus and the Airlines

Despite ten years of diversification, United Technologies is still considered an aerospace corporation by magazines like *Forbes*. At least 40 percent of its business revolves about power (engines) or flight (helicopters). Of its research and development expenditures, its own $736 million and the government's $469 million in 1981 were devoted principally to its power and flight businesses; elevators and air conditioners received minute funding in comparison. As for profit, fully 67 percent can be attributed to United's power and flight operations.[74]

United needs planes as a human needs a heart. The corporation could die if its aviation activities were threatened. And in the late seventies, that is exactly what happened. Airbus not only was making planes, but it was making them without Pratt & Whitney engines.

Airbus, funded and controlled by France, West Germany, and Great Britain, was established in 1966— a time when, ironically, airlines were pleading for an aircraft smaller than the 747. Although Airbus was created to fill the need for a sensible ship, orders were not forthcoming when its planes rolled off the assembly line in 1974. Two years later, only thirty-eight of the A-300's had been sold, and it seemed that the Europeans once again had failed to penetrate the world market for commercial aircraft.[75]

And then, to many a capitalist's dismay, the oil cartel continued to raise fuel costs at the same time that stiffer competition for passengers resulted in so many empty seats that the carriers had to cut costs somehow— and immediately. Airbus provided the answer with the right plane at the wrong time for American manufacturers. By the end of 1970, more than three hundred of the fuel-efficient A-300's had been ordered. What's more, the new two-hundred-seat Airbus offeed direct competition to Boeing's new entries, the 757 and the 767.[76]

Boeing was Harry Gray's best customer, purchasing $781 million of engines in 1979, $967 million in 1980, and $681 million in 1981.[77] The decline came because of deregulation, because of recession (Boeing, as of October 1982, had not sold a 767 in fourteen months), and because Boeing no longer supplied only Pratt & Whitney engines.

As Gray told stockholders, "Historically it was common to new aircraft programs for only one engine to be selected for a given airframe." As on the 727 or the DC-9, customers "must buy the engine originally selected for that aircraft."[78] Historically, this engine policy translated into a virtual monopoly for Pratt & Whitney —fully 92 percent of the commercial jet engines produced in 1966 came out of East Hartford, Connecticut.[79]

But by 1978, the figure was 62 percent and dropping. General Electric (24.6 percent) and Rolls Royce (12.7 percent) had entered the market in a big way because "of an increasing tendency on the part of airframe manufacturers to offer their airline customers a choice of engines from competing suppliers."[80] This had occurred, at least at the outset, because of Boeing's problems with the 747. Boeing disliked its total dependence on Pratt & Whitney so it created a contest for engine orders on the 757 and 767. Pratt & Whitney won that competition, but Boeing (and Airbus) had learned a lesson they were unlikely to ever forget: by focusing competition on the enginemakers, they probably increased the engine's performance and, equally important, shifted a good deal of the financial burden onto the shoulders of companies like United Technologies. For Delta's engine order on the 757, the competition was "the toughest and the most unbelievable Delta had ever seen."[81] The industry's hunger for orders meant lower prices, generous financing terms, hard-and-fast guarantees, or all three.

In its statements to stockholders, United complained about the new competition but, since that was now the name of the game, stated its intention to play to win. When its UTC Credit Corporation committed over $800 million in loans to Pratt & Whitney engine customers, United became reluctant owner of the airlines' airplanes. United bought planes, leased them back to the airlines and, with luck, would recover its investment "plus an anticipated return."[82]

Whether that return would ever materialize, of course, is another matter.

Throughout 1982, the worldwide recession threatened many already-endangered airlines. And even in the event of an economic upturn, United would still face new competition from Airbus and General Electric— competition that could intensify if foreign governments subsidized attempts to sell planes at or below cost. There was no doubt that Pratt & Whitney had lost its monopoly on commercial airplane engines. This in turn meant fewer of the more profitable spare-parts orders and, in sum, lower profits. In the new climate of the eighties, the best engine coupled with the best bid won the orders for planes.

In the long run Harry Gray had no reason to panic. Of the $80 billion the world's airlines were expected to spend on aircraft in the eighties, Pratt & Whitney was bound to get a substantial share.

Besides, he could sidestep his persisting airline problems by substantially increasing his reliance on military business. Ironically, instead of United's new subsidiaries paying for declining markets in defense, defense was paying for declining markets in commercial aviation, in construction, in automobiles and, of course, in semiconductors.

The reason for diversification —too much government business— was shoring up the now-diversified company. The military was paying for the consequences of the recession— and the consequences of Harry Gray's furious bidding wars.

The F-100 and Equitable Competition

In 1980, defense business equalled 22 percent of United's total sales. By 1981, the figure had climbed to 28 percent and, as of January 31, 1983, 33 percent. In dollar terms, this translated into an additional $1.1 billion in 1981 and another $650 million in 1982. Through 1982, United's military sales had climbed to a whopping $4.5 billion.[83]

Part of this dramatic increase can be traced to Sikorsky, whose military sales passed the one-billion dollar mark in fiscal 1982. Despite a nearly 250 percent "cost growth" in its helicopter program, from $2.9 billion in 1976 to a projected $7.2 billion in fiscal 1982,[84] the Army and Navy anticipated larger orders through 1992, indeed Sikorsky's record was so good that the military awarded the company the first of its new multiyear contracts assuring Sikorsky of military business for many quarters to come.

At Pratt & Whitney, however, the mainstay of its profits, the F-100 program, is threatened by what Pratt & Whitney President Robert Carlson calls "inequitable competition." As Carlson sees it, "Pratt and Whitney has one military engine of consequence to build in the next ten years, and it's the F-100."[85] Pratt & Whitney is sitting "on a one-legged milk stool," which the Air Force is trying to kick down by allowing arch-rival General Electric to compete for $8.5 billion worth of engine orders on very unfair terms. Because General Electric's F-110 engine has far greater thrust than the F-100, Carlson argues that General Electric is likely to win any fly-off. To make the competition equitable, he is requesting Air Force funding for improvements in the F-100's thrust.

Carlson failed to mention that the Air Force's unhappiness with the F-100 prompted it to subsidize General Electric's F-110. According to William J. Perry, under secretary of defense, the service had "ended up with engines of excellent performance but of very poor reliability, durability, and maintainability."[86] General Electric's success in developing an alternative power plant put Pratt & Whitney at a decided disadvantage in the competition for the multi-billion-dollar engine order. After erasing its design guarantees in 1975 and spending over a half billion dollars of federal funds in its Component Improvement Program, Pratt & Whitney expects Congress to authorize still more money for increased engine thrust.

So far, Washington has come through. The Senate Defense Appropriations Subcommittee earmarked $64.2 million for Pratt & Whitney in September of 1982.[87] With congressional approval, the engine manufacturer will receive the funding to upgrade the F-100 while continuing to draw its allowance from the Component Improvement Program. But in a bold business move on December 3, 1982, Harry Gray may have avoided an engine fly-off after all; he personally delivered to the Pentagon a proposal that exemplifies the essence of the United Technologies Corporation.

Instead of the $8.5 billion previously cited for 2,285 new engines, Gray offered to save the Air Force a full billion dollars over five years. Adroitly exploiting seven years of experience with the taxpayer-funded Component Improvement Program, he ensured that United Technologies would still earn 18 percent on its investment.

Then to cap his bid, Gray offered an extended warranty on the new engines. Instead of two hundred hours or two years, he offered three hundred hours or three years. On the high-pressure turbine, he doubled the warranty period from five to ten years.[88] With this proposal on the table, the Air Force will be hard pressed to reject Gray's bid; and General Electric, with no experience producing its F-110, will be even harder pressed to devise an offer that approaches United Technologies' generosity.

Thus, as of December 1982, things are looking up for Harry Gray and his company. If he wins the five-year F-100 contract, he assures Pratt & Whitney of many hundreds of millions of dollars in earnings over the contract's span; he will have beat General Electric with a warranty on an engine that once had guarantees; and, using his military profits to ride out the recession, he will be freer than ever to pursue any appealing corporate commodity that may appear on the merger meat market.

EPILOGUE

The United Technologies Corporation ended 1982 by playing a key role in one of the most bizarre takeover struggles in American corporate history, a role which provides clues to both the future of the corporation under Harry Gray's stewardship as well as some of the implications of his actions in the larger context of American business.

On August 25, 1982, William Agee, Chairman of the Bendix Corporation, attempted to seize control of Martin Marietta, the aerospace manufacturing concern, by increasing his 4.5 percent stock holding in that company. Agee stood prepared to buy up an additional 45 percent of Marietta's outstanding shares for $43 apiece, a $10 premium over their market value at that time. Agee's total bid came to $1.5 billion. Martin Marietta's president, Thomas Pownall, was opposed to such a merger, but instead of applying the usual "shark repellent," Pownall entered a bid to purchase 11.9 million shares of Bendix —a controlling 50.3 percent— at $75 a share, an $18 premium over market price. Wall Street wags promptly dubbed this attempt to mutually engulf each other the "Pac Man Takeover."

However, the prospects for either corporation winning the struggle could be disastrous in terms of their respective debt to assets ratios; in short, both Bendix and Marietta were ready to risk financial suicide for the sake of standing their ground.

Both companies had placed themselves at a disadvantage when Harry Gray entered the picture. Allying himself with Pownall, the two devised a scheme wherein United Technologies would make a separate bid for the majority of shares in Bendix. Then, whether

United or Marietta came out the winner, they would divvy up control of Bendix between themselves.

In what some analysts have seen as a fatal loss of nerve, Agee then summoned a white knight of his own in the person of Edward Hennessy, Gray's former number-two man at United and now president of the Allied Corporation. Hennessy's tender offer for Bendix's stock was $85 a share — a whopping $28 over the market price. Moreover, even though Agee had managed to buy 39 percent of Marietta by this time, Hennessy and Agee agreed to let Marietta go its own way in their merger.

Everyone seemed to come away with something in this deal. Allied acquired Bendix, and, if Bill Agee had needlessly exposed himself to takeover, at least he made big stock profits when Allied paid so much for Bendix's shares. Thomas Pownall kept Martin Marietta independent for the time being. And again, the Wall Street investment bankers had a heyday in commissions which totalled in excess of $8 million. Curiously, only Harry Gray came away from the negotiating table empty handed.

After all the publicity and criticism (one Bendix director termed the battle nothing more than a "struggle between a few ambitious men"), United Technologies wound up with nothing. Harry Gray, moreover, had suffered a conspicuous defeat at the hands of his former associate, Edward Hennessy. Some analysts even suggested that Hennessy's satisfaction in winning the battle was doubled by his besting Gray.

But Harry Gray will persist in his merger attempts, for his program for United allows him little latitude from this acquisitive course. If he is to achieve his announced sales goal of $20 billion in 1985 when he is due to retire, he can only significantly boost United's $14 billion volume for 1982 by buying up more companies.[1]

Herein lie the lessons, but more importantly the questions that make this whole story of United Technologies significant, because the future of this corporation —and so many other large American corporations— is inextricably bound up with the future federal policies of this nation. As the realities of competition in a global economy continue to erode our security day by day, we may finally have to face the hard questions that have been so conveniently swept under the carpet time and again throughout this account of one corporation.

First, at least in United Technologies' case, investment decisions are made with little sense of business or social vision. Billions are spent to rack up larger sales in the service of larger sales. By Harry Gray's own sworn admission, synergy between buyer and seller is a peripheral consideration. The key factor is whether managements will get along, not whether their merger will generate discoveries and jobs for more Americans.

Can we continue to let such huge investments be made on such a narrow basis? Or should we follow the advice of Gray's banking associate Felix Rohatyn and demand that Washington channel investments where Federal agencies decide they are most necessary? So far, Rohatyn's suggestions relate to troubled industries like steel. But if the government has the obligation to help where trouble occurs, shouldn't it also have the responsibility to prevent problems before they arise? When a billion dollars is put on the line with nothing more than a cursory examination of an annual report —as in the case of Otis Elevator— shouldn't the government at least review investments with the careful deliberation that United Technologies failed to exhibit?

Second, at a corporation like United Technologies, it's not a question of whether the federal government is going to become involved. The American people have long been a full partner in United Technologies. But, at a time when politicians from both parties are suggesting that Washington give billions to commercial as well as defense industries, we must achieve a consensus about the terms, amounts and direction of Federal funding.

What are we going to do about profit? If the government funds new or old industries, and those industries make (as Fred Rentschler did) substantial amounts of money, does that money belong to the industrialists who made it? Or, does the public —which underwrote the investment— deserve part of the profits? For example, given its investment in research and development alone, the government could demand a part of United Technologies profits, and use those funds to upgrade pay scales in the military, which would make the service more attractive to those who leave it to collect higher salaries for doing the same work in the civilian sector.

Third, what responsibility does the government have for the industrial capacity —especially the military capacity— it creates? As United Technologies' story shows, the recent dramatic increases in the defense budget have substantially increased the defense side of the company's business. What happens if President Reagan loses the 1984 election? Is the Federal government obligated to keep United Technologies' machines running to the tune of four billion defense dollars a year? If the government says no, isn't it predictable that the executives who run United will seek abroad the customers they cannot get at home? And will we ever be able to guarantee that these foreign customers will always be friendly to America? We should not forget the lessons of Teheran in 1980.

Finally, and most important, even if we solve the problems of how Federal funds should be invested in industries and how potential profits should be handled, we are still faced with the problem that America has formulated no clear vision of its industrial or national defense future. Right now, billions are poured into national defense without enough consideration given to longterm impacts. Congressional committees debate the pros and cons of MX missile systems and B-1 bombers that will draw huge appropriations from the Federal treasury and monopolize the best scientific minds of many parts of the industrial sector in the development of new arms systems. Meanwhile, Japan, for instance, with a population half the size of the United States graduates five times as many scientists and engineers each year, and puts almost all of them to work developing superior commercial products for the world market. The budget drain exemplified by the F-100 alone belies the larger problem for America. For better or worse, we go about "business as usual" —business that continues to regard conglomeration as an acceptable form of growth— with the end result being troublesome products, a weak defense, and no social or business vision.

To get that vision, we need to root future Federal policy in the wise counsel of President Eisenhower, who said: "The relationship between military and economic strength is intimate and indivisible."[2] Each depends on the other, and the best way to build a strong America is to base our national security in a commercial economy able to compete fairly with any nation on earth.

America is a business civilization and in partnership with the government there is no reason why capital and labor cannot provide the long-range vision so essential to any revitalization of the troubled American economy.

NOTES

Prologue

1. For Rentschler's testimony, *see* U.S. Senate, Special Committee of Investigation of Air Mail and Ocean Mail Contracts, *Investigation of Air Mail and Ocean Mail Contracts*, 73rd Cong., 2d sess. 1934, pp. 1795–1828.

2. John Kenneth Galbraith, *The Affluent Society* (Boston: Houghton Mifflin, 1958) p. 124–30.

1. Right Company, Right Place, Right Time

1. On the number of airplanes built, *see Historical Statistics of the United States*, U.S. Department of Commerce, (Washington: Government Printing Office, 1957), p. 466; on the early companies, *see* Harold Mansfield, *Vision* (New York: Duell, Sloan and Pearce, 1956); Elsbeth Freudenthal, *The Aviation Business* (New York: Vanguard, 1940); Henry Ladd Smith, *Airways* (New York: Knopf, 1942).

2. On modern war, *see Makers of Modern Strategy*, Edward Earle Mead, ed. (Princeton: Princeton University Press); J.F.C. Fuller, *The Conduct of War* (New Brunswick: Rutgers University Press, 1961): on the planes, *see* Bernard and Fawn Brodie, *From Crossbow to Atom Bomb* (Indianapolis; Indiana University Press, 1973), pp. 177–78; on American attitudes, cf. William Tinsley, "*The American Preparedness Movement*", Ph.D. dissertation, Stanford University, 1939, pp. 150–51.

3. On Colonel Deeds, *see The Hughes Report: U.S. Justice Department, Report of Aircraft Inquiry, 1918.* Reprinted in U.S., Congress, House, *Expenditures in the War Department: Aviation, The Graham Report,* 66th Cong., 2d sess., H. Rept. 637 (hereafter cited as Hughes and Graham Reports). The material on Colonel Deeds comes from Hughes Report, pp. 82–87, and Graham Report, pp. 18–19.

4. *See* Arthur Sweetser, *The American Air Service* (New York: Appleton and Company, 1919), p. 48; *see also* I.B. Holley, *Ideas and Weapons* (New Haven: Yale University Press, 1953).

5. Sweetser, *American Air,* pp. 74–78; *see also The New York Times,* "First of All Airplanes," June 10, 1917, editorial.

6. *See* Hughes Report, esp. pp. 83, 87.

7. Hughes Report, esp. 103–9; *see also* Freudenthal, pp. 35–61; Smith, pp. 35–49.

8. Hughes Report, pp. 85–86; Graham Report, p. 18.

9. Graham Report, p. 10.

10. Hughes Report, p. 122.

11. Graham Report, p. 19.

12. *See* testimony of Paul Henderson, Former Second Assistant Postmaster General, in *Aircraft,* Hearings Before the President's Aircraft Board, vol. 4 (October 14, 15, 1925), pp. 303–18.

13. Charles Lindbergh, *We* (New York: Putnam's, 1927), pp. 190–91.

14. Smith, *Airways,* p. 84; Historical Statistics, p. 466.

15. *See* the *Aircraft Yearbooks* for 1923 and 1924 (New York: Aeronautical Chamber of Commerce), pp. 106–18, 112–21. Both these volumes are full of stories about the need for air safety and government regulation.

16. Cf. Admiral Moffett's testimony before the Morrow Board in *Aircraft,* vol. 1, (1925) pp. 194–210.

17. *See* Robert Schlaifer, *The Development of Aircraft Engines* (Cambridge: Harvard University Press, 1950), pp. 165–66.

18. Schlaifer, pp. 174–75; *see also* Eugene Wilson, *Slipstream* (New York: McGraw-Hill, 1950), pp. 30–31.

19. On Mitchell, *see* Burke Davis, *The Billy Mitchell Affair* (New York: Random House, 1968); *see also* by Mitchell's commander, General Mason Patrick, *United States In the Air* (Garden City: Doubleday, 1928). For the raid on New York, *see The New York Times*, July 30, 1921.

20. Davis, *Billy Mitchell*, pp. 192–223.

21. Eugene Wilson, *Kitty Hawk To Sputnik To Polaris* (Palm Beach: Literary Investors Guild, 1960), p. 41.

22. *See* the biography of Morrow by Harold Nicolson, *Dwight Morrow* (New York: Harcourt, Brace and Company, 1935). The discussion of the Morrow Board appears on pp. 280–87.

2.   A New Firm: Pratt, Whitney, Rentschler, and Mead

1. *See The Story of Pratt & Whitney, a Condensed History* (Pratt & Whitney, West Hartford, Conn. 1960); also, "From The Rear Cockpit," *Beehive, Summer, 1950; on Colt, see* Brian Keating, *The Flamboyant Mr. Colt* (Garden City: Doubleday, 1978); *see also* Horace Horner, "Hartford's Happy Heritage," speech given on June 19, 1952, to the annual dinner of the Hartford Chamber of Commerce. Mr. Horner was then president of United Aircraft.

2. *See The Pratt & Whitney Aircraft Story* (East Hartford, Conn.: United Aircraft Corporation, August, 1950), pp. 18–19; also Cary Hoge Mead, *Wings Over the World: The Life of George Jackson Mead* (Wauwatosa: The Swannet Press, 1971), p. 63.

3. *See* Horace Horner, *The United Aircraft Story*, Hartford, 1958, p. 7; The American Encyclopedia of Biography on Frederick Rentschler; *see also* Frederick Rentschler, *An Account of the Pratt & Whitney Aircraft Group, 1925–1950* (Hartford: privately printed) 1950, p. 10. The

introduction to this volume indicates that only one hundred copies of the book were published. I have a photocopy of one of the originals. Each of the originals is bound in black leather and the pages are outlined in what appears to be gold. The name of each recipient is stamped in gold on the cover of his or her copy (hereafter called Rentschler, *My Story*).

4. *See* Robert Schlaifer, *The Development of Aircraft Engines* (Cambridge: Harvard University Press, 1950), **pp.** 187–88; *Eugene Wilson, Slipstream* (New York: McGraw-Hill, 1950), pp. 54–55; Rentschler, *My Story*, p. 12.

5. Interviews with Mrs. George Mead; Mead, *Wings Over the World; see also* Leonard Hobbs, "The Aircraft Engine," *Beehive*, Summer 1954, pp. 3–10.

6. In his account, Rentschler neglects to mention the colonel. Oddly, Deeds' role is discussed in the company's official history, *The Pratt & Whitney Aircraft Story*. For the meetings in New Jersey I have relied on interviews with Mrs. George Mead. She recalls the encounters held in *her* home and vividly remembers the colonel's essential role. *See also Wings Over the World*, pp. 62–63.

7. *See* United Technologies 10k report for 1981, p. 14. The exact figure is $469 million.

8. *See* testimony of Rentschler before the Temporary National Economic Commission, 76th Cong., 1st sess., p. 9, pp. 3633–50, esp. p. 3641.

9. For a summary of the original agreement, *see* U.S. Senate, Special Committee to Investigate the Munitions Industry, Pt. 6, 1934, pp. 1537–38 (hereafter cited as the *Nye Hearings*); on the value of Rentschler and Mead's stock, *see* U.S. Senate, *Investigation of Air Mail and Ocean Mail Contracts*, Hearings Before a Special Committee On Investigation of Air Mail and Ocean Mail contracts, 73rd Cong., p. 4, 1934, p. 1814 (hereafter cited as *Air Mail Hearings*).

10. Mead, *Wings Over the World*, pp. 65–68; *Pratt & Whitney Aircraft Story*, p. 40. *See also* the early numbers of *Beehive*. The paper began in December of 1926, and they underline the camaraderie of the early months.

11. Wilson, *Slipstream*, p. 66.

12. Rentschler, *My Story*, p. 19.

13. *See* testimony of Chance Vought, Aircraft Hearings Before the President's Aircraft Board, October 15, 1925, vol. 4, pp. 1466–71. Rentschler's written statement appears on pp. 1471–74.

14. Wilson, *Slipstream*, pp. 66–67; For an overview of procurement in the military services, *see* Harold Margulis and Harry Yospe, *Procurement* (Washington: Industrial College of the Armed Forces, 1964).

15. For the Morrow Board quotes, *see Aircraft in National Defense*, Message from the President of the United States Transmitting the Report of the President's Aircraft Board, December 10, 1925, Washington, esp. p. 8 and pp. 26–29.

16. For a recent discussion of these points, *see* Robert Heilbroner and Lester Thurow, *Five Economic Challenges* (Englewood Cliffs: Prentice-Hall, 1981), especially pp. 76–77.

17. *See Mead, Wings Over the World*, pp. 75–78; *see also Pratt & Whitney Aircraft Story*, pp. 41–43. Another source of information is the many hours Mrs. Mead graciously spent with me.

18. *See* U.S. Congress, House, *Hearings Before the Subcommittee on Aeronautics of the Committee On Naval Affairs*, Delaney Hearings, 1934. Donald Brown's testimony appears on pp. 858–912. The information on the first contract is on p. 865 (hereafter cited as *Delaney Hearings*).

19. Nye Hearings, pt. 6, p. 1537.

20. Mead, *Wings Over the World*, p. 79; on "sobersides" *see* Eugene Wilson, *Kitty Hawk to Sputnik to Polaris* (Palm Beach: Literary Investors Guild, 1960), p. 2; *see also* the company's eulogy to Rentschler in *Beehive*, Summer 1956, pp. 2–5.

21. Wilson, Delaney Hearings, pp. 742–63; the remark about the Wasp appears on p. 754.

22. Brown, Delaney Hearings, p. 865.

23. Wilson, *Slipstream*, p. 71; on the Navy's appropriations, *see* U.S. Congress, House, *Report of Select Committee of Inquiry into Operations of the United States Air Services*, appx. B, December, 14, 1925, p. 15; also Navy Five-Year Aviation Program, Public Law 422, 69th Cong., H.R. 9690, 1927.

24. Brown, Delaney Hearings, p. 865; Wilson, *Slipstream*, p. 71; for an overview of profits, *see* H.S. Hensel and Richard McClung, "Profit Limitation Controls Prior to the Present War," *Law and Contemporary Problems*, Vol. 10, 1943–44, pp. 187–214; *see also* Richard Osborn, Background and Evolution of the Renegotiation Concept, in J. Fred Weston, editor, *Procurement and Profit Renegotiation*, (San Francisco: Wadsworth, 1960), pp. 13–42.

25. Francis Spencer, *Air Mail Payment and the Government* (Washington: Brookings 1941), pp. 29–39; *see also* Henderson, Air Mail Hearings, 1934, p. 4, p. 1462.

26. On the abuses, *see* "U.S. Aviation and the Air Mail," *Fortune*, April 1934, pp. 85ff, esp. 140.

27. Harold Mansfield, *Vision* (New York: Duell, Sloan and Pearce, 1956) pp. 66–78 Rentschler, *My Story*, pp. 21–22; on the mail plane, *see Pedigree of Champions: Boeing Since 1917* (Seattle: Boeing Company, 1977), p. 18; Douglas Ingells, 747: *Story of the Boeing Super Jet* (Fallbrook: Aero Publishing Company, 1970), pp. 29–31

28. Wilson, *Slipstream*, pp. 76–77.

29. *See* Donald Brown, Statement of Views of the United Aircraft Corporation Pertaining to the Formulation of a National Policy Concerning the Munition Industry, published as pt. 6 of Nye Hearings, 1934, pp. 1599–1609, esp. p. 1601. When Brown wrote this statement he was president of United Aircraft.

30. On research and development funds *see* Brown, Delaney Hearings, p. 911; on the Hornet, *see Wings Over the World*, p. 83, and *Pratt & Whitney Aircraft Story*, p. 52; on the plant changes, *see Beehive*, February, 1928, pp. 16–19.

31. On Ponzi, *see* Arthur Leff, *Swindling and Selling* (New York: Free Press, 1976), pp. 61–76; on Florida, *see* Frederick Lewis Allen, *Only Yesterday* (New York: Harper & Row, 1931), pp. 225–40; on Ford, *see* Warren Sloat, *1929* New York: Macmillan, 1979), p. 41.

32. Herrick's comments on Lindbergh appear as a foreward to Charles Lindbergh, *We* (New York: Putnam's 1927); for the greeting in New York, *see The New York Times*, June 14, 1927; for a recent biography of Lindbergh, *see* Leonard Mosley, *Lindbergh* (Garden City: Doubleday, 1976); on the stock market, *see* Allen, *Only Yesterday*, p. 248; on Seaboard, *see* C. Morris and S. Smith, *Ceiling Unlimited* (New York: Macmillan, 1953), p. 281.

33. Rentschler, *My Story* p. 28; Brown, Delaney Hearings, pp. 870–71; "Plant Rearrangement," *Beehive*, February 1928.

34. On the competition question, *see* Charles Gragg, "Marketing Problems in the Aviation Industry," *Harvard Business Review*, 8: 4 (July 1930), pp. 490–500, esp. 493.

35. On profits and percentages—Army, Navy, and commercial *see* Brown, Delaney Hearings, p. 905.

36. G.R. Simonson, *Economics of the Aircraft Industry*, Ph.D. Dissertation, University of Washington 1959, p. 19; *see also Aviation*, October 5, 1929, p. 711.

37. Brown, Delaney Hearings, p. 880.

38. *Beehive*, February 1928, p. 19.

39. Ralph O'Neill, *A Dream of Eagles* (Boston: Houghton Mifflin, 1973, pp. 24–104.

40. Mead *Wings Over the World*, pp. 94–99.

41. On Boeing, *see* First Annual Report of the United Aircraft and Transport Corporation, 1929, pp. 42–43; on profits, *see* offering statement for stock of Boeing Airplane and Transport Corporation, *The New York Times*, November 1, 1928, p. 37.

42. Brown, Delaney Hearings, p. 905.

43. Cf. Robert Sobel, *The Great Bull Market* (New York: Norton, 1968); *see also* Arthur Stone Dewing, *Financial Policy of Corporations* (New York: Ronald, 1953), 5th ed.

3.   The United Aircraft and Transport Corporation

1. *See* testimony of Joseph Ripley, U.S. Congress, *Hearings Before a Subcommittee On Banking and Currency*, 72nd Cong., 2d sess., pt. 6, 1933, pp. 2324–43, esp. p. 2327 (hearafter cited as Banking Hearings).

2. Cf. M.R. Werner, *Privileged Characters* (New York: Robert M. McBride, 1935), pp. 450–51; *see also* Warren Sloat, *1929* (New York: Macmillan, 1979).

3. Banking Hearings, p. 2327.

4. *See* Ripley's testimony U.S. Congress, Senate, Special Committee On Investigation of Air Mail and Ocean Contracts, 73rd Congress, 2d sess., pt. 5, 1934, p. 2133 (hereafter cited as Air Mail Hearings).

5. The ad appears in *The New York Times*, November 1, 1928, p. 37.

6. Banking Hearings, p. 2332.

7. On Ripley's profits, *see* Banking Hearings, p. 2337; on National City's, *see* Air Mail Hearings pt. 4, p. 2124; on the list of friends, *see* Air Mail Hearings, pt. 4, pp. 2133–35; on the application to list, *see* Banking Hearings, p. 2332.

8. *See* U.S. Senate, *Investigation of Munitions Industry*, Special Committee to Investigate the Munitions Industry, pt. 6, September 17, 18, 1934, pp.1538–39 (hereafter cited as Nye Hearings); *See also* Rentschler's testimony before Air Mail Hearings, pt. 4, pp. 1800–1801.

9. For general information, *see* "Hamilton Standard: The Story of a Company and Its Products," as told in excerpts from *Beehive*.

10. *See* Rentschler, *My Story*, p. 27.

11. *Ibid.*, p. 27.

12. On the sixty-five thousand shares, *see* Ripley, Air Mail Hearings, pt. 5, p. 2166.

13. *See The Corporate History of United Airlines and Its Predecessors and Subsidiaries, 1925–1945* (Chicago: Twentieth Century Press, 1953) p. 159, fn. 19; *see also* Ripley, Air Mail Hearings, pt. 5, pp. 2167–68.

14. *See* William Boeing's testimony at Air Mail Hearings, pt. 5, pp. 2259–60; on Boeing's original purchase, *see* pp. 2250–51.

15. *See* Ripley, Air Mail Hearings, pt. 5, pp. 2127, 2161; *see also* Rentschler's testimony before Air Mail Hearings, pt. 4, p. 1801.

16. *See* letters of Philip Johnson, president of United Air Lines, in *Commercial and Financial Chronicle*, April 24, 1934, p. 2594.

17. Cf. Henry Ladd Smith, *Airways* (New York: Knopf, 1942) pp. 138–39; *see also.* Frank Taylor, *High Horizons* (New York: McGraw-Hill, 1951), pp. 50–51.

18. On Sikorsky, cf. Robert Bartlett, *Sky Pioneer* (New York: Scribner's, 1947), pp. 86–87; *see also* Frank J. Delear, *Igor Sikorsky* (New York: Dodd, Mead, 1976, rev. ed.).

19. Rentschler, *My Story*, p. 28; on the stock, *see Moody's Industrial Manual*, 1929, p. 1453.

20. *See* Eugene Wilson, *Slipstream* (New York: McGraw-Hill, 1950), pp. 154–55.

21. *Ibid.*, pp. 160–61.

22. *See* the first Annual Report of the United Aircraft and Transport Corporation, p. 8; *see also Beehive*, December 1929, vol. 3, pp. 4–7.

23. This quote is taken from a 1934 article by Donald Brown, then president of United, in *Aerodigest*, December 1934, p. 15ff.

24. For a description of the plant, *see* Moritz Kahn, "Aircraft and Engine Factory Layout." *Aerodigest*, January 1936, pp. 20ff. Mr. Kahn was one of the factory's principal architects.

25. *See* Eugene Wilson's testimony before U.S. Congress, House, Subcommittee on Aeronautics of the Committee on Naval Affairs. The Delaney Hearings, House of Representatives, 1934, p. 749 (hereafter cited as Delaney Hearings)

26. *See* "Curtiss-Wright: Warrior," *Fortune*, September 1938, p. 80.

27. On air mails, *see* United Air Lines Corporate History, p. 309; on Pratt

& Whitney, *see* Delaney Hearings, p. 905; on Hamilton-Standard, *see* Delaney Hearings, p. 652; on Vought, *see* Delaney Hearings, p. 749.

28. *The New York Times*, April 4, 1930.

29. Smith, *Airways*, pp. 138–40; Taylor, *High Horizons*, pp. 50–55; United Air Lines Corporate History, pp. 86–87; *The New York Times*, March 27, 1930.

30. United Air Lines Corporate History, p. 87.

31. Taylor, *High Horizons*, p. 53.

32. *Ibid.*, pp. 53–4.

33. *See* testimony of Colonel Paul Henderson, then a United vice president, in Air Mail Hearings, pt. 4, pp. 1471–72; on revenues from passengers, *see* United Air Lines Corporate History, p. 309; for an overview of the new law, *see* Francis Spencer, *Air Mail Payment and the Government* Washington: The Brookings Institution, 1941), pp. 40–56.

34. *See* The Boeing Corporation, *Pedigree of Champions* (Seattle: 1977), p. 21.

35. United Air Lines Corporate History, p. 290.

36. *Ibid.*, pp. 112–13.

37. Douglas Ingells, 747 (Fallbrook: Aero Publishers, 1970), pp. 48–52.

38. Rentschler, *My Story*, p. 30.

39. Carrie Hoge Mead, *Wings Over the World: The Life of George Jackson Mead* (Wauwatosa: The Swannet Press, 1971) p. 151.

40. Ingells, 747, p. 56.

41. Richard Hubler, *Big Eight* (New York: Duell, Sloan, and Pearce, 1960), pp. 34–35.

42. *See* "Success in Santa Monica," *Fortune*, June 1935, p. 83.

43. *See Flight Plan For Tomorrow, The Douglas Story, A Condensed History* (no date); Hubler, *Big Eight,* pp. 34–45; on the militarized 247, *see Pedigree of Champions,* p. 28.

44. United Air Lines Corporate History, p. 309; *see also* William Barclay Harding, *The Aviation Industry* (New York: Charles D. Barney, 1936), pp. 16, 24.

45. United Air Lines Corporate History, p. 309.

46. On Sikorsky and Trippe, *see* p. 523. *See also* Wilson's *Slipstream,* pp. 175–76. *See also* the extraordinary long interview given by Eugene Wilson in 1962. It runs to over nine hundred pages and is available from the Columbia University Oral History Project.

47. Wilson, Oral History, p. 523.

48. *See* testimony of Raycroft Walsh, then president of Hamilton-Standard, before Delaney Hearings, p. 653–58.

49. On the move from Pittsburgh, "Hamilton-Standard Story," *Beehive see* Walsh, the Delaney Hearings, p. 658; on Caldwell, pp. 62–64.

50. On Pratt & Whitney's profits, *see* Donald Brown's testimony at Delaney Hearings, p. 905; on number of engines sold, *see* Brown's testimony before Nye Hearings, p. 1511.

51. *See* "Profit Limitation Controls Prior to the Present War," *Law and Contemporary Problems,* 10 (1943–44), p. 201.

52. Brown, Delaney Hearings, p. 905.

53 *See* introductory statement of the Pratt & Whitney Aircraft Division of United Aircraft in Responding to Supplemental Questionnaire. House Naval Affairs Investigating Committee no. 6, 1942. On p. 1, the statement says that, since military and commercial support were insufficient the company "intensively campaigned" the early thirties' export market.

54. *See* Answers to Question 10 of Supplemental Questionnaire no. 6, House Naval Affairs, 1942. These are actual balance sheets of the corporation as a whole and for each of the subsidiaries. They are not

paginated. They do, however, indicate sales, customers, and net profits for the last four months of 1934 through the first three months of
1942.

55. *See* Wilson, Oral History, pp. 496, 626; *see also Time,* October 5,
1936, p. 65.

56. *See* Joseph Barr, *The Time of My Corporate Life* (Palm Beach:
Literary Investors Guild, 1978), p. 23. Barr was, for many years, president of United's export operations.

57. Rentschler's letter appears in Nye Hearings, p. 1585.

58. Hamilton's letter appears in Nye Hearings, p. 1584.

59. *See* Elsbeth Freudenthal, *Aviation Business* (New York: Vanguard
Press, 1940), p. 146; on what Rentschler and Hamilton did or did not
know about Hitler, *see* Nye Hearings, p. 1584. Hamilton writes on
March 15, 1933, that "Germany's determination to have an Air
Force, as previously recorded, is now taking definite form rather
rapidly."

60. *See* Nye Hearings, p. 1445; on the number of Corsairs, *see* pp.
1465–66.

61. Nye Hearings, pp. 1488–90, 1550–51.

62. For the guano deal, *see* Nye Hearings, pp. 1565–75.

63. See United's 1933 Annual Report.

64. For a copy of the letter, *see Commercial and Financial Chronicle,*
April 14, 1934, pp. 2593–94.

65. *See* Arthur Schlesinger, *The Coming of the New Deal* (Boston:
Houghton Mifflin, 1965), pp. 450–51.

4. Investigations: The Black, Delaney and Nye Committees

1. *See* "U.S. Aviation and the Air Mail," *Fortune,* April 1934, pp.
156–158ff; Arthur Schlesinger, *The Coming of the New Deal* (Boston:

Houghton Mifflin, 1965), pp. 446–55; M.R. Werner, *Privileged Characters* (New York: Robert McBride, 1934), pp. 380–433; Henry Ladd Smith, *Airways* (New York: Knopf, 1942), pp. 214–27.

2. "U.S. Aviation," p. 156.

3. Elsbeth Freudenthal, *The Aviation Business* (New York: Vanguard, 1940), pp. 306–307.

4. Mead's testimony appears in U.S. Congress, Senate, pt. 4 of *Investigation of Air Mail and Ocean Mail Contracts*, Hearings Before a Special Committee On Investigation of Air Mail and Ocean Mail Contracts, 73rd Cong. 2d sess., 1934, pp. 1848, 1855, 1856 (hereafter cited as Air Mail Hearings).

5. For Charles Deeds' testimony, *see* Air Mail Hearings, pt. 4, p. 1707.

6. For William Boeing's testimony, *see* Air Mail Hearings, pt. 5, p. 2285.

7. Smith, *Airways*, pp. 240–42; *see also* Francis Spencer, *Air Mail Payment and the Government* (Washington: Brookings Institution, 1941), p. 54.

8. For Brown's testimony, *see* Air Mail Hearings, pt. 6. This whole volume keys on Brown, esp. pp. 2349–52.

9. *See* Charles Kelly, Jr. *The Sky's the Limit* (New York: Coward-McCann, 1963), p. 92–94; *see also* Smith, *Airways*, pp. 249–51; Schlesinger, *The Coming of the New Deal*, pp. 450–51; *Fortune*, April, 1934, pp. 155–56.

10. Frederick Rentschler, *An Account of the Pratt & Whitney Aircraft Company, 1925#1950* (Hartford: privately printed), p. 32 (hereafter called Rentschler, *My Story*) *see also* Eugene Wilson's long interview with the Columbia University Oral History Project, 1962, p. 554.

11. Smith, *Airways*, p. 255.

12. *Ibid.*, p. 256.

13. Schlesinger, *The Coming of the New Deal*, p. 452.

14. *See The Corporate History of United Airlines and Its Predecessors and*

Subsidiaries, 1925–1945 (Chicago: Twentieth Century Press, 1953), pp. 173–75.

15. See *Commercial and Financial Chronicle*, April 24, 1934, p. 2594; the *Chronicle* reprinted the letters United's executives sent to stockholders. The letters were signed by Philip Johnson, then president of United Air Lines.

16. See United Air Lines Corporate History, p. 178; on the profits *see Moody's Industrial Manual, 1934*, p. 2757.

17. U.S. Congress, House, Subcommittee on Aeronautics of the Committee on Naval Affairs. The Delaney Hearings, 1934, pp. 1472, 1477.

18. Cf., "Profit Limitation Controls Prior to the Present War," *Law and Contemporary Problems*, vol. 10, 1943, p. 203.

19. *See* U.S. Congress, Senate, Investigation of the Munitions Industry, Special Committee to Investigate the Munitions Industry, September 17, 18, 1934, pt. 6, p. 1509 (hereafter cited as the Nye Hearings).

20. H.C. Englebrecht and F.C. Hanighen, *Merchants of Death* (New York: Dodd, Mead, 1934), p. 250; *see also* Charles Beard, *The Devil Theory of War* (New York: Vanguard, 1936).

21. Manfred Jonas, *Isolationism In America* (Ithaca: Cornell University Press, 1966), p. 145.

22. Wilson, Oral History, p. 660; Rentschler, *My Story*, p. 43.

23. Brown, Nye Hearings, pp. 1601; *see also* Donald Brown, "Export Volume and Its Relation to Aviation Progress and Security," *Aerodigest*, December 1934, pp. 15–18.

24. Elton Atwater, *American Regulation of Arms Exports* (Washington: Carnagie Endowment, 1941), p. 211; *see also* Richard Leopold, *Growth of American Foreign Policy* (New York: Knopf, 1966), pp. 504–5.

25. *See* the balance sheets provided by United for the parent operation and each of the subsidiaries. The material, with no pagination, was

presented to the House Naval Affairs Investigating Committee in 1942.

26. Rentschler, *My Story*, p. 32.

27. *See* Irving B. Holley, Jr., *Buying Aircraft: Material Procurement For The Army Air Forces* (Washington, D.C.: Office of the Chief of Military History, Department of the Army, 1964), pp. 113–31, esp. 113–16, 127.

28. *See* William Barclay Harding, *The Aviation Industry* (New York: Charles D. Barney & Company, 1936), p. 6.

29. Wilson, Oral History, pp. 622–23.

30. Eugene Wilson, *Slipstream* (New York: McGraw-Hill, 1950), p. 193; *see also* Oral History, p. 623.

31. *See* testimony of Clark MacGregor, vice president of United Technologies, in U.S. Congress, House, Subcommittee On Trade, Committee on Ways and Means, July 1978, p. 102.

32. Wilson, Oral History, p. 660; *see also,* letter from Charles Deeds, then president of United Aircraft Exports, to the secretary of state. The letter is dated June 9, 1936, and Deeds says " Chance Vought are extremely anxious to proceed with the fabrication of this material. Their shop had recently been closed due to lack of work, but. . . ." (My copy of the letter was obtained from the National Archives. The file is under the Office of Arms and Munitions Control, Department of State file no. 711.00111, Armament Control/145/Military Secrets [hereafter cited as Purport Files]).

33. Wilson, Oral History, p. 663–64 a summary of the Rentschler conversation appears in United Argentina file, dated April 3, 1936, in National Archives; Purport Files, entry no. 7½.

34. Wilson, Oral History, p. 664; *Slipstream*, p. 189–90.

35. On the losses, *see* the balance sheets presented to the House Naval Affairs Investigating Committee, 1942.

36. *Ibid.*, balance sheets for Hamilton-Standard.

37. Wilson, Oral History, p. 614; *see also* Frank J. De Lear, *Igor Sikorsky: His Three Careers In Aviation,* rev. ed. (New York: Dodd, Mead, 1976), pp. 168–73.

38. Balance Sheets, Naval Affairs Investigating Committee.

39. *See The Pratt & Whitney Aircraft Story* (East Hartford, Conn.: United Aircraft Corporation, August, 1950) p. 127; Wilson, Oral History, p. 742; *Slipstream,* p. 216.

40. Wilson, Oral History, p. 743.

41. *Newsweek,* December 25, 1937, pp. 10–11; on attitudes toward bombing, *see* Robert Batchelder, *The Irreversible Decision* (New York: Macmillan, 1961).

42. Purport Files, United Aircraft Shipments to Japan. (I am working from the summary files. The Japanese file which includes copies of the correspondence is the only file the National Archives was unable to locate. All the other material on United Aircraft is still in the State Department files.)

43. *Ibid.,* Purport Files, no. 18.

44. *Ibid.,* no. 34.

45. *Ibid.,* no. 39.

46. *See Hartford Courant,* January 15, 1939, p. 1.

47. Wilson, Oral History, p. 862.

48. Wilson, Oral History, pp. 862–63; Rentschler, *My Story,* pp. 34–38.

5.   The Fortunate Circumstance: World War II

1. Eugene Wilson, *Slipstream* (New York: McGraw-Hill, 1950), p. 218.

2. On Hamilton's saving the company, *see* Rentschler's letter to Thomas Finletter, September 25, 1947. Finletter was then head of President Truman's Air Policy Commission, and Rentschler told him

that United was "literally held intact through the French and later the British purchases. . . ." *See also* the statement of Eugene Wilson kept by the Truman Investigating Committee in 1942. Writing about United Aircraft, Wilson said that "the work of years was threatened when salvation came in the way of orders from France" the letters can be obtained from the records kept by the Truman Library.

3. Eugene Wilson, interview with Columbia University Oral History Project, 1962, pp. 746–47.

4. My copy of the French Contract was obtained from the National Archives, Diplomatic Branch; United's file no. 711.00111.

5. My copy of the letter was obtained from the National Archives. *See* file no. 711.00111, under "Germany."

6. On the various propeller agreements, *see* material submitted to the House Naval Affairs Investigating Committee in 1942, listing all licenses granted by United and dates the agreements were terminated. On Pratt & Whitney's new plant, *see* Jay P. Auwerter, "Pratt & Whitney Expands," *Aviation*, July 1940, p. 39.

7. *See* 1939 Annual Report.

8. Wilson, Oral History, pp. 750–54; *see also Slipstream*, pp. 221–28. On Morgenthau's role, *see* Irving Holley, *Buying Aircraft: Material Procurement For the Army Air Forces* (Washington, D.C.: Office of the Chief of Military History, Department of the Army, 1964), pp. 252–53.

9. Wilson, Oral History, pp. 754–55; *Slipstream*, pp. 224–28.

10. Hamilton's commissions were reported to the House Naval Affairs Investigating Committee in 1942.

11. *See* Donald Ross, *An Appraisal of Prospects for the Aircraft Manufacturing Industry* (New York: White Weld, 1940), p. 5.

12. *See* General Hap Arnold, *Global Mission* (New York: Harper & Row, 1949) pp. 172–73; Tom Lilley, Pearson Hunt, J. Keith Butters, Frank Gilmore, and Paul Lawler, *Problems of Accelerating Aircraft Production During World War II* (Boston: Division of Research, Harvard Business School, 1946), p. 14; Holley, *Buying Aircraft*, p. 230.

13. Max Hastings, *Bomber Command* (New York: Dial, 1979), p. 46; *see* J.M. Spaight, *Air Power and the Cities* (London: Longmans Green, 1930); *see also* Spaight, *Bombing Vindicated* (London: Bles, 1944).

14. Robert Batchelder, *The Irreversible Decision* (New York: Macmillan, 1962), p. 172.

15. Hastings, *Bomber Command*, p. 106.

16. Carrie Hoge Mead, *Wings Over the World: The Life of George Jackson Mead* (Wauwatosa: The Swannet Press, 1971), p. 196; *see also* Eliot Janeway, *Struggle For Survival* (New Haven: Yale University Press, 1952); Donald Nelson, *Arsenal of Democracy* (New York: Harcourt, Brace and World, 1946); Bruce Catton, *The War Lords of Washington* (New York: Harcourt, Brace and World, 1948).

17. On this period, *see* J. Carlyle Sitterson, *Aircraft Production Policies Under the National Defense Advisory Commission and Office of Production Management,* Historical Reports on War Administration: War Production Board, Special Study no. 21, Washington, D.C. 1946, pp. 22–49.

18. *Ibid.,* pp. 30–31.

19. *Ibid.,* p. 39.

20. Holley, *Buying Aircraft,* pp. 294–300.

21. Sitterson, *Aircraft Production Policies,* pp. 40–44; Holley, *Buying Aircraft,* pp. 297–98; Lilley, *et al., Accelerating Aircraft Production,* pp. 32–41.

22. Janeway, *Struggle For Survival,* p. 164.

23. *Moody's Industrial Manual,* 1945, p. 2420.

24. United Aircraft's 1940 Annual Report, p. 7.

25. *See* balance sheets presented to the House Naval Affairs Investigating Committee, 1942.

26. Wilson, Oral History, pp. 758–59; *see also Slipstream*, pp. 229–31.

27. Rentschler, *My Story*, p. 43; on Ford, *see* Charles Sorenson, *My Forty Years With Ford* (New York: Harcourt Brace) p. 273–300; "United Aircraft," *Fortune*, March 1941; *The Pratt & Whitney Aircraft Story*, pp. 127, 132.

28. Wilson, Oral History, pp. 660, 701, 772; on the denial of Colonel Deeds' role, *see* Henry Ladd Smith, *Airways*, (New York: Knopf, 1942) pp. 134, 420.

29. For Rentschler, *see* Frederick Rentschler, *An Account of the Pratt & Whitney Aircraft Company, 1925–1950* (Hartford: privately printed) 1950, p. 44 (hereafter called *My Story*); for Wilson's remark, *see* Oral History, p. 772.

30. Wilson, Oral History, p. 770; *see also* Navy's authorized history of these events in Robert Connery, *The Navy and Industrial Mobilization in World War II* (Princeton: Princeton University Press, 1951), pp. 266–92, esp. 270; *see also* U.S. Congress, Senate, Investigation of the National Defense Program, *Renegotiation*, Rept. no. 440, pt. 2, 80th Cong., 2nd sess., February 20, 1948. Both these sources confirm Wilson's statements about the results of renegotiation. One last point concerns the $13 million yearly profit United settled on with the Navy. In the Oral History Wilson said (in 1962) that the yearly profit at the time was $12 million. The actual figure was $13 million, and I have assumed that Wilson's memory was faulty on this item.

31. United Aircraft's 1941 Annual Report; no pagination, but quote appears in section titled "Operations and Finances."

32. Annual Report, 1941, final page of report signed by Wilson as president and Rentschler as chairman.

33. Wilson, Oral History, pp. 770–71.

34. *See* Robert Schlaifer, *The Development of Aircraft Engines* (Cambridge: Harvard University Press, 1950), pp. 461–66; Rentschler, *My Story*, pp. 46–47; Wilson, Oral History pp. 599–600.

35. On Sikorsky and the helicopter, *see* Charles Morris, *Pioneering the Helicopter* (New York: McGraw-Hill, 1945), pp. 80–91, 128; *see also* Frank J. Delear, *Igor Sikorsky* (New York: Dodd, Mead, 1976), p. 200; Charles Gablehouse, *Helicopters and Autogiros* (Philadelphia: Lippincott, 1969), p. 88; Wilson, Oral History, p. 617.

36. *See* Horace Horner's interview with staff of the Columbia Oral History Program, p. 13; *see also The Pratt & Whitney Aircraft Story*, pp. 132–36.

37. Wilson, *Slipstream*, p. 256.

38. United Aircraft's 1942 Annual Report, p. 3.

6.   The Pax Aeronautica

1. On Speer, *see* Albert Speer, *see* Albert Speer, *Spandau: The Secret Diaries* (New York: Macmillan, 1976), p. 80; on "terrific prang," *see* Max Hastings, *Bomber Command* (New York: Dial, 1980), pp. 152–53; *see also* on the human fascination with destruction, J. Glenn Gray, *The Warriors: Reflections on Men In Battle* (New York: Harper & Row, 1959), p. 79.

2. General Carl Spaatz, "Strategic Air Power: Fulfillment of a Concept," *Foreign Affairs*, March 1947, pp. 385–96, esp. p. 389; Hastings, *Bomber Command*, p. 150.

3. *See* Perry McCoy Smith, *The Air Force Plans For Peace* (Baltimore: Johns Hopkins University Press, 1970), pp. 5–7.

4. Rentschler discusses this meeting in Frederick Rentschler, *An Account of the Pratt & Whitney Aircraft Company 1925–1950* (Hartford: privately printed) 1950, p. 41 (hereafter called *My Story*); Wilson discusses it in *Slipstream* (New York: McGraw-Hill, 1950), pp. 260–62; and *Kitty Hawk to Sputnik to Polaris* (Palm Beach: Literary Investors Guild, 1960) pp. 1–6; and in Oral History, pp. 800–803. Rentschler and Wilson disagree on who initiated the meeting, but on the essential results of the encounter the two men are in full agreement.

5. Wilson, *Slipstream*, pp. 263–65; *Kitty Hawk*, pp. 14–16; Rentschler, *My Story*, pp. 41–42.

6. On Douglas, *see Time,* November 22, 1943, pp. 77–84; the remark about "shutting the damn shop up" appears on p. 77.

7. Wilson, *Kitty Hawk,* p. 18; *see also* Eugene Wilson, "An American Air Power Policy," *Aviation,* June 1944, p. 112ff; and *Air Power For Peace* (New York: McGraw-Hill, 1945).

8. Wilson, *Kitty Hawk,* p. 35.

9. Wilson, *Kitty Hawk,* pp. 38–39.

10. United Aircraft's 1943 Annual Report; on profits in aviation, *see* U.S. Congress, Senate, Hearings Before a Subcommittee of the Committee on Military Affairs, pt. 9, Aircraft, July 1944, p. 483 (hereafter cited as Aircraft Hearings).

11. Joseph Barr, *The Time of My Corporate Life* (Palm Beach: Literary Investors Guild, 1978), p. 53.

12. *See Aviation,* June 1944, p. 287.

13. Wilson, interview with Columbia University Oral History Project, 1962, p. 810.

14. Aircraft Hearings, 1944, p. 425.

15. *Ibid.,* p. 429; *see also* the pamphlet "Air Power" reprinted as appx. 3 of the 1944 Aircraft Hearings. The pamphlet summarizes the views which were adopted, due to Wilson, by the Aeronautical Chamber of Commerce.

16. For speeches by Wilson and others, *see Prospects and Problems in Aviation,* Papers Presented at the Chicago Forum On Aviation, University of Chicago, Chicago Association of Commerce, 1945.

17. Smith, *Air Force Plans For Peace,* esp. pp. 54–74: Kuter's comment is on p. 63.

18. David Irving, *The Bombing of Dresden* (New York: Holt, Rinehart, 1964), p. 155: *see also* Hastings, *Bomber Command,* pp. 340–44.

19. General Curtis Le May, *Mission With Le May* (Garden City: Doubleday, 1965), pp. 351–53, 375.

20. Robert Batchelder, *The Irreversible Decision* (New York: Macmillan, 1961), p. 227.

21. *Aviation*, June 1944, p. 287; *see also* Wilson's, "Air Power — The Key To Peace and Prosperity," *Aviation*, February 1945, p. 110ff; *see also* "The Aircraft Industry," in Wilson *Air Power For Peace*, 1945.

22. *See* United's Annual Reports, 1942 through 1945; balance sheets presented to the House Naval Affairs Investigating Committee in 1942; and United's 1945 Annual Report, p. 3.

23. On what United did with its funds in 1945, *see* the 1945 Annual Report, pp. 10–12.

24. Wilson, Oral History, p. 772; for the net worth figures, *see* material provided by Horace Horner to a Hearing before U.S. Congress, Senate, Subcommittee on Interstate and Foreign Commerce, 80th Cong., May 17, 1947, p. 81. These were Senate hearings about a bill to establish a National Air Policy Board (hereafter referred to as Air Policy Hearings); on White Weld, *see* George Bryant Woods, *The Aircraft Manufacturing Industry* (New York: White, Weld and Company, 1946), pp. 7, 90.

25. *See* Horner's testimony before U.S. Congress, Senate, a Special Committee Investigating the National Defense Program, 79th Cong. 1945, pt. 32, pp. 15891–93.

26. *Ibid.*, pp. 15887, 15895.

27. "Shall We Have Airplanes," *Fortune*, January 1948, p. 80.

28. *See* "Mr. Rentschler," *Beehive*, Summer 1956, p. 3.

29. On the jets, *see* Horace Horner's interview with the Columbia University Oral History Project, pp. 14–15; Rentschler, *My Story*, pp. 46–48; Wilson, Oral History, pp. 599–604; *see also* "United Aircraft, Success With a Wry Twist," *Fortune*, December 1963.

30. Charles Kelly Jr., *The Sky's the Limit* (New York: Coward-McCann, 1963), p. 168; also "The Airline Squeeze," *Fortune*, May 1947.

31. Annual Report, 1946, p. 5; *see also* p. 10–11.

32. Le May, *Mission with Le May*, pp. 396–98.

33. Horner, Air Policy Hearings, pp. 31–33.

34. *See Survival In the Air Age*, Report of the President's Air Policy Commission, Washington, D.C. January 1, 1948, p. 3.

35. *See* Rentschler's letter to Finletter dated September 25, 1947. The letters can be obtained from the Truman Library in Missouri. *See* ms p. 391.

36. *Ibid.*, September 25, p. 1.

37. Rentschler, letter to Finletter dated December 9, 1947.

38. Wilson, *Kitty Hawk*, p. 79.

7.   Saved by the Russians

1. *See* U.S. Congress, Senate, National Aviation Policy, From the Temporary Congressional Aviation Policy Board, 80th Cong., 2d sess., 1948, Rept. 949, p. 3 (hereafter cited as Congressional Aviation Policy Board); on grand strategy, *see* Bernard Brodie, *Strategy In the Missile Age* (Princeton: Princeton University Press, 1959); *see also* Russell Weigley, *The American Way of War* (New York: Macmillan, 1973).

2. *See* "Survival in the Air Age," Report of the President's Air Policy Commission, Washington, January 1, 1948, p. 12 (hereafter cited as President's Air Policy Commission).

3. *See* "The Wildest Blue Yonder Yet," *Fortune*, March 1948.

4. President's Air Policy Commission, pp. 45–70, esp. p. 46; Congressional Aviation Policy Board, pp. 33–43.

5. *Fortune*, March 1948, p. 96; *see also* "Shall We Have Airplanes," *Fortune*, January 1948.

6. For appropriations figures, *see* Charles H. Coates and Roland J. Pellegrin, *Military Sociology* (University Park: Social Science Press,

1965), pp. 86–87; *see also* Tom Lilley, *et al.*, *Problems of Accelerating Aircraft Production During World War II* (Cambridge: Harvard Business School, 1946), p. 14; President's Air Policy Commission, pp. 32, 34, 78.

7. President's Air Policy Commission, p. 67; *see also Business Week*, August 14, 1948; *see also* Annual Reports, 1947 and 1948.

8. Annual Report, 1949.

9. Herman O. Stekler, *The Structure and Performance of the Aerospace Industry* (Berkeley: University of California Press, 1965), p. 135.

10. Joseph Barr, *The Time of My Corporate Life* (Palm Beach: Literary Investors Guild, 1978), pp. 68–69.

11. *Ibid.*, pp. 58–59.

12. For net profit figure on other industries, *see* G. R. Simonson, *"Economics of the Aircraft Industry"*, Unpublished Doctoral Dissertation, University of Washington, p. 210; for sales and profit figures, *see Moody's Industrial Manual,* referring to the years in question.

13. Annual Report, 1954, p. 6; for budget figures, *see Military Sociology*, pp. 86–87; for Air Force awards, *see* Awards by Type of Contractor, By Fiscal Year, The Pentagon.

14. Stanley Blumberg and Gwinn Owens, *Energy and Conflict: The Life and Times of Edward Teller* (New York: Putnam's, 1976) pp. 218–19.

15. U.S. Congress, Senate, Report From the Special Committee to Investigate the National Defense Program, Renegotiation, 80th Cong., 2d sess., pt. 2, Rept. 440, p. 11.

16. Rudolf Modley, "Tax Hazards of Plant Expansion," *Aviation Week,* June 25, 1951, p. 40ff; Simonson, pp. 251–52.

17. Senate, Rept. no. 440, pp. 11–12; *see also* Irving B. Holley, Jr., *Buying Aircraft: Material Procurement for the Army Air Forces,* (Washington, D.C., Office of the Chief of Military History, Department of the Army, 1964), p. 295.

18. *Aviation Week,* June 25, 1951, pp. 40–41.

19. Annual Report, 1951, p. 10; John S. Day, *Subcontracting Policy in Airframe Industry* (Boston: Harvard Business School, 1956).

20. *See* U.S. Congress, House, Subcommittee For Special Investigations of House Committee on Armed Services, 1957, 81st Cong., 1st sess., pp. 1258–59; on amount of government-owned equipment, *see* 1951 Annual Report, p. 10.

21. *Time,* May 28, 1951, pp. 91–92.

22. *See Moody's Industrial Manual,* referring to the years in question.

23. *See The Economics of Defense Spending: A Look at the Realities* (Washington, D.C.: The Pentagon, July 1972), p. IV.

24. 1953 Annual Report, p. 6; *see also* Stekler, p. 159.

25. A copy of Talbott's statement was attached to United's 1952 Annual Report; on Talbott resignation, *see* William Manchester, *The Glory and the Dream* (Boston: Little, Brown, 1975), p. 670.

26. For Eisenhower's views, *see* Dwight D. Eisenhower, *Mandate For Change* (Garden City: Doubleday, 1963), pp. 446–47, 451–53; on critics, *see* "Is the H-Bomb Enough?" *Fortune,* January 1954; Raymond Aron, *On War* (Garden City: Doubleday, 1959); Maxwell Taylor, *The Uncertain Trumpet* (New York: Harper & Row, 1960).

27. "B-52 Pilot Speaks Out," *Beehive,* Summer 1952; "New Margin of Power," *Beehive,* January 1954.

28. On the number of engines, *see* Subcommittee For Special Investigations, 1957, p. 1259; on market share, *see* Stekler, p. 135.

29. 1955 Annual Report, pp. 8–9.

30. Barr, *The Time of My Corporate Life,* pp. 78–79; 1955 Annual Report, p. 9.

31. Horace Horner interview with Columbia Oral History Project, 1962, p. 19.

32. 1954 Annual Report, p. 10; 1956 Annual Report, p. 13; 1957 Annual Report, p. 11; 1958 Annual Report, p. 11.

33. John Newhouse, *The Sporty Game* (New York: Knopf, 1982).

34. "The Airlines' Flight From Reality," *Fortune*, February 1956.

35. *Business Week*, July 21, 1956, p. 170.

36. "The Selling of the 707," *Fortune*, October 1957.

37. *See* Robert Daly, *An American Saga* (New York: Random House, 1980), pp. 396–414, esp. pp. 408–9; Douglas Ingells, *747: The Story of the Boeing Super Jet* (Fallbrook: Aero Publishers, 1970), pp. 113–24; Charles Kelly, *The Sky's the Limit* (New York: Coward-McCann, 1963), pp. 187–99; Marylin Bender and Selig Altschul, *The Chosen Instrument* (New York: Simon & Schuster, 1982), pp. 467–76.

38. 1956 Annual Report, pp. 7; Daly, p. 410.

39. *Business Week*, June 30, 1951, pp. 72–75; 1956 Annual Report, p. 8; Daly, pp. 412–13; Kelly, p. 192.

40. U.S. Congress Aircraft Nuclear Propulsion Program, Subcommittee on Research and Development, Joint Committee on Atomic Energy, 86th Cong., 1959, p. 114 (hereafter referred to as Nuclear Propulsion Hearings).

41. Nuclear Propulsion Hearings, p. 29.

42. *See Aviation Week*, January 25, 1960, pp. 72, 114–16.

43. "CANEL Hot Lab," *Beehive*, Summer 1957, p. 29–30.

44. Nuclear Propulsion Hearings, p. 118; *see also* Herbert York, *Race To Oblivion* (New York: Simon & Schuster, 1970), p. 68.

45. U.S. Congress, Senate, Subcommittee on Civil Defense, Committee on Armed Services, 84th Cong., 1955, pt. 1, pp. 120–21.

46. Stekler, *The Structure and Performance of the Aerospace Industry*, p. 18; Coates and Pellegrin, *Military Sociology*, pp. 86–87; 1960 Annual Report, p. 2.

8. McNamara and Mistakes

1. United Aircraft's 1958 Annual Report, pp. 11–12; Max Hastings, *Bomber Command* (New York: Dial, 1979) p. 108; on Norden, *see* Michael Nisos, *Air Force* magazine, September 1981; *see also Moody's Industrial Manual*, 1957.

2. U.S. Congress, House, The Centaur Program, House Subcommittee No. 3 of the Committee on Science and Aeronautics, 87th Cong., 1962, pt. 3, pp. 1663–66; on research and development costs, *see* United's 1959 Annual Report, p. 3.

3. United Aircraft, Report of 1964 Annual Meeting of Stockholders, pp. 8–9.

4. The Centaur Program, pp. 28–29.

5. United Aircraft's 1960 Annual Report, p. 2; *Moody's Industrial Manual*, 1960.

6. Cf. Maxwell Taylor, *The Uncertain Trumpet* (New York: Harper & Row, 1960); Albert Wohlstetter, "The Delicate Balance of Terror," *Foreign Affairs*, 37 (January 1959), pp. 211–34.

7. Bill Gunston, *F-111* (New York: Scribner's, 1978). The "bow-tie bastards" remark appears on p. 16. *See also* Robert Art, *The TFX Decision* (Boston: Little-Brown, 1967); Charles Bright, *The Jet Makers* (Lawrence, Kans., Regents of the University of Kansas, 1972).

8. Richard Smith, "The $7 Billion Contract That Changed The Rules," *Fortune*, March and April, 1963; *see also* "McNamara's Expensive Economy Plane," *Fortune*, June 1, 1967.

9. U.S. Congress, Senate, TFX Contract Investigation, Second Series, Permanent Subcommittee On Investigations of the Committee on Government Operations, March 1970, p. 312.

10. *Ibid.*, p. 323.

11. United Aircraft's 1961–1963 Annual Reports, esp. 1962, p. 4; *see also* Harold Meyers, "United Aircraft: Success With a Wry Twist," *Fortune*, December 1963, pp. 111ff.

12. United Aircraft's 1963 Annual Report, p. 2; for profit figures, *see* *Moody's Industrial Manual* for the years in question.

13. Meyers, *Fortune*, December 1963.

14. Douglas Ingells, 747 (Fallbrook: Aero Publishers, 1970), pp. 133–35.

15. Taylor, *Uncertain Trumpet*, p. 64.

16. United Aircraft's 1962 Annual Report, p. 11; 1964, p. 11; *see also* Philip Siekman, "The Big New Whirl in Helicopters," *Fortune*, April 1966.

17. Robert McNamara, *The Essence of Security* (New York: Harper & Row, 1968), pp. 83–84; Berkeley Rice, *The C-5A Scandal* (Boston: Houghton Mifflin, 1971); John Mecklin, "The Biggest Cheapest Lift Ever," *Fortune*, November 1965, pp. 179ff.

18. John Mechlin, "The Ordeal of the Plane Makers," *Fortune*, December 1965; United Aircraft's 1964 Annual Report, p. 2.

19. United Aircraft's 1964 Annual Report, pp. 2–3; *see also* John Mecklin, "U.S. Airlines: Into the Wild Blue What?" *Fortune*, May 1966.

20. *Aviation Week*, March 15, 1965, p. 289; *see also* Gunston, F-111, pp. 25–27.

21. Rice, *The C-5A Scandal*, pp. 14–16.

22. Ingells, 747, pp. 140–41.

23. Laurence Kuter, *The Great Gamble: The Boeing 747* (University of Alabama Press 1973), p. 10; *see also* John Newhouse, *The Sporty Game* (New York: Knopf, 1981), pp. 117–20; Robert Daly, *An America Saga* (New York: Random House, 1980), pp. 432–33.

24. Kuter, *Great Gamble*, p. 11.

25. Eugene Wilson, interview with Columbia Oral History Project, 1962, p. 523.

26. United Aircraft's 1964 Annual Report, pp. 4, 23.

27. U.S. Congress, House, Hearings Before a House Subcommitteee of the Committee on Appropriations, 91st Cong., 1st sess. Part 3—Procurement, pp. 870, 866–82.

28. TFX Contract Investigation, p. 561; Tom Gervasi, *Arsenal of Democracy* (New York: Grove, 1980), p. 90; *Business Week*, June, 1968, p. 44.

29. TFX Contract Investigation, 2d Series, p. 562; Gunston, *F-111*, p. 35.

30. Senator McClellan's comments appear in U.S. Congress, Senate, *Congressional Record*, August 22, 1967, pp. 23493–97.

31. Kuter, *The Great Gamble*, p. 27 and pp. 33–36.

32. *Ibid.*, p. 36.

33. For money spent on the 747's engines, *see* the 1966 through 1970 Annual Reports.

34. United Aircraft's 1968 Annual Report, p. 3.

35. *Ibid.*, p. 4.

36. The percentages on sales of each subsidiary appear in United Aircraft's 1969 Annual Report, p. 18; the percentages on profits are based primarily on figures reported in United Aircraft's 1970 Annual Report, p. 18.

37. On the engine's problems, *see* Newhouse, *The Sporty Game*, pp. 164–67; Profits and losses are from *Moody's Industrial Manual* and the Annual Reports for the years in question; on the first flight, *see* *Aviation Week*, January 19, 1970, p. 27.

38. All figures are from the Pentagon publication *Prime Military Contracts by State, County, Contractor, and Place,* no pagination.

39. *See* "The TFX Verdict," *Aviation Week*, 94 (January 4, 1971), p. 7.

9. What's in a Name? The United Technologies Corporation

1. For losses on 747, *see* 1966–1971 Annual Reports. The losses cited for 1970 and 1971 alone total $183 million.

2. "Another Litton Man Wants to Run His Own Show," *Fortune,* November 1971, p. 33.

3. "Names and Faces," *Business Week,* December 10, 1979, pp. 77, 80.

4. Sworn deposition of Harry Gray in *Otis Elevator v. United Technologies Corporation,* U.S. District Court, Southern District of New York. The deposition, (hereafter cited as the Gray Depo) was taken at the offices of Skadden Arps, Slate, Meagher, and Flom on October 25, 1975. It runs to almost two hundred pages. The case number in the Otis suit is 75 Civ. 5150.

5. Gray Depo., p. 50; *see also* pp. 49–54.

6. Gray Depo., p. 51; *see also* p. 85.

7. Gray Depo., pp. 80–81.

8. Gray Depo., p. 82; for a sound analysis of takeovers, *see* Richard Phalon, *The Takeover Barons of Wall Street* (New York: Putnam's, 1981). On the "macho" spirit in takeovers, *see* the comment in Phalon: "It's like being in combat," or "it's like being a platoon leader on a beachhead," both on p. 71.

9. Cf. George Benston, "Conglomerate Mergers: Causes, Consequences, and Remedies," presented before the Subcommittee on Antitrust and Monopoly of the Senate Judiciary Committee, May 17, 1979; J. Fred Weston, "Mergers and Economic Efficiency," vol. 2, Industrial Concentration Mergers and Growth, United States Department of Commerce, June 1981.

10. *See* U.S. Congress, House, Hearings on Cost Escalation in Defense Procurement Contracts and Military Posture, House Armed Services Committee, May 22, 1973, p. 1433; *see also* p. 1416 (hereafter cited as Cost Hearings).

11. *See* U.S. Congress, Senate, Hearings Before the Committee On Armed

Services, "F-15 and F-16 Engine Problems," 96th Cong., November 27, 1979, pp. 75, 102 (hereafter cited as Engine Hearings).

12. "Prime Contract Awards Over $10,000 by State, County, Contractor, and Place," Connecticut, Directorate For Information, Operations, and Reports, The Pentagon, Washington, D.C. (hereafter cited as Prime Military Contracts).

13. *See* U.S. Congress, Senate, Committee On Armed Services, FY 1973 Authorizations, F-15 Program Review, 92nd Cong., p. 3606; on the two compressor designs, *see* p. 3605.

14. Engine Hearings, p. 102.

15. Cost Hearings, p. 1395.

16. Cost Hearings, p. 1372.

17. Cost Hearings, pp. 1388, 1390.

18. Cost Hearings, p. 1388.

19. *See* report to Congress, "Independent Research and Development Allocations Should Not Absorb Costs of Commercial Development Work," by the Comptroller General of the United States. Reprinted in U.S. Congress, Senate, Hearings Before the Subcommittee on Research and Development, Joint Economic Committee, 94th Cong., September 1975, p. 176 (hereafter cited as Independent Research and Development hearings).

20. *See* U.S. Congress, House, Hearing before a Subcommittee on Appropriations, 97th Cong., p. 327.

21. Independent Research and Development Hearings, pp. 229–31.

22. United Technologies Annual Report, 1973, p. 3.

23. United Technologies Annual Report, 1973, p. 21: on Essex, *see* The "Electrical World of Essex," *Beehive*, Spring 1974.

24. Prime Military Contracts, 1972, pp. 73, 74.

25. United Technologies Annual Report, 1974; *see also Moody's*, 1978, p. 3247.

26. Prime Military Contracts, FY 1974.

27. *Beehive*, Spring 1975, p. 3.

28. Gray Depo., pp. 72–74; p. 84–85, 90.

29. Gray Depo., pp. 99–100.

30. Gray Depo., pp. 101–2.

31. *See* affidavit of Ralph A. Weller, U.S. District Court, Southern District of New York, *Otis Elevator v. United Technologies Corporation*, p. 2 (hereafter cited as Weller Affidavit).

32. Gray Depo., pp. 136–37; *see also* Weller Affidavit, p. 2.

33. Gray Depo., pp. 139–40; *see also* Weller Affidavit, p. 5.

34. *See* sworn affidavit of Edward Hennessey, *Otis v. United Technologies*, pp. 2–3; *see also* 405 Federal Supplement 960 (1975), *Otis Elevator Company v.* United Technologies Corporation, pp. 968–69; *see also* p. 971.

35. Gray Depo., p. 180.

36. Gray Depo., p. 183.

37. On sales pitch, *see* "direct questioning" of Mr. Gray, enclosed with the case file, pp. 142–44.

38. 405 Federal Supplement 960 (1975), p. 974.

39. On rising cost of an F-100, *see Aviation Week and Space Technology*, December 2, 1974, p. 19; on problems, *see Aviation Week and Space Technology*, May 12, 1975, p. 18.

40. Testimony of Harry Gray, Capability of U.S. Defense Industry before U.S. Congress, House, Committee on Armed Services, 96th Cong., p. 53.

41. Engine Hearings, 1979, pp. 102–4.

42. Robert Carlson, "The Need For Equitable Competition," testimony

before U.S. Congress, Senate, Committee on Appropriations, May 25, 1982, p. 11; *also* Engine Hearings, 1979, p. 104.

43. United Technologies Annual Report, 1975, p. 1.

44. *See* Form 8k for the month of March 1976, Securities and Exchange Commission, Washington, D.C., pp. 2–3.

45. *See* Barry Bluestone, Peter Jordan, and Mark Sullivan, *Aircraft Industry Dynamics* (Boston, Auburn House, 1981), pp. 84–85; *see also* Anthony Sampson, *The Arms Bazaar* (New York, Bantam, 1977), pp. 294–304.

46. United Technologies Annual Report, 8k, April 20, 1977, p. 2.

47. "After Winning Otis, Wither United Technology?" *Business Week*, December 15, 1975, pp. 84–85.

48. NASA, One Hundred Contractors Listed According to Net Value of Direct Awards, Fiscal Year 1974–1976; *see also* Prime Military Contracts, 1974–1976.

49. *See The Babcock and Wilcox Company* v. *United Technologies Corporation*, Civ. A, No. C77-124A, U.S. District Court, N.D., Ohio, E.D., July 15, 1977, Federal Supplement 1249 (1977), pp. 1253–54.

50. Gray Depo., p. 82.

51. *Babcock-Wilcox* v. *United Technologies*, p. 1254.

52. "An Unwelcome Suitor Keeps Plugging Away," *Business Week*, April 18, 1977, p. 48; *see also Fortune*, May 8, 1978, p. 99.

53. "What Makes Harry Gray Run," *Business Week*, December 10, 1979, p. 75.

54. *Ibid.*, p. 76.

55. Rohatyn's comment appears in Phalon, *The Takeover Barons*, p. 120; for fees generated in Babcock case, *see* A.F. Ehrbar, "Corporate Takeovers Are Here To Stay," *Fortune*, May 8, 1978, p. 100.

56. U.S. Congress, House, Defense Procurement Policies and Pro-

cedures: Cost Management and Control, House Armed Services Committee Hearing, 97th Cong., 1981, pp. 416–17, 430–31.

57. Tom Gervasi, *Arsenal of Democracy* (New York: Grove, 1981), p. 189; also Bluestone, *et al.*, *Aircraft Industry Dynamics*, pp. 72–74.

58. Prime Military Contracts, 1976–1978.

59. Abraham Briloff, *The Truth About Corporate Accounting* (New York: Harper & Row, 1980), pp. 97–98.

60. *Ibid.*, p. 99.

61. Phalon, *The Takeover Barons*, p. 249.

62. Ehrbar, *Fortune*, May 8, 1978, p. 99.

63. *See Carrier Corporation* v. *United Technologies Corporation*, United States District Court, Northern District of New York, no. 78-CV-488, cited 1978-2 Trade Cases, Trade Regulation Reports, 76,364–76,365.

64. *Ibid.*, pp. 76, 378.

65. Briloff, *Corporate Accounting*, p. 100.

66. Telephone Interview with Mr. Sevin, July 24, 1982; *see also* A.F. Ehrbar in *Fortune*, September 22, 1980, p. 97ff.

67. *See* United Technologies, 1980 10k Report, p. F-9.

68. United Technologies Annual Report, 1979, p. 8.

69. Telephone Interview with Mr. Sevin; *see also* Gene Bylinsky, "Japan's Omnious Chip Victory," *Fortune*, December 14, 1981, p. 52.

70. Cf. "Japan's Strategy For the 80's," *Business Week*, December 14, 1981, pp. 39–120.

71. Telephone Interview with Mr. Sevin.

72. United Technologies 1981 Annual Report, p. 3.

73. United Technologies Third Quarter 1982 Report, p. 3.

74. United Technologies 1981 Annual Report, p. 38.

75. Cf. John Newhouse, *The Sporty Game* (New York: Knopf, 1982), pp. 123–25; *see also* pp. 23–25.

76. Newhouse, *Ibid.*, p. 28.

77. United Technologies, 1979 10k, p. 3; 1980 10k, p. 2; 1981 10k, p. 3.

78. United Technologies, 1980 10k, p. 6.

79. Bluestone, *et al.*, *Aircraft Industry Dynamics*, p. 62.

80. United Technologies, 1980 10k, p. 6.

81. Newhouse, *The Sporty Game*, pp. 185–86.

82. United Technologies Credit Corporation, 1981 10k, p. 3.

83. United Technologies 1981 Annual Report, p. 13; Third Quarter 1982 Rept. p. 4; 1982 Annual Report.

84. Defense Procurement Policies and Procedures, 1981, p. 426.

85. Carlson, Committee on Appropriations, 1982, pp. 4–5.

86. "The F-100 Engine has Double Trouble," *Business Week*, November 12, 1979, p. 46.

87. *See* Robert Waters, "Senate Panel Finds Funds For Pratt Engine," *Hartford Courant*, September 22, 1982.

88. *See Aerospace Daily*, December 7, 1982, p. 185; *see also* Robert Waters, "Pratt & Whitney Fights GE With Discount," *Hartford Courant*, December 8, 1982, p. 1.

Epilogue

1. For overview of the Bendix-Martin Marietta-United Technologies story, *see* Roy Rowan and Thomas Moore, "Behind the Lines in the Bendix War," *Fortune Magazine*, October 18, 1982, pp. 157–63; *see*

also Newsweek, September 20, 1982, p. 60, and October 4, 1982, pp. 67–68.

2. Dwight David Eisenhower, *Mandate For Change* (Garden City: Doubleday, 1963), p. 446.

INDEX

Gray, Harry
  acquisitions and mergers of
    Ambac, 260
    Babcock-Wilcox, 257-259
    Carrier Corp., 260-262
    Essex Industries, 244-245
    Otis Elevator Co., 246-251
    Mostek, 212-263
  as Chief Executive Officer, 245
  diversification and merger policy
    of, 239-241
  refusal to return funding on JT-9,
    244-245
  selection as President of United
    Aircraft Corporation, 237-241
  as "takeover artist," 3-4
Green, Joseph, 109
Gross, Courtland, 222
Grumman, and TFX program,
  211-212
Guano deal, 84
Gwinn, William, 192
  as president of United Aircraft, 198
  retirement of, 245

Hamilton, Charles, 60
Hamilton, Thomas, 50, 81, 83, 107, 121
  1940 commissions, 125
  and Pratt & Whitney Aircraft and
    Boeing Air Transport merger,
    53
Hamilton Aero Manufacturing Co.,
    merge with Boeing Aircraft and
    Transport Co., 60
Hamilton Standard Propeller
    Corporation, 66-67, 191
  1929-1930, 79
  1936, 1938, 111
  World War II, 134
Hanighen, F.C., 100
Harris, Arthur, 150
Hartford Courant, The, 2, 116
Hearst, William Randolph, 90
Helicopters, 112. *See also* Sikorsky
    Aviation
  early designs of, 142-144
Henderson, Paul, 15, 93

Hennessey, Edward, 238
  merger and diversification role
    of, 239
  and Otis Elevator Co. acquisition,
    247, 248, 249
Herald, The, 20
Herald Tribune, 45
Herrick, Myron, 45
Hewes, Thomas, 109
Hobbs, Leonard, 105, 167, 181
  Collier Trophy, 190
Holding companies, 53
Holm, Melvin, 261
Hooven, Owens, Rentschler Company,
    27
Horner, Horace
  air freight campaign, 219
  as chairman of United Aircraft, 198
  on postwar subsidies, 163-164
  on post-World War II aviation
    industry, 170
  on research and development, 206,
    207, 208
  retirement of, 230
  selection as president, 153
Hornet engine
  beginnings of, 36
  production of, 43-44
Hubbard, Eddie, 43
Hudson Motor Company, Howard
    Coffin and, 10
Hughes, Evan, 13
Hull, Cordell, 110
Hydrogen bomb, 184

Independent Research and
    Development Program, 244

Janeway, Eliot, 133
Japan
  exports to, 107-108
  moral embargo of, 114-116
Jeffrey, T. S., Jr., 225
Jet engines, Chance Vought's
    production of, 180-181
Jets
  early research programs, 141